TWO COMMUNITIES IN THE CIVIL WAR

A NORTON CASEBOOK IN HISTORY

TWO COMMUNITIES IN THE CIVIL WAR

A NORTON CASEBOOK IN HISTORY

Andrew J. Torget
and
Edward L. Ayers

W. W. NORTON & COMPANY

New York / London

W. W. Norton & Company has been independent since its founding in 1923, when William Warder Norton and Mary D. Herter Norton first published lectures delivered at the People's Institute, the adult education division of New York City's Cooper Union. The Nortons soon expanded their program beyond the Institute, publishing books by celebrated academics from America and abroad. By mid-century, the two major pillars of Norton's publishing program—trade books and college texts—were firmly established. In the 1950s, the Norton family transferred control of the company to its employees, and today—with a staff of four hundred and a comparable number of trade, college, and professional titles published each year—W. W. Norton & Company stands as the largest and oldest publishing house owned wholly by its employees.

The text of this book is composed in Baskerville MT with the display set in Cloister Openface.

Composition and maps by ElectraGraphics, Inc.
Manufacturing by the Courier Companies—Westford division.
Managing editor: Lory Frenkel.
Series design by Jo Anne Metsch.
Production manager: Benjamin Reynolds.

Library of Congress Cataloging-in-Publication Data

Two communities in the Civil War: a Norton casebook in history / edited by Andrew J. Torget, Edward L. Ayers.
  p. cm.
  Includes bibliographical references and index

ISBN-13: 978-0-393-92738-2 (pbk.)
ISBN-10: 0-393-92738-5 (pbk.)
  1. Augusta County (Va.)—History, Military—19th century—Sources. 2. Franklin County (Pa.)—History, Military—19th century—Sources. 3. Augusta County (Va.)—Social conditions—19th century—Sources. 4. Franklin County (Pa.)—Social conditions—19th century—Sources. 5. Virginia—History—Civil War, 1861–1865—Personal narratives. 6. Virginia—History—Civil War, 1861–1865—Social aspects—Sources. 7. Pennsylvania—History—Civil War, 1861–1865—Personal narratives. 8. Pennsylvania—History—Civil War, 1861–1865—Social aspects—Sources. 9. United States—History—Civil War, 1861–1865—Personal narratives. 10. United States—History—Civil War, 1861–1865—Social aspects—Sources. I. Torget, Andrew J., 1978– II. Ayers, Edward L., 1953–

F232.A9T89 2006
973.7′455916—dc22

                                                                            2006046849

W. W. Norton & Company, Inc., 500 Fifth Avenue, New York, N.Y. 10110-0017
www.wwnorton.com
W. W. Norton & Company Ltd., Castle House, 75/76 Wells Street, London W1T 3QT
1 2 3 4 5 6 7 8 9 0

CONTENTS

THE VALLEY OF
THE SHADOW PROJECT

All the documents for this casebook were drawn from the *Valley of the Shadow: Two Communities in the American Civil War* project (http://valley.vcdh.virginia.edu) based at the Virginia Center for Digital History at the University of Virginia. The Valley Project is an online digital archive that documents life in two communities, one Northern and one Southern, along the border between free and slave states throughout the era of the American Civil War. In addition to the sources in this casebook, readers can explore thousands of other records—including letters and diaries, newspapers and speeches, census and government documents, soldier and church records—available in the Valley Project's archive that document the rhythms of life in these two communities during the turbulent years of the Civil War.

The Valley of the Shadow Project and this casebook are only possible because of the work and dedication of a team of researchers at the Virginia Center for Digital History. A full listing of the people who gathered, processed, and digitized the numerous records that make up the Valley's archive is available on the project's Web site. We would also like to thank Gary W. Gallagher, who commented insightfully on the introduction to this casebook.

A Note to the Reader: Asterisks (* * *) are used in this book to indicate material that the editors have omitted. Ellipses (. . .) are used if they appear in the original document.

INTRODUCTION

Despite all that has been written about it, historians continue to battle over the causes and consequences of the American Civil War. Understanding how white Southerners came to believe secession was their only recourse, how Abraham Lincoln and the Republican Party turned a war for Union into a war against slavery, and how black Southerners built new lives in the wake of emancipation remain some of the greatest challenges facing historians today. Part of the difficulty lies in the fact that Americans lived in such a complex and turbulent world during the years between 1861 and 1865. Faced with the secession of half the country, battles that killed more than 620,000 Americans, and the destruction of the most powerful slave society ever formed, men and women—both black and white—struggled with momentous questions throughout the era of the Civil War.

People living along the great border between the slaveholding and non-slaveholding regions of the country found themselves at the heart of those struggles. Abraham Lincoln's election in 1860, for example, hinged on his ability to win crucial votes in Pennsylvania. During the secession crisis, Virginia's early unionism shaped Lincoln's approach to the crisis and prompted the new Confederacy to send commissioners to the state in hopes of convincing its leaders to leave the Union. Once the fighting began, many of the bloodiest battles of the war played out in Virginia, Maryland, and Pennsylvania. This casebook provides a new window into the experience of life during the Civil War by taking a deep look into two communities living along this border between North and South: Augusta County, Virginia, and Franklin County, Pennsylvania. By following the experiences of people from these two counties during the course of the war—from the uncertain days before secession

1

through the aftermath of the Confederacy's defeat—the sections of this book offer an opportunity to see the era through the eyes of those who lived it.

This casebook is divided into ten sections, each delving into a different aspect of life during the Civil War era—such as the place of slavery along the border, the experience of fighting on the front lines, and the aftermath of emancipation. The voices that emanate from the letters, diaries, and newspaper articles in this book describe the hopes, fears, elation, and despair shared by the residents of border communities like Augusta and Franklin. The Civil War, for both counties, was a period of profound confusion and uncertainty. Throughout the war, people made decisions based on what information they had at the time, relying on the limited and often inaccurate reports they received from newspapers and neighbors. Some looked ahead with confidence, believing that the upheaval of the country would bring a better future. Other saw their deepest fears fulfilled by the destruction brought on by four years of desperate struggle. None, however, could have known how drastically the war would change their lives by April 1865.

Within each section you will find the writings, both public and private, of people from Augusta and Franklin as they grappled with the issues that consumed their world during those difficult years. In their letters and diaries, people in the nineteenth century tended to dwell on personal and family concerns—such as the health and fortunes of family members—rather than the great political questions of the day. Here discussions of events like the secession crisis or great battles were often brief, frequently paired with news about crops and local weather. In the editorials and articles of the county newspapers, however, heated political debates took center stage. Americans at the time of the Civil War had a voracious appetite for newspapers, and by the 1860s presses churned out weeklies in almost every community. Nearly every paper boasted a political affiliation—Democratic, Whig, or Republican—and each sought to help their readers see the world through their own partisan lens. Through these writings, whether intended for a personal or public audience, we gain a glimpse of the lives of Americans immersed in a great war with one another.

Augusta and Franklin Before the War

Situated only 200 miles from one another in the Shenandoah Valley, Augusta and Franklin counties shared similar geography, economies, and histories. The Valley was a twenty-mile-wide swath of rich farmlands, nestled between the Blue Ridge and Allegheny mountains, that ran the entire course of Virginia and Pennsylvania. People in both counties tended to live in the countryside, relying primarily on farming for their income and planting grains (such as corn, wheat, oats, and rye) that grew so well in the Valley's rich soil. Franklin was slightly more urbanized, centering around the county seat of Chambersburg, with villages spread throughout the county. Augusta's county seat in Staunton was nearly as large as Franklin's and boasted a railway connection that linked the county to the rest of Virginia. People in both communities ate the same foods, read the same sorts of books, worshipped in the same kinds of churches. The two counties seemed to have almost everything in common, with one crucial exception. Slavery existed in Augusta but not Franklin, separating the two counties in their politics and national outlook.

Slavery provided the economic backbone for Augusta's farms. More than 5,000 enslaved men, women, and children worked the fields that made Augusta one of the wealthiest counties in Virginia. About one in every four white families in Augusta owned at least one slave at the time of the war, an average that held throughout the South. Many more families, however, rented slaves from their neighbors and the practice touched every aspect of life within the county, where slaves were bought and sold on the steps of the county courthouse, whipped and punished when they displeased their masters, and chased when they ran away. In every measurable way, slavery fused itself into all aspects of Augusta's society. Indeed, the slaves of Augusta's residents, worth nearly $7 million in 1860 dollars, represented the county's primary source of wealth.

While it held no slaves, Franklin County did have a significant free black population. Almost 2,000 free blacks lived in the county (giving Franklin County the fifth-largest black population in Pennsylvania), 500 of whom lived in Chambersburg, where they crowded into dilapidated housing in the poorer parts of town. Free blacks in Franklin supported themselves as best they could in an uncertain world, working as day laborers, cooks, maids, tanners, chimney sweeps, brickmakers, and any other occupation they could find. Even without slaves, the issue of slavery held a prominent place in Franklin's politics, where newspapers and politicians from every party vilified blacks. Some whites in the county made a living by catching slaves who escaped from the South, returning them for a reward. Other whites, along with the free black community, helped runaway slaves make their way north toward freedom. Living so close to the line between slave and free states, Franklin County residents of all colors could not escape the long shadow cast by slavery along their southern border.

By 1860 slavery had become the central political issue in the nation. The Republican Party had risen to prominence during the 1850s by opposing the expansion of slavery into the new western territories of the United States. White Southerners found themselves outraged at the prospect of being barred from taking their property into the western states. More viscerally, they feared that if slavery were successfully banned from states carved out of the west, Republicans would then seek to outlaw the institution where it already existed in the east. Slaveholders, and those who hoped one day to own slaves, became increasingly alarmed at the prospect of a Republican one day winning the presidency.

In October 1859, a man named John Brown presented Southerners with something even more fearsome. An abolitionist whose bloody acts in Kansas had gained him national notoriety, Brown had plotted for years to incite a slave uprising in the South in hopes of sparking a war that would end slavery in the United States. Eventually his plans settled on raiding the Federal arsenal at Harpers Ferry, Virginia, which he hoped to use as a base for arming local slaves and beginning his race war. In the months before the raid, Brown rented a house under a pseudonym in Franklin County—because of its proximity to Virginia—where he spent the summer gathering accomplices and weapons for the raid. Brown and his party finally launched their attack on October 16, 1859. After initially gaining control of the armory, the rebellion began to fall apart when slaves did not rise up as Brown had hoped, allowing

U.S. Marines led by Robert E. Lee and J. E. B. Stuart to surround and capture the conspirators.

John Brown's failed raid sent shock waves throughout the country. Southerners were outraged that Brown had hoped to start a slave rebellion that would likely kill thousands of whites, and worried that his efforts represented common sentiments among Northerners. Many Northern communities, it turned out, were just as outraged as the South, and many people in Franklin County were particularly appalled and embarrassed that Brown had planned much of his raid while living in their county. In other places in the North, however, people publicly expressed sympathy for Brown and his efforts. Indeed, a series of letters between Brown and some Northerners that surfaced immediately after the raid seemed to suggest a widespread conspiracy within the North to destroy Southern slavery. Though Brown was quickly hanged in Virginia for his actions, some Southerners, particularly those in South Carolina, began to speak of seceding from the Union if the Republican candidate for president won the November 1860 election.

When the Democratic Party met in April 1860 to select its nominee for president, the effects of Brown's raid were readily apparent. Northern Democrats coalesced around Stephen A. Douglas of Illinois, who advocated using popular sovereignty as a way of settling the vexing issue of slavery in the western territories. Southern Democrats, however, would accept no less than a candidate who explicitly endorsed the rights of slaveholders to take their property into the west, and they walked out of the convention rather than support Douglas. Suddenly split as a party, the Democrats ultimately nominated two candidates for president: Stephen Douglas for the Northern Democrats and John C. Breckinridge of Kentucky for the Southern Democrats. The Republicans nominated Abraham Lincoln on a platform promising to outlaw the expansion of slavery into the American West, but also to leave it alone where it already existed. Unionists disturbed by the prospect of such a sectional election, many of them former members of the now-defunct Whig party, nominated a fourth candidate. Calling themselves the Constitutional Union Party, they offered John Bell of Tennessee on a platform promising to maintain the status quo by strictly interpreting the Constitution.

As summer gave way to fall in 1860, Abraham Lincoln appeared certain to win the four-way race. The fractured nature of the Democrats meant that neither Douglas nor Breckinridge could muster enough national support to threaten Lincoln. Similarly, Bell had not managed to build any significant following beyond the border states, and many of his supporters hoped to divide the national vote enough for the race to be forced into the House of Representatives (where Bell would win, they believed, as the best alternative to the more sectional candidates). In contrast to his opponents, Lincoln appeared ever stronger as the election approached. All indications pointed toward him winning most Northern states, whose large populations would give Lincoln enough electoral votes to win the presidency even without carrying a single Southern state.

The results of Election Day, November 6, 1860, indeed brought victory to the Republicans. Lincoln won handily in the Electoral College, taking every Northern state except New Jersey, which he split with Stephen Douglas. Douglas had placed a close second in the national popular vote, but was pummeled by Lincoln in the electoral vote. Beyond a share of New Jersey, Douglas had won only Missouri and could claim a mere 12 electoral votes to Lincoln's 180. For his part, John Bell won Virginia, Kentucky, and Tennessee, but he also mustered only 39 electoral votes. John Breckinridge had fared better than either Bell or Douglas by winning most of the South, but his 72 electoral votes fell far short of challenging Lincoln.

The election totals in Augusta and Franklin reflected the general sentiment in the two counties. In Augusta, Unionist candidate Bell won with 2,553 votes, compared to the 1,094 cast for Douglas and 218 for Breckinridge. Voters in Augusta had responded to Bell's message of preserving the Union, largely ignoring Douglas while rejecting outright the sectional appeal of Breckinridge. In Franklin voters had tended toward either extreme, 4,151 voting for Lincoln and 2,515 for Breckinridge. The moderate candidates fared poorly in the county, with Douglas claiming 822 votes and Bell only 76. No one in Augusta or Franklin was surprised by these results, though neither could anyone in the two counties now be sure what Lincoln's election would mean for the country. Everyone along the border watched with trepidation as states in the lower South began taking active steps toward leaving the Union.

Few people in Augusta or Franklin relished the prospect of a war between the North and South. Men and women in both counties understood that living along the border meant that their farms and homes would become the battlefields of any sectional war. In Augusta County, most people now opposed secession just as actively as they had once opposed Lincoln. As long as Augusta remained in the Union, they reasoned, there were protections for slavery built into the U.S. Constitution that not even the Republicans could destroy. If Virginia were to leave the Union, however, those protections would disappear along with the slaves who would run away to the North (which, as a separate country, would no longer be required to return runaways to their owners in Virginia). The best course, most agreed, would be to wait and see what the Republicans would do once Lincoln was inaugurated as president.

Residents of Franklin County worried that a war would put their local economy and future at grave risk. People living just north of the Mason-Dixon Line knew all too well how deeply intertwined their economy was with the economy of their neighbors in the South. Even those unswayed by economics feared the prospect of having their homes overrun by marauding soldiers and armies—not that any of that stopped the county's political parties from sniping at one another. Franklin's Democratic newspaper took the opportunity to rail at the county's Republicans, blaming the precarious state of the nation on Lincoln's party and sympathizing with the complaints of discontented Southerners. Local Republicans, meanwhile, defended Lincoln and celebrated his victory. Despite the rhetoric, most in the county believed that some sort of compromise could be reached that would calm the nation and avoid war. What proved most frustrating, however, was that Franklin residents had little choice but to watch as Virginia and the South considered the question of secession.

In the first few months after the election, states from the lower South began to put the machinery of secession into motion. South Carolina acted first, quickly calling a state convention and voting to secede on December 20, 1860. Six other states soon followed, as

Mississippi, Alabama, Florida, Georgia, Louisiana, and Texas each voted to leave the United States. By moving swiftly and decisively, and before Lincoln could be inaugurated, they hoped to strike a preemptive blow in defense of slavery and force other slaveholding states (which would otherwise be outnumbered by the free states in the U.S. Congress) to join them. With unparalleled speed the new Confederate states formed a provisional government at Montgomery, Alabama, and by early February 1861 had elected Jefferson Davis of Mississippi the new nation's first president.

While all this happened in the deep South, slaveholding states along the border continued to resist secession. As the winter wore into 1861, Virginia, North Carolina, Tennessee, Kentucky, Maryland, Delaware, Missouri, and Arkansas each debated their options in the crisis. It was to Virginia, however, that all eyes turned. The state held more slaves and slaveholders than any other in 1860 and, just as important, housed the majority of the South's industrial capacity. Both Abraham Lincoln and Jefferson Davis recognized that if Virginia left the Union several other states would likely follow, and both men sought to sway the Old Dominion's decision. Most early indications of Virginia's actions seemed to be in Lincoln's favor. When the state held a vote in February 1861 for delegates to a state convention to determine whether Virginia would secede, residents from across the state (including Augusta County) voted overwhelmingly for Unionist candidates.

As Virginians debated, events farther south pushed the crisis to a breaking point. After the secession of South Carolina, U.S. Major Robert Anderson moved his troops into Fort Sumter, a Federal garrison off the coast of Charleston, South Carolina, from the less-defendable Fort Moultrie. Sitting in the middle of the Charleston harbor, Fort Sumter could control all naval traffic into and out of the Southern port. More important to both Confederate and Union leaders, the fort had become a crucial test of how the Federal government would respond to secession. Lincoln hoped to hold Federal property in seceded states, but by early April 1861 the garrison had run dangerously low on supplies and soon would have to be either reinforced or abandoned. Lincoln refused to abandon Federal property and Confederate authorities in Charleston refused to allow him to resupply the fort. Events came to a head in the predawn darkness of April 12, 1861, when Confederate cannons opened fire on a Federal ship attempting to resupply the fort. The American Civil War had begun.

Living the Civil War in Augusta and Franklin

Lincoln responded to the shelling of Fort Sumter by calling for 75,000 troops to be raised for putting down the Confederate rebellion. All states, including Virginia, would be required to supply men and munitions for the new army. Furious that Lincoln had apparently forced a fight at Sumter, and recoiling at the thought of providing soldiers for a campaign against fellow Southerners, Virginians voted on April 17, 1861, to secede from the United States. The shift in sentiment throughout Virginia was dramatic, as men and women across the Old Dominion suddenly found themselves enthusiastic supporters of secession. As Lincoln had feared, the state was soon followed by Arkansas, North Carolina, and Tennessee, bringing vast new stores of manpower and materiel into the Confederacy.

Once the war came, everything in Augusta and Franklin changed. For two communities that had resisted such a war so stridently, both Augusta and Franklin threw themselves into the fighting with remarkable speed and commitment. Newspapers in both counties, which had generally preached calm deliberation during the secession crisis, suddenly demonized their new enemies and exhorted local men to enlist in the new armies. Men on both sides of the border raced to join local regiments. Several hundred men in Augusta enlisted within the first few weeks after Virginia seceded, and more than 1,500 would sign up by August 1861. While fewer men signed up in Franklin to fight during these early months, the U.S. established a military base, Camp Slifer, to the southeast of Chambersburg, which soon flooded the county with Union soldiers.

Those in both counties who did not enlist threw themselves into supporting the armies. Women sewed uniforms and flags, often presenting them to local regiments in elaborate ceremonies, along with any other item a soldier might find useful in the field. Men who had not signed up themselves offered encouragement to their friends who had, wrote patriotic articles for the newspapers, and predicted that victory would be both glorious and quick. In the years to come, people on the home front would be asked continually to sacrifice by purchasing war bonds, giving up food so the army could eat, and sending new men to the front in order to replace those who had died. Indeed, throughout the war, people at home played a crucial role in supporting the armies on both sides by sending supplies and soldiers to the front lines. Perhaps just as important, the letters and newspapers they sent their soldiers brought news of home and allowed them to connect with loved ones fighting far away.

Soldiers wrote home often, describing the hardships, terror, and tedium that marked army life during the long years of war. The earliest letters often evoked the romance of war as young men on both sides waited eagerly for their chance to prove themselves in battle. Some described camp life in elaborate detail for their families back home; others speculated when the first great battle of the war would take place and predicted with confidence who the victor would be. Men from both communities comforted themselves and their families with their firm belief that God favored their side in the conflict. Confident in the righteousness of their cause, soldiers on both sides could not wait for the fighting to begin.

Only three months after the firing on Fort Sumter, these soldiers got their wish. On July 21, 1861, Union and Confederate armies clashed in the first major battle of the war at a place called Manassas Junction, near Bull Run Creek, just 30 miles southwest of Washington, D.C. After initially being pushed back, the Confederates eventually overran the Union lines and forced the Federals to retreat toward Washington. Casualties had been roughly similar on both sides, but the fact that the Union retreated was all that mattered to most people. In Augusta, people cheered as news poured in across the telegraph wires of their victory at Manassas. Augusta's regiments had been at the heart of the battle—losing five men killed and 16 wounded—and the county took pride in the role their soldiers played in the victory. Franklin County residents, for their part, were stunned by the news. No local regiments participated in the battle, but that did little to soothe the humiliation of defeat.

Confederates rode the emotional wave of their victory at Manassas through the rest of the year. Their hastily assembled army had proven that the Southern states could defend their claims to independence, bolstering hopes that the new nation could survive. Chagrined by defeat, Lincoln decided to find a better military leader and appointed Major General George B. McClellan head of the Union armies. McClellan spent the fall and winter of 1861–62 organizing and training his army in preparation for an assault on Richmond, Virginia, the new capital of the Confederacy. By taking the seat of the Confederate government, McClellan hoped he could end the war in a single decisive campaign.

While McClellan's men massed for an assault on Richmond, Confederate General Thomas "Stonewall" Jackson received orders to go on the offensive in the Shenandoah Valley. Jefferson Davis's military advisor in Richmond, Robert E. Lee, hoped Jackson would be able to occupy Union armies in the area long enough to prevent them from joining McClellan's force in the march on Richmond. The longer Jackson distracted Federal troops in the Valley, reasoned Lee, the fewer soldiers McClellan would have at his disposal for the planned assault. Lee also believed that it was crucial for Jackson to prevent the Union from occupying the Valley, where counties like Augusta teemed with crops and supplies that Confederate armies would need during the war.

Jackson marched his men up and down the Valley in a mystifying series of moves designed to baffle the Federals. The Confederates (made up, in large measure, by men from Augusta and neighboring counties) confused their opponents by marching over the Blue Ridge Mountains and then, after loading soldiers onto trains waiting on the other side, mysteriously reappearing in the Valley the next day. By relying on local farmers (who knew the terrain intimately) and his mapmaker (Jedediah Hotchkiss of Augusta County), Jackson could navigate the Valley better than any Union army. Indeed, Jackson's Confederates won all their battles in the Valley—though the fighting sent a constant stream of wounded men into Staunton, giving the town the appearance of one large hospital—and prevented Federal troops from joining McClellan's army. Jackson's masterful campaign in the Valley cemented his status as a hero among Confederates, particularly those in Augusta County who knew he had saved their homes from being overrun by Union soldiers.

While Jackson won engagements in the Valley, McClellan began lumbering with his army up the peninsula that led to Richmond in the spring of 1862. Though his men eventually came within six miles of the city, close enough to hear the ringing of Richmond's church bells, the Union general hesitated to attack. As he would time and again, McClellan overestimated the strength of his opponents, mistakenly believing his own force badly outnumbered. The new commander of the Army of Northern Virginia, Robert E. Lee, seized the opportunity presented by McClellan's hesitation. Attacking the Federals in a bold offensive campaign, Lee defeated McClellan in a series of clashes that became known as the Seven Days Battles, pushing the Union army away from the gates of Richmond.

Having won Richmond a temporary reprieve, Lee and Jackson moved north to challenge the other Union army in Virginia, this one commanded by General John Pope, before McClellan could reinforce it. After a series of flanking maneuvers on both sides, the two armies clashed for a second time near Manassas Junction. Fighting on the same ground where they had met a little more than a year before, Confederates and Federals savaged one another for three days in late August 1862. A series of miscalculations by Pope—combined with McClellan's refusal to reinforce him—allowed Lee to gain another decisive victory for the Confederates, who lost 9,200 men in the battle while the Union lost 16,000. Units from Augusta and Franklin counties suffered greatly in the fighting. Augusta's 5th Virginia Infantry lost 14 killed and 91 wounded; Franklin's 107th Pennsylvania Infantry lost 11 killed and 106 wounded and missing.

His victories over McClellan and Pope having pushed Union forces back to Washington, D.C., Lee decided to invade the North in the late summer of 1862. During the previous spring, the Confederacy had been defeated in several battles in the western theater of the war, losing control of Tennessee, New Orleans, and most of the Mississippi River in the process. Lee believed an invasion of Union territory would help turn the tide of the war and possibly prompt countries such as Britain and France to grant the Confederacy diplomatic recognition. Moreover, by menacing Washington, D.C., Lee knew he could draw more Union troops away from Richmond. Just as crucial to the Confederate war effort, the invasion would also allow his army to forage in Northern territory rather than continue to strip what was left on Virginia's farms. That September, Lee pushed his way into southern Maryland, forcing McClellan to chase him.

McClellan finally caught up with Lee's army in Maryland near a creek called Antietam on September 17, 1862. The battle that followed produced the bloodiest single day of the war, with nearly 6,000 men killed and 17,000 wounded. The 107th Pennsylvania from Franklin County found itself in the middle of some of the most vicious fighting, leaving 19 dead on the field and 45 wounded. Augusta's regiments endured nearly as much, accounting for five of the dead and 37 of the wounded. As night fell on the battered Confederates, Lee retreated to the edge of the Potomac River. When McClellan did not renew the attack the next day, Lee took advantage of the respite by slipping back across the river into Virginia. Though the battle killed more Union soldiers than Confederate, Lee lost a higher percentage of his army than McClellan, and the Confederate retreat across the Potomac granted the U.S. a strategic victory.

Lincoln seized on the costly victory as the opportunity he needed to issue a preliminary Emancipation Proclamation. On September 22, 1862, only days after the Battle of Antietam, Lincoln announced that all slaves residing in states still in rebellion on January 1, 1863, would be declared forever free. At its base, the proclamation was primarily a war measure. Lincoln hoped to entice states in rebellion to return to the Union by promising that their slaves would be exempted from emancipation if they returned before 1863, thereby bringing the war to an end sooner. Slave states still in the Union, such as Kentucky and Maryland, were exempted from the decree, as were parts of the Confederacy already under Union control. In effect, the Emancipation Proclamation would free no slaves immediately but promised to make the Northern war effort after 1863 as much about ending slavery as preserving the Union.

Lincoln's announcement drew strong reactions. For many Confederates, the decree only proved what they had always believed about the Republicans' plans for slavery. People in Augusta County already had no intention of returning to the Union, Emancipation Proclamation or no, but the measure steeled their resolve. Secession had clearly been the wisest course, they said, and now only Confederate victory could preserve their Southern way of life. Some even believed that Lincoln hoped his decree would encourage slaves to rise up violently against their masters. In Franklin County, Republicans faithfully defended and supported Lincoln's measure. Democrats in the county, however, balked at the idea of fighting for anything other than restoring the Union and questioned whether the president had the authority to issue such an order. Even as a war measure, Franklin Democrats feared, the proclamation could have the unintended effect of uniting the South more tightly than ever before.

Franklin's men and women had more immediate concerns, however, when 1,800 Confederate cavalrymen under the command of J. E. B. Stuart rode into Chambersburg in October 1862. Stuart's cavalry had been sent on a scouting mission by Lee and slipped into Pennsylvania undetected by riding around the entire Union Army. With no Federal troops in the immediate area, the citizens of Chambersburg could do little but watch as Stuart's men pilfered food, clothing, horses, and other supplies from the town. A shoe store was emptied immediately and a storehouse for U.S. military arms was torched. The Confederates also rounded up several free blacks in Chambersburg to take with them south, likely as slaves. Finally, after they had stolen all they could carry, the raiders set fire to several buildings in town and returned to Virginia.

Many of Franklin's soldiers were only a dozen miles away during the raid and felt humiliated when they heard the news. Rather than rail against the Confederates, however, most of the soldiers (and even the civilians in the county itself) blamed their inept political and military leaders for allowing such an invasion. Indeed, displeasure with Lincoln had been mounting in the county (and the

North as a whole) since the loss at Bull Run. When the November 1862 congressional elections arrived, they brought widespread victories for the Democrats in the North. The Republicans retained control of the U.S. House and Senate, but voters' discontent with the course of the war—and Lincoln's Emancipation Proclamation in particular—had sent more Democrats to Congress.

Lincoln, too, felt it was time for a change. Immediately following the November elections, he sacked McClellan as head of Union armies in the East and placed Ambrose E. Burnside—a major general who had enjoyed some modest battlefield victories—in his stead. Burnside immediately began to march his army toward Richmond, but had trouble crossing the Rappahannock River just outside Fredericksburg. Robert E. Lee, who had arrived on the other side of the river with his Army of Northern Virginia, took up a strong position at Fredericksburg and waited for the Union to advance. Burnside's army finally crossed the river on December 11, 1862, and began assaulting the Confederate positions two days later. Lee's men, however, had taken positions on high ground that proved nearly impossible to penetrate. Wave after wave of Union regiments attempted to break the Confederate lines, most of them assaulting Marye's Heights, and each failing. By nightfall, nearly 13,000 Union troops lay dead or wounded (approximately the same number lost at Antietam), while the Confederates lost 5,000 men. Regiments from both Augusta and Franklin participated in the fight. Franklin's 126th Pennsylvania made the final charge up Marye's Heights, losing 12 men killed, 57 wounded, and 14 missing. Augusta's 5th Virginia lost no men, although 11 were wounded.

The winter of 1862–63 brought with it both celebration and despair. Northerners were appalled by their loss at Fredericksburg. Burnside was soon removed as commander, to be replaced by Joseph Hooker as head of the Army of the Potomac. Southerners were elated with the outcome at Fredericksburg but also found themselves preoccupied with a more ominous development. As promised, Lincoln issued his Emancipation Proclamation on January 1, offering freedom to all slaves residing in territory not yet controlled by the Union. People in Augusta, as throughout the Confederacy, denounced it as a political move designed to distract attention from Lincoln's failures and the Confederacy's victories. Many Northerners denounced the proclamation as well, while others hoped it would help speed the war's end. As the opposing armies settled into camps as they usually did during winter, preparing for the campaigns that would return with the warmth of spring, people in both counties debated what the war would bring next.

In the North, some of the most vicious debates centered around the proposed arming of blacks. Thaddeus Stevens, a Franklin resident and prominent Republican, led the fight in Congress for arming the Union with black soldiers. Stevens, with many of the Radical Republicans, argued that arming former slaves who ran away from the South could turn a Confederate asset (its enslaved labor force) into a tremendous liability. Northern Democrats, however, vehemently opposed the measure. Democrats argued that black men could not be counted on in battle, or in anything else for that matter, and to hand them rifles would be to invite a race war. While the Federal government debated the wisdom of such a measure, Massachusetts began raising the first black Union regiment: the 54th Massachusetts. When news of the new regiment reached Franklin's black neighborhoods, men rushed at the opportunity to fight for the Union and black freedom. Forty-five men from Franklin signed up for the 54th Massachusetts and another 13 enlisted in its successor, the 55th. Confederates responded to the creation of the new regiments by promising to kill every captured black soldier, along with any white officers who commanded them, or sell them into slavery. White Southerners would not accept armed blacks as legitimate soldiers.

African Americans in Augusta County also seized every opportunity for freedom. Wherever Federal troops went, slaves throughout the South used their presence as an opportunity to throw off the shackles of slavery and abandon the plantation, rushing to Union lines by the thousands. Indeed, of the blacks who would fight for the Union during the war, including those serving in the 54th and 55th Massachusetts, many had only recently escaped slavery and enlisted at the first opportunity. Union troops had marched throughout the Valley during the campaigns of 1862, providing enslaved men and women in Augusta the chance to escape their bondage. Even when no Union armies were near, slaves in the county ran away in ever increasing numbers as the war progressed. Word of the Emancipation Proclamation had reached black ears as well as white, and living so close to the border afforded Augusta's slaves more opportunities for escape than their counterparts toiling in states farther south.

Even with their slaves running away at every opportunity, the institution of slavery remained at the heart of the Confederate war effort. Over the course of the war, the Confederacy managed to send more than 80 percent of its eligible white males into the army, a feat possible only because enslaved men and women remained on Southern plantations growing the food that fed and the cotton that clothed those soldiers. Some of the more wealthy soldiers, often officers, brought their slaves with them into the army, to wait on them in camp and provide some of the comforts of home while on campaign. As the years progressed, the Confederate government began requiring masters to lend their slaves to the war effort, using them to dig trenches, build breastworks for defenses, and toil in Richmond's Tredegar Iron Works (which produced more than half the cannons used by the Confederacy). Confederates used their slaves to every advantage they could during the war, even debating in 1865 whether to force them to fight in Confederate battalions.

When spring came in 1863, Hooker crossed the Rappahannock River and encamped at a place called Chancellorsville, a few miles west of Fredericksburg. Hooker believed he could compel the Confederates to fight by taking up this position only ten miles from Lee's entrenched army, in a place nicknamed the Wilderness by locals because of its dense forest and thick undergrowth. The Union's superior numbers (they outnumbered the Confederates two to one) proved of little use, however, in such heavily wooded areas. In a daring move, Lee divided his force and attacked separated portions of Hooker's army one at a time, killing or wounding 17,000 Federals while driving the rest back to the Rappahannock. The 126th Pennsylvania from Franklin lost four killed and 38 wounded or missing in action. The Confederate victory, though, had come at great cost to Lee's army: 13,000 killed, wounded, or missing. Augusta's 5th Virginia lost nine men killed, with another 116 wounded in the battle. More distressing, Stonewall Jackson had been accidentally shot in the arm by Confederate soldiers as he rode through the woods. When Jackson succumbed to pneumonia several days after having his arm amputated, Lee lost his most trusted and gifted general.

Lee took another gamble after his costly victory at Chancellorsville. Marching northward, the Confederates made a second invasion of the North with the same hopes that had brought them there in 1862. If they could forage on Northern farms, they would be able to relieve the already ravaged Virginia countryside. If they could threaten Washington, D.C., they would be able to draw Federal troops away from Richmond and possibly out of Virginia. And if they could bring the ravages of war to Union states, perhaps the North's will to continue the fight would break and thereby bring the long war to an end. In the meantime, the Union Army was forced to pursue Lee across the Potomac, on his way to Pennsylvania.

The Army of Northern Virginia marched into Chambersburg, in Franklin County, in late June 1863. Lee issued orders that civilian property was to be respected by all troops, though that did not stop Confederates from rounding up local African Americans as "runaway slaves" to be returned to Virginia. Terrified blacks hid in the woods, in barns, in wheat fields, and anywhere else that might offer shelter from the invaders, who seemed to be capturing every African American they could find. Even women and children were not spared, and soon wagons full of "recaptured runaways" began carting blacks from Franklin down to slavery in Virginia. For local white residents, the return of Confederates proved less destructive than J. E. B. Stuart's raid in 1862—no buildings were burned this time—although they again found that they could do little but watch as the Confederates seized whatever they thought useful and paid for it in worthless Confederate scrip.

Union troops caught up with Lee's army near the town of Gettysburg, Pennsylvania. Cavalry scouting for the Union Army, now commanded by General George Meade who had replaced Joseph Hooker only three days before, stumbled upon a group of Confederates on the morning of July 1, 1863. Over the next three days, more men would die in the Battle of Gettysburg than in any other battle on American soil. Confederate and Union soldiers slaughtered each other in places whose names would become infamous for the savagery of the fighting that took place there: Devil's Den,

Cemetery Ridge, Little Round Top, the Wheatfield. Both armies lost tremendous numbers of men—23,000 casualties for the Union and 28,000 for the Confederates—but it was Robert E. Lee who could least afford the carnage. After losing more than a third of his soldiers, Lee pulled back and retreated once again into Virginia, much of his army again passing through Franklin County on their way south.

At almost the same moment, news arrived in the east of a great Union victory in the West. On July 4, the last major Confederate holdout on the Mississippi River, Vicksburg, fell to Federal guns under the command of Ulysses S. Grant. Control of Vicksburg meant the Union now controlled the entire Mississippi River, and most of the western portions of the Confederacy. Northern sentiment was buoyed by the twin victories at Gettysburg and Vicksburg, which had dealt harsh blows to their enemies. Indeed, the news struck Confederates hard; they had followed the long siege at Vicksburg in the newspapers and believed that Lee's invasion of the North would succeed in 1863 where it had failed in 1862. Despite recent losses, however, many white Southerners maintained a tenacious faith in the Confederacy born of the long years of hardship they had endured. After all they had sacrificed for their new nation, few in Augusta or elsewhere in the Confederacy could conceive of the war ending in anything less than rebel victory.

Lincoln, for his part, believed that he had finally found in Grant a general who could match the military cunning of Robert E. Lee. Following another Union victory at Chattanooga, Tennessee, Lincoln brought Grant east in March 1864 and placed him at the head of all Union armies. Grant set up his headquarters with the Army of the Potomac and immediately began making plans to attack Lee's Army of Northern Virginia. Bitter campaigns and bloody battles had reduced Lee's force to 64,000 men, while Grant's ability to draw soldiers from the North's larger population meant that his own army remained 115,000 strong. Rather than focus on capturing Richmond, as other Union commanders had, Grant intended to use his numerical advantage to pursue Lee relentlessly, wearing down the Confederacy's most powerful army through what became a war of attrition.

Upon arriving in Virginia, Grant also decided that something must be done about the Shenandoah Valley. For most of the war,

Confederate armies had relied on the Valley's rich resources for food and supplies. Indeed, railroads lines that ran through Staunton and Lynchburg allowed Confederates throughout Virginia to depend on crops and munitions gathered in places like Augusta County. If they were going to subdue Lee's army, Grant believed, the Union would have to destroy the resources that sustained them. Accordingly, Grant ordered General Franz Sigel to march his 6,500 men into the Valley and capture Staunton in Augusta County. Sigel, however, never made it that far. On May 15, 1864, Sigel's men were defeated at the Battle of New Market, north of Augusta, by a Confederate force of 5,000 commanded by John C. Breckinridge, the Southern Democratic candidate for president in 1860.

After relieving Sigel of command, Grant ordered General David Hunter to mount another campaign in the Valley to destroy the railroad depots that supplied the Confederate armies. Marching 15,000 men into Augusta County, Hunter captured Staunton and then proceeded south toward Lynchburg, another center of Confederate supply. Hunter's men ravaged much of the countryside as they marched, taking what they needed from local civilians and often burning what they did not. The harsh tactics of Hunter's men came in part from their earlier experiences fighting Confederate guerrillas in West Virginia, where distinctions between soldiers and civilians often blurred. Upon reaching the town of Lexington, just south of Augusta County, Hunter ordered his troops to burn the Virginia Military Institute and the home of John Letcher, governor of Virginia. Hunter's campaign ravaged the Valley, leaving barren fields and destroyed homes where some of the richest farms in all of North America had once stood.

The Confederates responded in kind to the desecration of the Valley. Lee ordered General Jubal Early to sweep into the Valley to counter Hunter's marauding troops and end the destruction. After successfully defeating Hunter near Lynchburg (the Federals subsequently retreated into West Virginia), Early turned north and marched on Washington, D.C. Early's battle-hardened troops appeared just outside the Federal capital in early July, producing panic in the city and forcing Grant to dispatch troops to help defend the capital. The Confederates remained on the outskirts of

Washington for two days before passing through sections of Maryland and Pennsylvania on their way back to Virginia. In addition to distracting Union forces currently dogging Lee, Early decided to retaliate against the North for the destruction wrought in places like Augusta and the brutality that had been shown to citizens in the Valley.

On July 28, 1864, General John McCausland received orders from Early to capture Chambersburg and burn it, unless the citizens paid $100,000 in gold or $500,000 in Federal greenbacks. McCausland immediately began marching his troops northward, entering the town on July 30. Already having sustained two previous Confederate incursions, many people fled the town when word came of the approaching troops. Those who remained in Chambersburg were rounded up by McCausland's raiders and read the ransom demands. When the town refused to accede, McCausland ordered his men to set Chambersburg ablaze. Most of the damage concentrated on the center of town along Main Street, where the courthouse was destroyed. Homes and businesses throughout Chambersburg, however, burned to the ground as the fire spread rapidly from rooftop to rooftop and gutted the city.

Northerners were outraged at the burning of Chambersburg. Grant immediately placed Major General Philip H. Sheridan at the head of a newly created Army of the Shenandoah, ordering him to chase Early down and turn the Valley into a "barren waste." Picking up where Hunter had left off, Sheridan swept through the Valley, destroying everything that could be of use to the rebels. In their relentless march up the Valley, Sheridan's troops burned or consumed nearly every barn, field, crop, and animal they came upon. Jubal Early's troops clashed with the Federals in several engagements but never were able to dislodge Sheridan from the Valley as they had Hunter. The Confederates came close once when they surprised Sheridan's troops in an attack near Cedar Creek in October 1864, overrunning and scattering the Union soldiers. When Early's exhausted men stopped to forage in the Union camps, however, they were routed in a counterattack led personally by Sheridan. With only Confederate guerrillas left in the region to challenge him, Sheridan controlled the Valley until he rejoined Grant's forces in 1865.

As Sheridan stripped the Valley of what little remained, Grant continued to chase Lee and his army. In early May 1864, the two generals fought each other to a standstill at the Wilderness, on the same battlefield where Lee had defeated Joseph Hooker a year earlier. Unlike Hooker, though, Grant refused to retreat and only two days later slammed his army into Lee's at Spotsylvania, where each side again endured tremendous casualties without either emerging victorious. As both armies moved closer to Richmond, they clashed again in early June at the Battle of Cold Harbor, where Grant attempted to dislodge the Confederates from entrenched lines by ordering a frontal assault on Lee's troops. The result was a Union disaster, with 7,000 killed and wounded while the Confederates lost only 1,500. Grant finally pinned Lee down at Petersburg, where the Confederates dug trenches and settled in for a siege that would ultimately last nine months. In seven weeks of unprecedented bloodshed, Lee had lost 35,000 men killed, wounded, and missing, while Grant had lost an astounding 65,000 men.

The immense casualty lists generated by Grant's dogged campaign soon proved to be a political liability for Lincoln. With the November 1864 elections approaching, Democrats in the North seized on the massive death tolls and the war-weariness of the Northern public as their opportunity to retake the White House. They nominated the deposed general George McClellan as their candidate for president, promising to end the war's push for emancipation—and possibly the war itself. Confederates, just as weary after four years, followed the election as closely as any Northerner, hoping that a defeat of Lincoln would mean peace between the two nations. Indeed, with Grant mired in a standoff with Lee and the war stretching into the foreseeable future, Lincoln's reelection prospects appeared bleak. Then, in early September 1864, Union general William Tecumseh Sherman captured the city of Atlanta after a protracted campaign. The news shot across the North and abruptly changed Lincoln's election prospects. With reports of Sheridan's successes in subduing the Valley adding to renewed Northern optimism, Lincoln won a landslide victory in November, taking 212 electoral votes to McClellan's 21.

After Lincoln's reelection, Confederates resigned themselves to resuming the fight. The Army of Northern Virginia, however, could not sustain more bloodletting. Grant's relentless campaigns in 1864 had bled Lee's army nearly dry, and the nine months of siege warfare that followed had further eroded the Confederate ranks. On April 2, 1865, Lee escaped from his confinement at Petersburg with the tattered remnants of his once great force, hoping to revive his army by joining it with Joseph Johnston's troops in North Carolina. At the same moment, the Confederate government abandoned Richmond and fled south, burning part of the city in their retreat. Within two days, Abraham Lincoln walked through Richmond's charred and empty streets, escorted by a few armed guards and greeted by jubilant freed slaves.

The momentous events of the next two weeks came in rapid succession. Grant's men pursued Lee until the Confederate general could run no more. With his army dissolving in front of him, and no prospects for reinforcements, Lee finally surrendered the Army of Northern Virginia to Grant on April 9, 1865. Every unit from Augusta and Franklin counties still in the field witnessed the historic moment, which marked the end of the war for both sides. Joyous celebrations broke out across the Union, as telegraphs sped news of the surrender to Northern communities like Franklin County. Confederates from Lee's army began making their way home, straggling into places like Augusta County to begin rebuilding the lives they had left behind four years before. Less than a week after Lee's capitulation, a frustrated Confederate sympathizer, John Wilkes Booth, assassinated Lincoln on April 14 as the president relaxed at a play in Ford's Theater in Washington, D.C. Both sides of the Mason-Dixon Line mourned that April, Northerners for their lost president and Confederates for their lost nation.

The Aftermath of War in Augusta and Franklin

By the time Lee surrendered, the war had wrought vast changes in Franklin and Augusta counties. Franklin had sustained incursions from three separate Confederate forces, the last of which left only after having burned much of the town to the ground. Many of Franklin's black residents had been kidnapped during these invasions and taken to Virginia when the rebels retreated. Now that the war was over, their families sought desperately to find those who had been stolen and bring them home. Soldiers from the county who had survived, both black and white, came home as soon as they could. Their return celebrated by family and friends, these soldiers found a county that had been ravaged by the demands of war. Many, however, would not return, and with more than 620,000 men from both sides killed in only four years almost everyone in the nation mourned at least one person who would never come home again. It would take years, even generations, to rebuild what the war had destroyed.

The changes that reshaped Augusta County were even greater than those in Franklin. More than 5,000 enslaved men and women had been freed in Augusta, upending the county's entire prewar economic, social, and political systems. To help these former bondsmen make the difficult transition from slavery to freedom, the U.S. government established the Freedmen's Bureau at the close of the war, charging the agency with providing assistance to ex-slaves and mediating between the freedmen and their former masters. An agent of the Bureau set up an office in Staunton in July 1865, a presence that rankled most white residents in the county until the Bureau shut down in December 1868. While the freed slaves sought to assert their newfound political rights in the county, defeated Confederate soldiers returned to Augusta to rebuild their homes and lives. Many found that their farms and businesses had been destroyed, either by the foraging of Confederate armies or the raids of Hunter and Sheridan. For these defeated soldiers, everything about the county they left in 1861 had changed by the time they returned in 1865.

The years that followed were difficult ones for both communities. Whites and blacks in Augusta clashed repeatedly—sometimes violently—as whites attempted to resurrect much of the old social order and blacks sought to live as free people. The continued Federal presence, both in the county and in Virginia, proved a tremendous comfort to the freedmen and a painful reminder to local whites of the struggle they had lost. For those in Franklin, rebuilding Chambersburg proved the most daunting task. Leaders from the county repeatedly petitioned state and Federal officials for assistance in reconstructing the city (the only Union town burned by the Confederates), usually without success. While they worked to rebuild, many in Franklin found themselves as outraged by the early course of Reconstruction as people in Augusta, although their anger was instead directed at President Andrew Johnson's forgiving approach toward the defeated Confederates. One of the most painful tasks of the postwar period, however, was shared by people from both counties. For years after the fighting ended, families in Augusta and Franklin sought to locate the remains of loved ones who had died and been hastily buried on battlefields far from home, reinterring them when they could in more familiar surroundings.

Even after the rifles were silenced, the Civil War continued to echo across Augusta and Franklin. For those who lived through it, the war was something they would spend the rest of their lives trying to understand. Veteran organizations throughout the country grew with each passing decade, with groups like the Grand Army of the Republic in the North and the United Confederate Veterans in the South boasting tens of thousands of members. Veterans held reunions, wrote articles about their wartime exploits, told their stories to the young men and women of the next generation. Committees erected statues and dedicated parks to memorialize the dead and inspire the living. Flag and memorial days became annual events in the country, when graves of veterans would be decorated with U.S. or Confederate banners. On the anniversaries of great battles, ex-soldiers gathered with friends and former enemies in ceremonies that ranged from solemn to celebratory.

More than anything, people continued to debate the causes and consequences of the war. In time, the white South would come to imagine the days before the Civil War as an idyllic world of loyal slaves and refined society that had been needlessly destroyed by Lincoln's armies. Northerners, for their part, came to accept much of this Southern myth, as white men and women from both sections found ways to reunite in their shared disdain for African Americans willing to assert their political rights in the postwar era. Black Americans—whose lives, more than any others, had been

changed by the war—never stopped championing the righteousness of emancipation, the contributions of black soldiers to Union
successes, or the central role slavery played in the conflict. As the
twentieth century approached, however, their voices were increasingly drowned out by competing interpretations of the war and its
legacy.

Historians continue to debate how communities like Augusta
and Franklin came to find themselves on opposite sides of the battlefield at places like Antietam, Gettysburg, and the Wilderness. Indeed, our attempts to understand the descent of the nation into
four years of brutal war continue to defy easy explanations. The
documents in this casebook provide a way into the discussions and
debates that raged in both communities during those uncertain
times. They provide a window into the difficult and often painful
choices that confronted people throughout the Civil War.

I
Slavery

1. Augusta County

Charlottesville Oct 8th 1852

Dear Husband I write you a letter to let you
know of my distress my master has sold albert to a trader
on monday court day and myself and other child is for sale also
and I want you to let hear from you very soon before
next cort if you can I dont know when I dont want you to
wait till chrismas I want you to tell dr Hamilton and
your master if either will buy me they can attend to it
now and then I can go afterwards I dont want a trader to
get me they asked me if I had got any person to buy me
and I told them no they told me to the court house too they
never put me up a man buy the name of brady bought
albert and is gone I dont know whare they say he lives in scott
esville my things is in several places some is in staun
ton and if I should be sold I dont know what will be
come of them I dont expect to meet with the luck to get
that way tell if am quite heart sick nothing more I
am and ever will be your kind Wife Maria Perkins
To Richard Perkins

Maria Perkins to Richard Perkins, October 8, 1852

Maria Perkins, a slave, writes to her husband Richard in Augusta County about the sale of their son, Albert, and the imminent sale of herself with their other child. Maria hoped that Richard would be able to convince his master to purchase Maria and their child. While very few slaves could read or write, most would face the sale of themselves or a loved one at one point in their lives.

Charllotesville Oct 8th 1852

Dear Husband

I write you a letter to let you know of my distress my master has sold albert to a trader on monday court day and myself and other child is for sale also and I want to you let hear from you very soon before next cort if you can I dont know when I dont want you to wait till christmas I want you to tell dr Hamelton or your master if either will buy me they can attend to it know and then I can go afterwards I dont want a trader to get me they asked me if I had got any person to buy me and I told them no they took me to the court houste too & they never put me up a man buy the name of brady bought albert and is gone I dont kow whare they say he lives in Scottesville my things is in several places some is in staunton and if I should be sold I dont kow what will become of them I dont expect to meet with the luck to get that way till I am quite heart sick nothing more I am and ever will be your kind Wife

Maria Perkins

Diary of Joseph A. Waddell, October 15, 1856

Owner and editor of the Staunton Spectator *until 1860, Joseph Waddell catalogues his possessions, including his two slaves, in his diary and declares his*

revulsion at the buying and selling of human beings. While he said that he ab-
horred slavery, Waddell also did not believe the institution could be ended soon
in the United States. Like many Southerners, Waddell believed that the efforts
of abolitionists to end slavery immediately in the South endangered the lives of
white Southerners and made the gradual end of slavery more difficult.

Wednesday night, Oct. 15th 1856
     * * * This morning the ground was covered with snow, and everything without wore a wintry aspect. It commenced snowing yesterday afternoon, and continued, at intervals, till late to-day I have no recollection of such a storm so early in the season before.
     Mr. Tate and Mary returned from the wedding this evening, having been detained by the storm. Mr. T. + Mary acted as attendants—father and daughter!—but he only took the place of one who failed to be there.————I was at the Corporation office to-day, and looked over the report of the assessment of real estate in town, lately made. I find quite a difference between the assessment and the appraisement by commissioners of my father's property. The brick house was appraised at $3000, and assessed at $2500; the stone house was appraised at $1700 and assessed at $2000; the garden cot + stable assessed at $800 and appraised $900 respectively. This reminds me to enter a list of *my* possessions here, at this date, for the gratification of curiosity hereafter. First, I presume my interest in the Printing office, accounts and all, is worth at least $3000; then I have 10 shares in the Central Bank—worth at this time probably $900—I have a Central Railroad Coupon bond for $1000—worth $800. I have bonds, which with interest and dividends coming due, will amount to about $1000 on the 15th of January next; the balance of my interest in the estate (exclusive of the property in which the widow has a life estate) is some $1500 to $2000; Selena is valued at $1000 (I have been offered that for her), and Moses is probably worth $200 to $300. Our furniture, silver +c (including Virginia's) is worth some $200—Besides I have books and pictures—the former accumulating rather too fast for my means—which might bring $100 to $150. Aggregate of *my wealth*—$8700. I think this rather under than above the real value. The following is an inventory of our furniture made out for the Commissioner

of Revenue, on Feb. 1st 1856: Bureau $30—2 tables $3—2 chairs $8.—Andirons Shovel + Tongs and Fender $5.—Bedstead $13. Bedding $41.50.—Lamps $5—Washstand, $5.—old Bureau $3.— Wardrobe $3.—Bowl + Pitcher $1.50.—Book stand (called What-not) $10.—2 Lounges $5.—Watch $15.—1/2 doz. Table Spoons $20.—1/2 doz. Tea Spoons $6.—Other Silver $9.—Jewelry (Va's) $20.

Dr McGill proposed to buy Selena to-day, and offered me $1000—I would not have sold her for $20,000, unless she desired to go, or had grossly misbehaved. This thing of speculating on human flesh is utterly horrible to me—the money would eat into my flesh like hot iron. Slavery itself is extremely repulsive to my feelings, and I earnestly desire its extinction everywhere, when it can be done judiciously, and so as to promote the welfare of both races. Yet I am no abolitionist. The day for emancipation with us has not come, and we must wait God's time. For the present all that the most philanthropic can do is to endeavor to ameliorate the institution; but it is hard to do this in the midst of the mischievous interference of outside fanatics. * * *

Staunton Spectator, "Export of Slaves from Virginia," October 11, 1859

The Staunton Spectator *discusses the practice of selling slaves from Virginia to plantations in the lower South states, such as Mississippi and Alabama. The cotton and sugar plantations of the lower South required vast amounts of labor, driving up the price of slaves and creating a lucrative market for slaveholders in states like Virginia to sell their slaves to the lower South for higher prices than they could get at home. While a common practice, it raised questions within Virginia about whether the continued selling of slaves to the lower South would weaken the institution in Virginia.*

The immense exodus of slaves from Virginia and North Carolina is beginning to attract the attention of the press, and serious apprehensions are expressed as to the effect upon the agricultural interests of these States. The "Petersburg Express" states that in Eastern Virginia the places of the thousands of slaves who are annually sold for the cotton fields of Alabama, Mississippi, Arkansas and Texas, are not filled by other laborers, which so disables that section of the State from working its lands profitably, as of necessity to retard seriously its progress and prosperity. In view of the extensive and costly system of internal improvements now in operation and under construction in this State, a new impetus has been given to development and production, an adequate supply of labor is demanded, and yet we are continually subjected to a drainage of our slave labor to supply the wants of the extreme Southern States.

The subject is certainly one of the very highest importance to the people, especially the slave owners of Virginia, and should receive earnest attention and calm deliberation. It opens up a wide field of enquiry as to the probable consequences of this drainage upon the border slave States, not only as it may effect their material progress, but especially as to their political bearings. The effect upon the agricultural interests of the State, though of course important, is not the matter of highest public concern. Where labor is in great demand, it will gradually find its way, and the experience of other States establishes the fact that agricultural interests may prosper, and every other branch of industry and enterprise flourish when there is no slave labor. Eastern Virginia may suffer temporary inconvenience by a diminution of slaves, because her wants are not widely known; but when her necessities become so pressing that she is forced to seek labor, laborers will be found in abundance flocking to her uncultivated fields. But it will be *white* labor—white labor of the North, and of foreign countries. It seems to us that this is the striking aspect of the question. As slave laborers are diminished white laborers, anti-slavery by education and from interest, will supply their place, and it becomes a question of prominent interest what is to be the effect of the exchange upon the cherished and peculiar institution of slavery.—Negroes will continue to be sold at enormous prices as long as they are needed in the Cotton States, where white labor will not answer the purpose. Slave dealers will buy and transport them from the border States to the extreme States just as long as they command high prices, and we agree with the "Express" that there seems to be no prospect of their receding. The consequence will be a steady and constant drain of slaves, and for every one that goes out a white man from the North will in all probability come into Virginia and the neighboring States. It requires no prophetic vision to foresee the result of this kind of operation, in the course of time.

Taking this view of the matter under consideration, it becomes a question for the reflection of the people, and the grave deliberation of political assemblies, what can be done to remedy the evil? The owners of cotton and sugar plantations of the extreme South would prefer to obtain their labor upon cheaper terms by reopening the African slave trade, and there are doubtless those in our own State who would resort to this inhuman traffic for the purpose of "providing for the great and growing deficiency" of negroes to work the tobacco and grain-fields in Eastern Virginia. However effectual this remedy might be, we are loath to believe that any considerable portion of the people would sanction such a movement, even under cover of the Jesuitical plea that "the end justifies the means."

There is still another question brought into view by the consideration of this subject which may assume a different phase from that which it presents in the abstract, when contemplated in connection with the exodus of slaves from Virginia. We allude to the acquisition of territory. When the demand for slaves is already so great, as to effect the constant and perceptible diminution of slaves in the border States, how many would be left in a few years if that demand were quadrupled by the acquisition of Cuba, or other extensive territory requiring slave labor? Is it not the true interest of Virginia and the South generally to oppose the acquisition of territory, that her slaves may remain in her own limits, instead of being exported by thousands to supply the wants of new slave territory?

These are questions of practical importance and should be decided according to the dictates of common sense. There are many in the State of Virginia and throughout the Southern States—men whose devotion to the interests of the South are above suspicion—

who conceive that the permanency of the institution of slavery can only be secured by confining slave labor to its present limits. Not preventing it by prohibiting laws, Wilmot provisos, or even Squatter-sovereignty, from going wherever the Constitution and the laws entitle it to go; but voluntarily declining, as a matter of policy and interest, to take it outside of the area upon which the negro now toils.

Staunton Vindicator, "The Results of African Labor in the New World," February 10, 1860

Responding to criticism of Southern slavery, from both Northern abolitionists and nations such as Great Britain, the Vindicator seeks to demonstrate that slavery has produced tremendous benefits for worldwide civilization. African slavery, argues the newspaper, has allowed nations in the New World to prosper, improved the lives of the slaves, and produced a global market for the products of slave-based agriculture. In contrast, the paper asserts, emancipation has had the opposite effect on countries, producing political instability and destroying black populations.

When Columbus discovered the New World the fact became disclosed that there existed a vast intertropical region, extending from twenty to thirty degrees on each side of the equator, which contained the richest and most prolific soil to be found on the face of the globe, but the immense resources of which, without the employment of African labor, could not be developed.—Africa was populous, teeming with millions of the darkest skinned and wildest tribes, whose prisoners captured in war were continually destroyed. When a field was opened in the hot latitudes of America—the only climate suitable for their employment—their captives, instead of being killed, were purchased and sent hither, where their services have been attended with the most important results.

The Negro races of Africa are estimated at about 60,000,000. Since the commencement of the slaves trade only about five millions have been imported into the New World which amounts to but a small per centage of the numbers slain in their savage warfare. And the exportation of the five millions was, to a great extent, a mere question of death or deportation. Of the whole number of Africans introduced into the New World, 1,700,000 were landed in the British West India possessions, 375,000 (up to 1808) in the United States, and the remainder were sent to other European possessions in the New World. African labor in the tropical regions of the West has done more to advance and extend commerce and the arts of civilization over the world than any other cause that we know of; and to day civilization is from one or two centuries ahead of what it would have been without it—because white labor could not have accomplished what it has performed.

There exist at the present time in the New World, including the United States, Brazil, Cuba and Porti Rico, about 7,000,000 of African slaves, the results of whose labor exceed those of any similar number of persons, white or black, bond or free, to be found anywhere else on the face of the earth. Without descending into particulars, we may state that the annual value of products raised by African slave labor amounts to not less than $400,000,000, nearly $240,000,000 of which is supplied by the United States. In this estimate we include cotton, coffee, sugar, tobacco, rice, naval stores and indigo. The consumption of these articles by the white races of the temperate latitudes has become an immense necessity. Of the general aggregate, the cotton crop of the United States for 1859–60, estimated at 4,200,000 bales may be put down at $200,000,000. The transportation of these immense supplies, their transformation by manufacturing [illegible word] and men [illegible word], in changed forms, give employment to millions of tons of shipping, and afford support to millions upon millions of free white laborers all over the civilized world. By the increase and expansion of commerce civilization has been spread to the remotest corners of the globe, while steamships have been multiplied, railroads extended, and communication of all kinds increased to an extent they would not have reached in a century without the development of the agricultural resources of the tropics in the West by African labor. * * *

* * * If African labor is evil, the North and the civilized world have extracted an immense and incalculable good out of it. This may be said not only of the whites, but of the blacks also. The cotton bales of the United States have kept England and America at peace for forty years, and prevented the whites from mutual slaughter. Emancipation is not only the destruction of African labor, but the extermination of the negroes themselves. All those [illegible word] communities of the New World in which emancipation has been enforced have gone to the dogs, which the blacks among them are gradually dying out, those, on the contrary which have preserved African labor continue to be prosperous, powerful and progressive. Thus, the island of Cuba, though oppressed by an effete monarchy, is worth more to its government and to the world at large than all the other West India islands put together. * * *

* * * The Southern States have a great duty to perform, and one which they owe alike to themselves, to the African laborers committed to their charge, to the stability of government, to commerce, to civilization, and to the happiness and progress of the human race generally, to discharge with fidelity and humanity. The tendency of all communities, but more especially in the enervating climate of the tropics, where African labor is overthrown, is to anarchy on the one hand, and to the one man power on the other. The destruction of African labor by emancipation and the final extinction of the race are synonymous. * * *

* * * When the first census of the United States was taken in 1790, there were 40,000 African slaves in the free States of the North, and 27,000 free negroes, making a total of 67,000. The increase of the slaves of the South has been at the rapid rate of about thirty per cent each decade. Now, had the negroes at the North increased as fast as the negroes of the South, by the end of sixth decade, or in sixty years, they should have amounted to about 326,000; but instead of this, we find that the census of 1850 only gives a total of about 113,000; a part of which was supplied by recruits from the South. What has become of the missing negroes? Some masters, probably to prevent their loss by emancipation, sold their slaves to the South; yet this does not account for their whole disappearance. Every New Yorker and Jerseyman of four score and ten can recollect the time when negroes were more numerous than they are now. He can remember when they [illegible word] [illegible word] docks loading and unloading vessels, inspiriting each other by their loud and sonorous songs; when they labored in the streets; waited in [illegible word] and served in private families.— Where are they now? Where have they mysteriously disappeared? If you want an answer, examine the tumuli in our petterfields [potter's fields], or consult the dissectors in our medical colleges— places to which pneumonia, typhus fever, varioloid, consumption; scrofulous affections, and other wasting diseases engendered often amidst want and filth, have consigned them.

Staunton Spectator, "The Late Slave Murder Case," October 16, 1860

The Spectator *provides an account of the murder trial and conviction of a master who whipped his slave to death. While slaveholders rarely whipped their slaves to the point of death or permanent injury, whippings and other forms of physical punishment were common methods of control on Southern plantations. Local communities sometimes punished slaveholders who treated their slaves with unusual violence, in part as an effort at regulating the practice of slavery by preventing the worst abuses.*

At the term of the Circuit Court of Mecklenburg county, Va., Charles Hudson was tried for the murder of his slave woman Jane, convicted of murder in the second degree, and sentenced to the Penitentiary for eighteen years.

The Tobacco Plant says very truly that it is one of those cases which thoroughly vindicate the Southern character against the aspersions cast upon us by our enemies at the North. It develops what is as true of us as of any other people on the civilized globe, that we utterly detest and abhor cruelty and barbarity, whether to whites or blacks.

The evidence in the case was that on the morning of the 4th of July last, at 8 o'clock, one of the hottest days of the past Summer,

Hudson stripped the woman, naked as she came into the world, tied her to a persimmon tree, and whipped her for three consecutive hours, with occasional intermissions of a few minutes, until he had worn out to stump fifty-two switches, and until the bark of the body of the tree was rubbed smooth and greasy by the attrition of the body of the victim. The ground around the tree for seven or eight feet, though it had been freshly plowed, was trodden hard. One witness testified that he heard distinctly, at the distance of six hundred yards, both the noise of the switches and the screams and entreaties of the woman. The poor creature was buried the same afternoon only some ten inches beneath the ground, in a rough box, without any shroud. The overseer suggested that the neighbors had better be sent for to see the body before burial, but Hudson dissented.

The body was exhumed on Friday, two days afterwards, but was in such a state of decomposition that the external marks of violence were well nigh obliterated. But the testimony of the physician, who dissected the body, and of several other physicians, who were examined as experts, was distinct and positive that the violence used was sufficient to produce death. It was also in evidence that, after the protracted punishment, Hudson untied the woman and sent her to the creek, some one hundred and fifty yards distant, to wash herself, accompanied by a negro boy, with instructions to bring her back to him; that she complained of great thirst, and was seen to go down to the water's edge; that she remained there about fifteen minutes; that on her return she stopped two or three times, and complained of having a severe colic; that finally she stopped and could proceed no further, when the negro boy, at the command of his master, took hold of one hand and Hudson of the other, and dragged her towards the tree.

The main argument of the defense was based upon the idea that the woman went into the creek, remained there fifteen minutes, drank to great excess, and that this, in all probability, brought on a congestion of the vitals and produced death.

Such is an imperfect account of this horrible transaction. The jury hesitated much between a conviction for murder in the first and murder in the second degree. But finally they agreed and ascertained the term of imprisonment in the Penitentiary at eighteen years—the longest term known to the law. Hudson is now sixty-eight years old, and there is scarcely a probability that he can survive his confinement. Indeed he is already exceedingly prostrated. * * *

Staunton Vindicator, "Census of Augusta County," November 11, 1860

The Vindicator *reports on the 1860 census returns, arguing that increases in the enslaved population demonstrate that slavery remained strongly entrenched in Augusta County. The cultivation of cotton in new states like Mississippi and Alabama during the previous 40 years had created a large and profitable market for selling slaves from places like Virginia to plantations in the lower South. Some, like the* Staunton Spectator, *argued that this practice threatened to weaken the institution in Virginia by reducing the number of slaves in the state. The* Vindicator, *however, pointed out that the local slave population had actually grown since 1850, despite the growth of the internal slave trade.*

We are indebted to Robt. W. Burke, one of the Deputy Marshals to take the census, for the following census returns of this county: Whole population, 27,705, of which 5,553 are slaves, and 569 free negroes.—As compared with the census of 1850, these figures show an increase of 8,152, of which 300 are slaves. It will thus be seen that notwithstanding the plaintive appeals of demagogues as to the decrease of slave population in Virginia, here in Augusta county there has been really an increase. We believe, further, that in Western Virginia, notwithstanding the extensive trade in this species of property, the result will exhibit that we have more slaves than in 1850.

2. *Franklin County*

Diary of Reverend Abraham Essick, June 6, 1857, and September 8, 1857

Abraham Essick comments in his diary on the differences between Virginia and Pennsylvania farms, concluding that Pennsylvania farms enjoy an advantage that can be accounted for "on the grounds of Slavery." Raised in Franklin County, Reverend Essick served in various churches in the Valley of Virginia during the 1850s, when he closely observed the differences between Virginia and his native Pennsylvania. Farms in both Augusta and Franklin counties, like the majority in Virginia and Pennsylvania, produced mostly grains such as corn, wheat, and oats. Although farmers in Franklin grew more wheat and less corn than their counterparts in Augusta, the differences that Essick observed were largely those of farm organization and population densities rather than of crops.

June 6

Left Baltimore at nine o'clock, arrived at Winchester at five PM. During my visit to Pennsylvania I was deeply impressed by the contrast between the general appearance of the country and this. Naturally they are similar, both lying in the same valley, and presenting many of the same characteristics. But in Virginia the farms are large and the population sparse. The differences in cultivation, productiveness, and the general indications of thrift, are immensely in favor of Pennsylvania. It is usual to account for this on the grounds of Slavery.

Sept 8

Tuesday morning. I left home in company with my brother Hiram and his wife—their destination being their home in Farmerville, Louisiana, and mine being our old home in Franklin Co., Pa. Brother and his wife spent two weeks with us. They came north in April and have been visiting their friends all summer, spending most of this time with her friends in Columbia, but part of it at our old Homestead in Franklin Co. We travelled together as far as Martinsburg, Va. where I left the cars and took a coach for Hagerstow[n].

The ride was pleasant, through a rich and well improved country. The corn crops are very abundant in this region. Farming seems to be much better done in Maryland and Pa. than in Virginia. * * *

Franklin Repository, "Where Is Judge Black," November 2, 1859

The Repository *criticizes the political motivations of Northern politicians who enforce the fugitive slave law of 1850, arguing that Southerners who illegally import African slaves into the South commit a far worse crime than Northerners who shelter runaways. Passed as a part of the Compromise of 1850, the fugitive slave law was intended to calm Southern fears about the future of slavery by allowing slaveholders to recover slaves who escaped to Northern states. Unpopular in the North because it impinged on state sovereignty, the law required federal agents to arrest runaway slaves hiding in Northern states and provided harsh penalties for anyone who aided a runaway.*

A short time since some overzealous advocates of human liberty at Oberlin, Ohio, assisted a fugitive slave in escaping from a greedy negro catcher—a violation of the infamous law of 1850, commonly called the "Fugitive Slave act," which compels every freeman to become a blood hound. The watchful Attorney General, ever on the alert to see that no impious wretch lays violent hands upon Congressional enactments, hurried to the rescue and urges the Marshall, for the district wherein occurred the unlawful act, to spare no efforts to bring the offenders to condign punishment, and, if necessary, the whole army and navy would be sent to back him. How very fearful lest somebody should trample upon so sacred a thing as an act of Congress! Doubtless the like was never done till then, and the horrified Attorney General was eager to make an example of the audacious being who could raise his puny arm against the immaculate United States Government, with so terrific a cabinet officer as he!

We might admire the zeal of Judge Black, if we did not know that it is nothing but time-serving sycophancy—place-hunting subserviency to the all powerful (with his own party) oligarchy. In defense of our condemnation of the weak-kneed Jerry, we quote from a Southern newspaper, the *Memphis Avalanche*, the following:

"Three of the six native Africans brought here a few days since, were sold yesterday at the mart of Mr. West, and brought respectively, $750, $740 and $515. The latter sum was paid for a boy about fifteen years old, who seemed to possess more intelligence than any of the others. These negroes are a part of the cargo of the yacht Wanderer, landed some months since."

This is an open, undisguized violation of an Act of Congress; but the moon-eyed Attorney General cannot see anything wrong in the South. The highest crime known to the laws—Piracy—is carried on by the propagandists of slavery, unblushingly, yet the very sensative Judge Black, (sensative when a Northern man dares to give a cup of cold water, or a crust of bread, to a famishing fellow mortal, in opposition to the Fugitive slave law) can not see or hear anything to condemn in that section of the country.

We would like to see the Congressional law prescribing the duties of his office—Perhaps it is worded so as to justify his watching, with sleepless vigilance, the shortcomings of Northern men; and requiring him, under severe penalties, to close his eyes to every outrage, no matter what be its character, which Southern men may commit. If such is its phraseology he may, possibly, hide behind *it* to screen him from a charge of dereliction of duty. If, however, it requires him to arrest and arraign *every* offender against the national statutes, no matter where he may reside, or what may be his name, then we would like to know how he can, as an honest man, allow these pirates to go unwhipt of justice.

There can be no higher offense against law, good government and human safety, than that odious, diabolical, indefensible crime—piracy. The laws of Congress have pronounced the slave trade to be piracy, and have said that those concerned in the inhuman trafic shall be punished as pirates. Accordingly, it becomes the duty of the

Attorney General to see that no person, either as a principal or an accessory, shall engage in this unholy business. By the foregoing declaration from the *Memphis Avalanche*, which is so flauntingly thrown into the face of the Attorney General by that paper, the unrighteous, piratical traffic is openly conducted throughout the South. Why does not the Attorney General issue an order to the Marshall of the district in which the *Avalanche* is printed, commanding him to ferret out these foul offenders against every principle of justice, decency, and humanity, as he did so eagerly, at the instance of the lords of the lash, in the case of the Oberlin rescuers? Where is he now? Why does he not offer the army and navy to crush out these foul violators of Congressional laws?

The difference is that Jerry has an eye to the succession, and the Convention is to meet away down South—in Charleston, South Carolina; in the State where Tories were so thick during the Revolution that, it has been alleged, their toes stuck out over the State lines; in the State which sends to Congress brave, valiant, chivalric men who steal up behind an unarmed, unprotected United States Senator, while at his desk in the Senate Chamber, and strike him to the floor for no offense but loving freedom better than slavery. It is not safe then for timid men to oppose these desperate characters, and then ask office or a nomination from a convention meeting in their State.

Franklin Repository, "The Nigger Democracy," March 7, 1860

The Repository *denounces the* Valley Spirit *and all other Democratic Party newspapers for publishing articles in favor of Southern slavery, arguing that slavery is a degenerate labor system that threatens to reduce the white working classes of the North to the status of poor Southern whites. The* Repository *had no sympathy for African Americans but, like most Republican Party newspapers, wanted to prevent slave labor from competing with white labor in the North and in the western territories of the United States, where it could drive down the wages of free whites.*

A baser or more subservient stooping to lick the dust from off the shoes of wealthy aristocrats, never exhibited itself to the astonished gaze of a race of freemen, than is to be found in the columns of the *Valley Spirit.*

Nigger, nigger, nigger, is their only theme. The interest of the nabobs of slavedom, the only rights worth battling for—the only principles worthy the support of the party of which the *Spirit* is the organ in this county. Everything freemen of the North do in behalf of free white-men and the interests of free labor, is denounced by this advocate of the labor of the woolly head—the friend to the extension of free labor, with its necessary result; the crushing out of white laboring men.

Who, among working men, that has any respect for himself and for his wife and children, wishes to see this free State of Pennsylvania overrun with Slavery; every branch of industry, which now affords support for thousands of white people, who are willing to work for a living, supplied with the labor of negroes whose bodies and souls (while in the flesh) belong to their masters—recognized as such by law? Who, among the high-minded, independent, intelligent mechanics of Franklin County, desires to see his means of supplying the wants of those who are dependant upon him, degraded by the competition of Slave labor? Who, among all the different branches of industry, so multifarious in its form wishes to be reduced to the level of the poor whites of the South; those wretched beings of whom Locofoco United States Senators says: "they are not fit to associate with a Southern *gentleman's* body servant?" No man, not even a voter with the Nigger Democracy in the North, among poor working, white men desires to witness any of all of these calamities to befall the beautiful hills and dales of the dear old Keystone of the Federal arch—beloved Pennsylvania. Yet there is nothing more certain to happen—not even the setting sun to follow its rising—than that of Slavery, with all its blighting effects, will again be introduced into every Northern State, if the policy of the Nigger Democracy is suffered to be carried out to the conclusion the oligarchs are hastening it as fast as circumstances will permit. The Editor of that, and the Editor of every other locofoco paper, knows as well as do we, that the object of the leaders of the odious dogma of Slavery extension is to carry their system of labor not only into the Territories, but into all the Northern States. The bolder among the hotspurs have, over and over again, declared that slavery is the *best* form of labor which *capital* can employ. Certain leading Southern locofoco orators have had the impudence to declare that "*color* had nothing to do with slavery;" and that the "rightful and normal condition of *all poor laboring* men is slavery." All these abominable teachings fall from the lips of the Southern leaders of the Nigger Democracy; their Northern allies see and hear the disreputable language and have not the manhood to speak out in reprobation thereof in suitable terms.

Some of the purse-proud lords-of-the-lash have publicly declared "that the great cause of the violent agitation in this country, is, to decide whether it is better for capital to own or to hire its labor." Thus saying, as plainly as language could express it, that there is an "irrepressible conflict" between capital and muscles, at this time, going on in the land. In this struggle the Republicans, like Jefferson, and all his compeers [*sic*], are on the side of labor. The Nigger Democracy like the enemies of poor working men in every age of the world, is on the side of capital.

If the Northern dough-face *followers* of the Slave-owning, man-stealing, man, woman and children selling, Southern leaders of the Nigger Democracy, in all their wicked assaults upon poor white working men, can find satisfaction in giving aid and comfort to these bitter, unrelenting foes to the genuine interests of the industrious sons of toil in the free North, they can go on in their dark, fiendish attacks upon free labor till they bring about its necessary fruits, when, it is to be expected, they will be assigned their wished-for position—will be made overseers, their proper post.

Valley Spirit, "How Our Negroes Live," March 30, 1859

The Spirit *provides a graphic description of a black slum in Chambersburg, Pennsylvania. Around 2,000 free blacks lived in Franklin County, more than*

500 in Chambersburg, and they were forced to live in the worst sections of town. The Valley Spirit *took this as evidence of the hopelessness of free blacks as U.S. citizens, emphasizing the squalor of their homes as proof of their inferiority to whites.*

* * * UGLOW'S ARCADE.—In one of the back streets of our town there may be seen a long low range of buildings, of a *sui generis* style of architecture—baffling description in itself, and without a parallel for comparison. Come, reader, let me take you by the collar and drag you into this abode of crime and wretchedness of destitute and degraded humanity. We know you will not come willing, so come *nolens volens*. Now, take your stand in this corner and observe the "sights to be seen." Here, in this wretched apartment, eight by ten feet square, you may see by the light of that dim lamp, twenty human beings—fourteen women and six children—from a babe a week old to the urchin just entering its teens. Observe their actions and listen to their conversation. What disgusting obscenity! What horrid implications! Their licentious and blasphemous orgies would put to the blush the imps of pandemonium. Drinking whisky and inhaling tobacco smoke you would hardly suppose would keep soul and body together; yet you perceive no indications here that would lead you to suppose they subsist on anything else. You seem impatient to get out of the atmosphere of this room; mount that ladder and take a look in the room above. One look will be sufficient. Here huddled promiscuously together, on beds—no, not on beds; there is an idea of ease and comfort attached to a bed, that would never enter your mind on looking at these heaps of filthy rags—are men, women and children; arms, heads and legs, in a state of nudity, protrude through the tattered covering in wild confusion. Poverty, drunkenness, sickness and crime, are here in all their most miserable and appalling aspects. But, come, we have twenty rooms of this description to visit in this building, and we cannot devote any more time to this set. What! twenty rooms filled with beings of this kind? Do not let it startle you in the least, my friend, or disturb the serenity of your christian equanimity. *They do not know they are accountable beings,* and a society has been formed in this place to keep them in "blissful ignorance." Its satellites are very

active in the good work, and we will one day furnish you with a copy of the report of their proceedings. As the exhibition you have just witnessed has no doubt prompted you to do something to meliorate the condition of this benighted portion of your race, we would [advise] you to go home, while in the mood, and make a generous donation to the *Foreign* Missionary Society, which will be gladly received and appropriately expended in a string of beads for the Heathen!

Valley Spirit, "The Slavery Question in Congress," July 25, 1860

The Spirit *asserts that Republicans are purposefully arousing agitation between the North and South by repeatedly raising the issue of slavery in the U.S. Congress. The Republican Party rose to power in the late 1850s by opposing the expansion of slavery into the western U.S. territories, producing heated political battles in Congress over the future of slavery in the country. A Democratic Party newspaper, the* Valley Spirit *opposed efforts by the Republicans to limit the expansion of slavery and to make the future of the institution a central political issue.*

Every true friend of our country must depreciate the agitation of the slavery question. It matters not how and what measure may be brought before the people, the eternal nigger question is certain to be mixed up with it. Look at the action of Congress, for instance. Has there been a question brought before that body in which the nigger had no hand? No man will deny that some of the greatest measures—measures intending to promote the happiness and welfare of the country—have suffered by again and again dragging this *dark* question into the foreground.

But, it may be asked, who is the cause of all this strife and animosity, of this delay in our public business? This question is easily solved. When men like Hale, Wilson, Seward, Sumner, and other leaders of the Republican Abolition party, get up in the halls of

Congress, avowing their determination to leave no stone unturned in agitating this great humbug slavery question; when men, *professing* to be friends of the *whole* Union continue to throw one fire brand after another into the slaveholding States, exciting their negroes to rebellion and to cause domestic strife, war and bloodshed—as has been the case heretofore—we say, that when we see the leaders of the Republican Abolition party—and will any one deny that the Republican party is not abolitionized?—using all their power and influence to not only free the negroes, but to put him on an equal footing with the white man, and not to rest until they have accomplished their base and treacherous design, we do not then wonder that our Southern brethren, belonging to the same Confederacy that we do, living under the protection of the same Constitution, become alarmed and excited. Why all this bitter feeling between the different sections of one common country? It is high time that there be a stop put to this slavery agitation.—The welfare of the country suffers by it, whilst our people are made the laughing stock amongst foreign powers.

Franklin Repository, "Strike for Freedom," May 2, 1860

The Repository *exhorts its readers to vote Republican in the upcoming presidential election, believing that Abraham Lincoln's victory will inspire poor Southern whites to vote for the Republican Party. Many Republicans believed that poor whites were held down by the slaveholding elite of the South and that non-slaveholders would join their party if given an opportunity. By securing a constituency among white laborers in the South, Republicans hoped to become a national party and ensure the future of free white labor.*

REPUBLICANS OF FRANKLIN!—You have a part to perform in the grand achievement—the enfranchising of your Southern brethren. Every right which a freeman holds dear, has been there stricken down by the co-horts of Slavery. Liberty of speech is

unknown; the Press—which is formidable only to tyrants—is muz-
zled; and every impulse that ennobles humanity and beautiful freedom, is dwarfed, smothered, crushed out by the reign of terror
which has been inaugurated by the Southern leaders of the Locofoco party. It therefore behooves every lover of Freedom to buckle
on his armor to do many battles in the great contest for Free Principles that we are now about entering upon. Truth has often been
stricken down, but "truth, crushed to earth, shall rise again." Give
your best exertions to exalt her, and if victory crown our combined
efforts, one very satisfactory reflection will be, not that we have asserted and maintained our own rights as freemen, but that we have
assisted in giving others the same boone—clothed others with the
same mantle of glorious freedom.

The election of a Republican President would be the signal for
the uprising of Republicanism in the South. The masses, who have
been so long down-trodden by the Slave Oligarchy, would arise in
their might and emancipate themselves from a bondage that is even
worse than slavery of the body—the loss of their birth-right as
American citizens. As an evidence of this, we will here quote the
language of Mr. JENKINS, of Virginia, who but a few days ago,
while addressing Congress, deprecating the success of the Republican party, as a misfortune, said:

> "Another misfortune would be the dispensation of patronage
> throughout the South by a Republican President, in such a
> way as to build up and strengthen Republicanism. It was a
> great mistake to suppose that southern men would not be
> found to take office under a Republican President, and thus
> the germ of a Republican party would spring up in the very
> bosom of the South."

This accounts for the violence of the Nigger Democracy against
the organization of the White Man's Republican party in the
South—"men would be found to take office under a Republican
President, and thus Republicanism would spring up in the very
bosom of the South"!—Like Demetrius of old, the leader of the silver smiths who made silver shrines for Diana, apprehending that
the Apostle's teachings would interfere with their trade, assembled
his co laborers and addressed them thus:—"Sirs, ye know that by

this craft we have our wealth," and they were filled with wrath and cried out, "Great is Diana of the Ephesians," and a mob was raised to assault Paul, similar to that raised in Baltimore, and other localities in the South, against peaceable assemblages of Republicans. They fear the organization of a Republican party in the South— not that it would conflict with the development of their resources, mechanical, manufacturing, agricultural, or commercial—but the Government patronage would slip out of their hands, and it is by that "craft they have their wealth." This is the secret of the whole opposition; but you might as well try to dam up a rapidly flowing stream of water with sand as to attempt to prevent the spread of truth, religious or political. Republicanism is political truth, and the fates have decreed its triumph over the combined opposition of ignorance and fanaticism, backed by the corrupt patronage of the General Government and the misrepresentation of the Nigger Democracy.

The Republican Conventions held in Maryland, Missouri, Virginia, Delaware and Kentucky, to send Delegates to the Chicago Convention, are the entering wedges that will eventually split the log that has heretofore interposed as a barrier to the propagation of political truth in the South, and when the triumph is complete, no people will rejoice more than the Southern people themselves, when fully clothed in the glorious habiliments of political freedom.

II

John Brown's Raid

1. *Augusta County*

B. S. Brooke to John T. Blake, November 14, 1859

B. S. Brooke writes to a friend of his safe arrival in Staunton and notes the unsettled nature of Augusta County almost a month after John Brown's raid at the Federal arsenal at Harpers Ferry, Virginia. As Brooke observed, Brown's failed attempt to incite a slave revolt on October 16, 1859, struck deeply held fears among white Southerners of black insurrection. While most slaveholders focused on dealing with abolitionists like Brown in the aftermath of the raid, a few decided to send their slaves to the lower South as a precaution.

Staunton Nov 14, 1859

My Dear Friend

I am happy to inform you of my safe arrival in this place, found all well and glad to see me.

I have nothing of importance to communicate the times seem hard, money scarce, but not quite so bad as in Greenbriar for here you can get plenty to eat for the money and at rather reasonable prices. I see by the paper this morning that Cook has been convicted—Stevens has been handed over to the U.S. authorities and will doubtless be tried in Staunton. There is considerable excitment here in reference to this insurrection. Many persons are selling, and sending their negros to the South.

My kindest regards to your mother & sister. I have no news to give you & read none. I thought I would write you a line, to let you know of my safe arrival—Love to all

I remain
Truly Yours,
B. S. Brooke

Staunton Spectator, "Danger of Insurrection," November 29, 1859

The editor of the Spectator *mocks the idea that white Southerners live in fear of slave insurrections, attempting to use the failure of Brown's raid as evidence that Virginia's slaves (referred to in this article as "Cuffee") have no desire to rise up against their masters. Rather, the* Spectator *asserts, the real danger comes from radical Northern abolitionists such as William Lloyd Garrison and Harriett Beecher Stowe. There were certainly white Southerners who shared this editor's opinion, particularly his faith that God favored the practice of slavery. Yet fears of slave revolts were far more prevalent in the South than the* Spectator *suggests, particularly in Virginia where the largest slave revolt in U.S. history occurred in 1831.*

While the crazy fanatics of the North imagine that the poor negro, smarting under a galling sense of his degradation, and inspired by a noble impulse of resistance to tyranny, is ready at a moment's warning to grasp the murderous pike and fight for his freedom, the people of the South feel the most perfect security in the full assurance that they possess not only the willing obedience but the strong attachment of their slaves. It is a most egregious blunder to suppose that we who live in the enjoyment of all the benefits of the "peculiar institution," live also in constant dread of insurrection and rebellion, and go to our beds at night with the terrible apprehension that our throats may be cut before morning. Not a bit of it. We sleep as soundly and sweetly as though we were surrounded by an armed body guard of chosen defenders, in the confident belief that

our ebony friends will not feel the slightest disposition to "rise" until we [illegible word] them up with a long pole at the break of day.
Some of them sleep so soundly after the toils of the day that nothing can arouse them from their slumbers short of the most vigorous
shakes and downright pummeling. It is a fixed fact that Cuffee is an
unleavened and unleavenable lump. Garrison and Giddings may
call upon him at a respectable distance; Beecher and Cheever may
exhort him in the highest strains of their eloquence; Old Brown
may even thrust pike staffs into his hands; but "nigger will be nigger still"—he won't *rise*. This *fact* has been demonstrated beyond a
cavil by the experience of the negrophilists at Harper's Ferry. Col.
Washington's negro man took the murderous weapon, but expressed his determination to watch which side "Mass Lewis" fought
on, and do battle beside him, and the other poor creatures penned
with Old Brown in the Engine House, snoozed away their hours of
confinement in comfortable slumbers. With the hour of deliverance
at hand, surrounded by professed friends, prepared to lead them
to the Canaan of deliverance, with arms and ammunition in abundance within their reach, there Cuffee snored, and in defiance of
entreaties and exhortations and commands positively refused to
"rise."

The state of public feeling at present establishes the fact that no
apprehension of danger from servile insurrection is felt by the people of the South. The danger is apprehended outside of the State,
from the insane crew who entertain such unfounded opinions in regard to the condition of the slaves, and their disposition to free
themselves from bondage. In the prospect of further invasion of
our state for the purpose of rescuing those who have already
stained its soil with blood, we see the people of Virginia leaving
their wives and children in the hands of their faithful domestics,
and repairing to the borders of Virginia, far away from their
homes, to repel the insolent foe. They leave their families behind
without an apprehension of danger from those who are supposed
at the North to be ready to massacre them at the first favorable opportunity. On the contrary they feel confident that their little ones
are safe in the hands of their "Mammys," and that Sambo and
Cuffy will fight to the death in defence of "Missus and the children."

But in addition to their confidence in their own servants, the people of the South place their trust in a higher power, whose protecting care they expect in time of peril. They believe that the institution of slavery is ordained of Heaven, and that the slaveholder who trusts in the Almighty arm will find that arm a refuge and a fortress. They expect to be delivered from the snare of the Abolition howler and the noisome pestilence of fantaticism. * * *

Cyrus Alexander to John H. McCue, December 12, 1859

A member of Augusta's Whig Party, Cyrus Alexander comments on local affairs and Brown's raid in his letter to John McCue, a local attorney. Alexander blames the raid on the Democratic Party's willingness to use debates over slavery as a political tool and their practice of denouncing Whig candidates as unwilling to defend the rights of slaveholders. Slavery had been a touchstone of political battles in the U.S. Congress for decades by 1860, developing in the 1850s into a debate primarily between Republicans and Democrats over the institution's future in the western territories. Many Southerners like Alexander believed the debates encouraged abolitionists such as Brown by giving the impression that some Southern whites were less committed to the institution than others.

Waynesboro Dec. 12, 1859

Dr Jno
    Yours of—is to hand, and I am sorry to say that your friend Miss Lucy is no longer an inhabitant of this Commonwealth, for some unknown cause—probably because the *"Species"* were not propagated fast enough in this region. She emigrated to Ohio last Spring, with no intention of *ever* returning. Does it not make you *weep* to think that you have forever lost the services of Lucy & her *"Catnip"*. As she has always been a necessary *institution* in your Domestic affairs, I see no other channel for you in the future, than to "shut up shop" and discontinue the Business. Tell Liz. that I have some idea

of paying her a Visit about the first of the new year, & that if she will make her *arrangements* to that time, that I will carry with me some Catnip, & that you & I will put her thro all the phases of Lucy & the Catnip.

I know of no one whose services as nurse could be had, except your Aunt Ginnie Martin—she is a fine woman & an excellent nurse, but I do not know whether she could be induced to go so far from home. Sarah is quite smart, but is slightly afflicted with the same epidemic under which Liz is labouring.

No news of interest. Times are Dul & weather cold. There is considerable War Spirit in this country. We are seeing in the Harpers Ferry affair, the legitimate consequences of the Jno Letchers election—that result justified Old Brown & friends in believing that a Majority of Virginians were ready to join them. The Democracy are responsible for it, & should be held so, for all this slavery agitation they have kept it alive for years. Elect Millard Fillmore President, & I would guarantee that before the expiration of his term all would be quiet. I would like to see Wise, Seward, Douglass and a few others Hanged as high as was Jno Brown.

Why Dont you come over. all Well. Love to Liz & children

Yours
C. Alexander

William McCue to John McCue, December 25, 1859

William McCue writes to his brother, John, to discuss Virginia's military preparations for defending the state against future attempts by abolitionists to incite slave revolts, describing debates about secession and his own determination "to maintain our rights at the point of a bayonet" if necessary. While most Virginians did not consider secession a real option in the wake of John Brown's raid, McCue's sentiments express much of the frustration Southerners felt with the public displays of sympathy for Brown that emanated from some Northern communities at the time of his trial and execution.

Fincastle Dec 25th 1859

Dear Brother
    Your kind favor bearing date Dec 16th was received yesterday &
read & reread with more than usual interest, so replete was it with
interesting items & good advice. Permit me in the commencement
of my letter, to express my very high appreciation of the motives
which prompted you to give expression to those feelings of pater-
nal affection, so beautifully & affectionately set forth in your communication. * * *
    * * * The late excitement occasioned by the foray of John Brown,
& his infamous coagitators, is about to bring our school more
prominently before the public, Owing to the disturbed state of the
public mind & the dangers that threaten the distinction of our once
glorious honor, the citizens feeling the importance of fostering the
military spirits now aroused, and of giving the growth of the country instruction in military [illegible word] on last court day drew up
a petition to the Legislature asking an appropriation to assist them
in establishing a military Professorship, in the [illegible word] [il-
legible word] Academy,—believing that the prosperity & usefulness
of the institution would be greatly promoted thereby. which was
signed by a number of the most prominent citizens of the county
& sent to their delagates, accompanied with a petition from the
"Board of Directors," If the petition should be granted, we may expect a large acquisition to our school.
    9 of our students, members of a volunteer company, in obedi-
ence to Executive orders were in public service at Charlestown during the execution of Coppie & Cook. If the said petition passes the
Legislature the school will at once be converted into a military
school. Wilson & I will uniform & take a regular course of military
training. Since the excitement a large company of volunteers has
been raised in Fincastle & a Company of cavalry is now being
raised, to which I belong I think it more than probable that I will
be elected to one of the offices, as I have the reputation of being
one of the best horsemen in this section of country, At the public
meeting of which I spoke, there were a number of resolutions
adopted similar to those adopted throughout the state,—declaring
their intention to cut off all trade with the north to preserve the

Union if possible & if not to maintain our rights at the point of the bayonet. A number of warm & eloquent speeches were made some were in favor of an immediate secession but the prevailing sentiment seemed to be that contained in the resolution adopted—which you will see in the Richmond papers—I for my part love & cherish the Union, & do wholy & heartly endorse that sentiment of Webster "Union now & forever, one & unseparable" but if this cannot be, I am ready to should[er] my musket at a moments warning & die if need be in defence of my country's rights. * * *

* * * Give my love to sister Liz & the children & remember very kindly to Mrs Wills & write

Your brother
Billy

Staunton Spectator, "Democracy and Slavery," February 7, 1860

The Spectator, *a Whig Party newspaper, blames the Democrats for complicity in creating the circumstances that led to Brown's raid. In their zealousness to protect slavery and win elections, argues the* Spectator, *the Democrats denounced the position of Whig candidates on slavery and thereby encouraged abolitionists like Brown. Like almost all nineteenth-century newspapers, the* Spectator *interpreted nearly all events, big and small, through its particular political lens and sought to carve out partisan advantages whenever it could.*

John Brown embarked in his insane enterprise against Virginia under the mistaken notion that he would find sympathizers in the State, who would gather around his standard at the first sound of a bugle. He did not anticipate accessions to his small band of desperate and determined men from the negro population alone, but confidently believed that many of the free white citizens of the Commonwealth, who he imagined to be anti-slavery in sentiment, were ready and anxious to rally under the banner of a bold leader and strike for the liberty of the slaves. It is an admitted fact that such was the impression of the deluded man in regard to the state of sentiment in Virginia, and although the delusion may seem strange at first blush, we are constrained to admit when looking back upon the political struggles of the past in this State, that John Brown was in some degree justified in the belief that Virginia was ripe for the "irrepressible conflict." The leader of the army of invasion was the old *old* John Brown,—a man well up in years—who had watched with the keen eye of fanaticism the progress of political events in this country for the last twenty years, and marked their bearings upon the great idea of his life—the one grand object of his aspirations and efforts—the liberation of the slaves from their bondage. It is not reasonable to suppose that he was an indifferent spectator to the fierce conflicts of parties in Virginia. On the contrary, the last steps of his career upon the soil of our State, as the avowed leader of a crusade against slavery and slaveholders, even to bloodshed and death, is of itself sufficient to establish the fact that he had been watching the course of affairs in the State of Virginia with special and peculiar interest. And what had he learned from the conflicts of the last twenty years, and heard with exultation from the lips of politicians and papers of the Democratic party? To those who are familiar with the political history of the State it is scarcely necessary to say that from them he heard, probably for the first time, of a difference of sentiment among the people of Virginia on the subject of negro slavery. From them he learned, not that a few of the people, but that a large and imposing party, led on by men of acknowledged talents and ability, were regarded with distrust by their fellow citizens and denounced as unsound and unworthy to be trusted by the South with the power of either the Federal or State government. He heard it as far back as 1836 when the "great Commoner" of Kentucky, a Southern man and slave owner, was denounced as unworthy of Southern confidence and support, and those who sustained him were charged with disloyalty to their section and its "peculiar institution." He heard of it again in 1840, and 1848, and 1852, when the same groundless and unjust charges were proffered against Harrison and Taylor and Scott, together with all who sustained those true and loyal sons of the South in those memorable contests. He heard it in still louder tones in the gubernatorial election of 1851, when Geo.

W. Summers, the gallant standard bearer of the Whigs, was held up for his inspection and admiration as an abolitionist "to the manner born," and the thousands who gathered around the banner which he bore so gallantly, were denounced and defamed as affiliating with and lending aid and comfort to the enemies of the South.

But not only during the political campaigns had John Brown heard this cheering intelligence of the progress of anti-slavery opinions in the State of Virginia.—Pending the discussion of every measure bearing upon the question of slavery, he had heard the same charge ringing from the hustings and the press against many of the greatest and best of Virginia's sons. The sound had been listened to so long that it grew familiar, and it is not surprising that it received credit. When so many concurred in the statement that a vast number of the people of Virginia, were "doughfaces" and "submissionists," and thousands of other sympathisers with the anti-slavery sentiment of the North, is it to be wondered at that John Brown believed the thing to be true, and addressed himself to the consummation of his grand project with the confident expectation of finding all things ready for the crisis? Like many others who have put faith in the Democracy, however, he was most egregiously deceived.

Without holding the Democratic party directly responsible for the bloody scenes at Harper's Ferry, we are fully persuaded that it is responsible to a certain extent for that delusion in regard to the sentiments of Virginia, which lured old Brown to his doom. We had hoped that the men of that party would have seen the civil consequences of such a mode of warfare, counterbalancing in our opinion all the advantages to be derived from a mere party success, and that the scenes of the bloody drama on our borders, to which men of all parties rushed for the defense of a common soil, would have put an end to all aspersions upon the soundness of Virginia on this question of slavery. But we have been disappointed. We find the Democratic papers still virulent in the abuse of all who do not square up to their ideas of what a Southern man should be. We find them setting up an "armory bill" in the Legislature of the State as a test of soundness on the slavery question, and holding up those who resist it as an unnecessary and extravagant measure, as recreant to the State that gave them birth; and especially are they violent against those who are most likely to be in their way in the effort to perpetuate the power of the Democratic party. Thus do they endeavor to perpetuate a "reign of terror" under which so many destitute of "back-bone" have been dragooned into their ranks. We are mistaken, however, if such treatment will do any good either to the Democratic party or the South. Men of sense will not be driven into all sorts of folly because John Brown invaded Virginia, nor frightened from their propriety by charges of unsoundness that have been rung against them all their lives.—The Democracy may turn the Harper's Ferry affair to their advantage, as they have generally managed everything connected with slavery for the furtherance of their party schemes; but they will find it a mere temporary advantage. The conservatism of Virginia cannot be thus crushed out. * * *

2. Franklin County

Valley Spirit, "Insurrection at Harper's Ferry," October 26, 1859

The Valley Spirit *characterizes John Brown's raid as "the beginning . . . of more serious troubles" for the nation. The newspaper was particularly upset that Brown and his accomplices planned much of their raid while living in Chambersburg under pseudonyms, and categorically denied that any white resident of Franklin had any advance knowledge of the plot. Most whites in the county, of all political affiliations, denounced Brown and proved eager to distance themselves from his raid. Some in the county, including the editor of the* Valley Spirit, *strongly suspected that Franklin's black population might have had a hand in supporting Brown and his plan.*

In the present issue of our paper will be found full and accurate details of the recent Abolition insurrection at Harper's Ferry. This attempt to subvert the Government of the United States by a handful of crazy fanatics may seem ridiculous, and hardly worthy of serious attention for a moment. But there is another light in which the matter is to be viewed and one that presents a more alarming aspect. This outbreak is only the beginning—the foreshadowing of more serious troubles. That an extensive organization exists, in various States, to overthrow the Government by means of a general and servile insurrection there can no longer be a doubt. The frustration of this rash beginning has not by any means broken up the organization. It will only have the effect to make the conspirators more cautious in their working, and more desperate and determined in their next attempt. * * *

* * * It is not, however, at this time, of the general character, or political tendencies of the insurrection that we wish to speak. Our community has by some means, of which we were entirely unaware, become mixed up with this insurrection. While we were harbouring, for months these desperadoes among us we do not believe that a single one of our white citizens was in any way connected with them, or even suspected their designs. In regard to our blacks it is believed that a portion of them knew the object of these men, were associated with them, and would have joined them if successful. There is no sympathy in this community for the fugitives, and if any of them should come this way they will receive no assistance or protection from any of our citizens. It is the sentiment of one and all, in this community, to have the outlaws arrested and receive that punishment which their crimes demand.

The first trace we can find of these men among us was in the month of July last. They were doubtless here previous to that time. Old Brown, passing by the name of Smith, and a couple of men he called his sons. A man by the name of John Henrie, who Brown on one occasion said was his son, was also among the first comers and was the last to leave. This man is among the killed by the name of "Capt. Kagi." Mrs. Cook, wife of Col. John E. Cook, gave us the information that this man's name was John Henrie Kagi, and that he had been one of Brown's men in Kansas. Large quantities of arms, and munitions of war, were received at our warehouses, from time to time, upon which Brown paid the freight, which in some instances amounted to seventy dollars.—Some of the boxes containing Sharps Rifles came through from Kansas, and other freight from Connecticut. The lance handles were shipped from that State. Henrie remained here pretty much all the time superintending affairs. [Line illegible] at a time, or merely passing through to Harrisburg, or other points. While here he transacted business through our Bank having had several drafts cashed on New York. He was here at the time Fred Douglas lectured and was in the Hall that night with Henrie and several others of the party. Our citizens had little idea how strongly Fred Douglas was backed up on that occasion. Brown had no doubt an interview with Douglas at the time and the object of Douglas' visit to the place is now fully explained. Henrie was with Douglas at the house of the colored man at which Douglas stopped. When Douglas left he gave out that he would return in October, about the time the outbreak took place. It is quite likely he will postpone his visit now to the *great disappointment* of some of his admirers here! The last time Brown was known to have been in this place was on the 7th of October, when he brought the wife of Col. John E. Cook here and left her at a private boarding house. The man Henrie (Kagi) was the last of the gang known to have been here. He left for Harper's Ferry on Friday the 14th just in time to meet his just doom. Brown or Henrie do not seem to have made the acquaintance of any of our white citizens while among us, though it is known they were intimate with some of our negroes.

The whole number of white men engaged in the insurrection were no doubt sojourners with us at different times during the summer. Nine white men and two negroes can be identified as having been here. Brown and his two sons, Henrie, Leeann, Tided, Mermaid, Taylor and Coppice, were well known by name in the neighborhood where they boarded. Other strangers of whose appearance we have a full description were also seen in their company—The negro called "Emperor of New York"—taken prisoner is said to be the black man who was upon the stage with Douglas the night he lectured in this place. He did not go back with Douglas and was not seen in this place afterwards. Brown frequently visited here with a horse and wagon. The man called Tidd was also here at one time for freight with a mule and wagon. Merriam was here a week or ten days before the outbreak. He was very active in writing letters, and telegraphing to different points. Some of his dispatches to Boston cost him as much as $6. He hired a horse and buggy and in company with Henrie, it is supposed, visited Harper's Ferry. He returned and left in the cars. This man was not at the Ferry at the time of the insurrection. * * *

* * * It will no doubt seem to many impossible that these men lived among us for months—transacted business through our Bank and Warehouses, kept up an extensive correspondence through our Post Office, and using the Telegraph occasionally and yet no one suspected their real character or designs. As incredible as this may seem, it is nevertheless true. Our community can scarcely be brought to realize it even now, and seem astounded at their own blindness. We feel very confident they have no aiders, abettors or sympathizers among us and this may account for our complete ignorance of their true object. They found none here to whom they could express their opinions or make known their intentions. It is true that at one time, during their stay among us, they were thought to be a gang of burglars.—This was after the robbery of the Warehouse, and from certain circumstances connected with that affair it is not at all unlikely that some of the gang may have had some hand in the robbery. There was not sufficient proof, however, to justify the arrest of any of the parties, and that suspicion against them seems to have died out. While residing here they kept to themselves—expressed no insurrectionary opinions to any one—paid their bills regularly, and in every respect behaved themselves in such a correct and orderly manner as to attract little attention. Our community can certainly rest under no blame for not discovering and thwarting the schemes of these rebels. We cannot be accused of being more blind than the people about Harper's Ferry who knew more about them than we did and never mistrusted them until they found themselves in pretty much the same fix that Paddy had the Hessians—"surrounded!" We will stand no imputations against Chambersburg until Harper's Ferry defines its position!

Valley Spirit, "Fruits of Black Republicanism," November 2, 1859

The Valley Spirit, *a Democratic Party newspaper, blames the Republicans for inciting John Brown's raid and argues that such horrific events will continue if Northern voters do not abandon the Republican Party. Citing a visit to Franklin*

County two months before the raid by Frederick Douglass, an ex-slave and prominent abolitionist, the paper argues that Brown enjoyed widespread support among Republicans and abolitionists (which the Spirit *considers synonymous). The result of continued Republican political success and abolitionist agitation, warns the paper, will be civil war.*

We have already laid before our readers a full account of the attempt made at Harper's Ferry lately, by a score of emissaries of the Abolition party, to inaugurate a civil war in the very heart of the Republic. From the developments already made, there can be no doubt that this treasonable and murderous movement had the previous sanction of a large number of prominent opponents of the Democratic party at the North. The ridiculous failure of the hellish scheme will prevent the names of many of its chief abettors from coming to light. The principal villains who laid the plans and furnished the means will either preserve [illegible word] or mildly condemn the attempt, now that it has not succeeded; but if the slaves of Virginia and Maryland had arisen and murdered their indulgent masters by tens of thousands, the envenomed wretches who now conceal their disappointment at the miscarriage of their plot, would have openly rejoiced at its success. * * *

* * * Our own peaceful town, it appears, was made the rendezvous of the rascals employed to lead off in what the Abolitionists doubtless hoped would grow into a formidable insurrection. We have but little doubt that the visit of Fred. Douglas to this place two months ago, had reference to this very matter. His violent speech against the South was probably intended to create among our people a sympathy with the cause of Abolitionism, that would lead them to extend shelter and protection to the gang of cut-throats selected to begin the work of blood at Harper's Ferry, and to such slaves as might be induced to join them, in the event of their not being able to sustain themselves south of the Potomac.

This Harper's Ferry outbreak is the legitimate consequence of the crusade against slavery preached by the Republican leaders of the North. The rank and file of the Republican party can now see the dangerous tendency of the doctrines they have been honestly supporting. The people of this valley can now appreciate the risk they run in giving countenance to declaimers against the South. Suppose Brown and his associates had succeeded in inciting to insurrection several thousand slaves. The insurgents would have been driven North through this valley. They would have entered our houses, plundered us of our property, and perhaps murdered our wives and children. They would have been pursued; and driven to desperation, they would have turned and fought when overtaken, and all the calamities of *war* would have been brought to our very doors. What has taken place at Harper's Ferry is but a trifle in comparison with what will some day occur, if conservative men of all political creeds do not unite with the Democracy to put down the sectional party that has disturbed the peace of the country.

Franklin Repository, "The Harper's Ferry Insurrection," November 2, 1859

The Repository, *a Republican newspaper, denounces Brown's raid as the work of madmen. More than that, the paper hopes to dispel the belief common among many in both the North and South that Republican leaders were somehow involved in the plot. Evidence that Brown received assistance, mostly financial, from some Northerners (Frederick Douglass in particular) surfaced in the weeks following the raid, raising suspicions in the South of conspiracies among Republicans and abolitionists to eradicate Southern slavery.*

The idea of calling the farce at Harper's an "insurrection" says the Pittsburgh *Gazette*, is ridiculous—as ridiculous as the mustering of thousands of soldiers by the government to put down a squad of seventeen crazy white men and five negroes. It had none of the characteristics of an "insurrection." Not one of the numerous slaves of the neighborhood had a hand in the crazy attempt. It was not an uprising of oppressed but misguided men, nor an attempt to throw off a burdensome yoke; but a foolhardy adventure of a handful of monomaniacs, as audacious as Col. Blood's celebrated attempt to carry off the crown jewels from the Tower of London.

The whole project appears so perfectly unreasonable, wild and insane, that, but for the stern record before him, one could hardly suppose that such was the dream of even a fanatical renegade like Brown. He certainly has had too much to do with warfare life not to know how suicidal such a project would be. The idea of anything save a mad house lunatic ever expecting to organize a wide spread insurrection at the head of a raw improvised band of twenty-two white men and negroes, on a public thoroughfare, easily accessible by telegraph and railroad to important and powerful military aid, is so wild and foolish as almost to defy belief. It was simply a purposeless and senseless riot, the leader of which, well known as "Old Ossawatomie Brown," has been driven to frenzy by the persecutions he endured on the Kansas border. Ever since the death of his son Frederick, who was shot down at his own door in Kansas, by a Missouri mob tenfold more revengeful and bloody than that which lately filled Virginia with terror, and since the old man witnessed, on the same occasion, the destruction of property that he had been a life time in accumulating, he has been a monomaniac. * * *

* * * The first feeling excited by the telegraphic account of the affair, and the one which continues after all the facts are known, is that of profound amazement. It is difficult to believe that there were a handful of such fanatics and fools as Brown and his men are represented to have been. A gang of escaped maniacs could not have stumbled upon a freak so horribly foolish. The utter madness of their scheme—the absolute certainty of their sudden destruction—does not seem to have occurred to him. They have paid for their criminal folly with their lives, and it is to be hoped there are no more of the same sort.

The attempt will be made, of course—nay, has already been made—to make political capital out of the affair. There will be a vast amount of political twaddle manufactured out of it. The fire-eaters will be more fierce than ever. The whole North will be charged with the responsibility for the crack-brained doings of a handful of madmen. There are paltry politicians who seek to make capital out of it, but the common sense of the country will be proof against so far-fetched a slander.

There is not a man in the Republican ranks who is at all connected with, or has given any sympathy to this silly movement.

That it has had some northern aid, is plain; but the men who have assisted it have never heretofore been and are not now, identified in any way with the Republican party. Frederick Douglass and Gerrit Smith were never Republicans, but were leaders in a little party of their own, polling two or three thousand votes. They ran an electoral ticket against Fremont in New York in 1856, and last year Gerrit Smith ran as an independent candidate for Governor and stumped the State, against the Republican candidate. They have always been the bitterest opponents of the Republican party, because it was not ultra enough; and all attempts to hold our party responsible for their acts will fail. The Republicans disapprove, as heartily as any others can, all attempts to put an end to Slavery, by force. It is no part of their mission to make war upon slavery in the States, either through the powers of the government or by force of arms; and the responsibility for this silly act must rest solely upon the heads of the few wild zealots who conceived it and have perished in trying to carry it into execution.

Valley Spirit, "Food for Mercantile Digestion," February 1, 1860

The Valley Spirit, *commenting on the recent victory of a Republican Party candidate in an election in Pittsburg, Pennsylvania, argues that Southerners have a right to be alarmed by Republican political victories in the wake of John Brown's raid. Emphasizing the connections between the North and South, the* Spirit *asserts that Republican electoral victories in the aftermath of Brown's raid are a repudiation of the South and hypocritical of people who denounced the raid. Many Democratic newspapers, like the* Spirit, *sought to use Brown's raid to discredit their primary political rivals, the Republicans.*

* * * These Republican victories have certainly a peculiar significance to Southern people. Passing by all that was said and done prior to the Brown outrage, that last event was quite sufficient to cause the belief that the people of the North would be most anx-

ious to repudiate *practically* all sympathy with the party which had *doctrinally* provoked that foray. A reaction was anticipated. The Union sentiment was thought to have been aroused. In fact Union sentiments [were] proclaimed and resolved. The Southern people, good easy people as they are, anticipated that good fruits would be gathered from these demonstrations in the way of conservative ballots for conservative candidates. They did not for an instant conceive, honorable men as they are, that there was no intention to carry out in practice what was resolved in theory. They did not think of placing all the fine things said about sympathy, assistance and brotherly affection to the credit side of Bosh, Sham & Co. They did not think it was lip service, nor any thing but pure, genuine, conservative talk, which was to be followed by practical, conservative voting.

The Pittsburg election has done much to undeceive them. They are now forced to ask themselves and us, which of the two and the greatest effect as expressed at the ballot box, Union meetings, or Brown sympathizing meetings? Let the business classes of Philadelphia answer this question next May. They have an interest in it which cannot be too seriously considered. A walk through Market street will convince any one of that. Stores are found filled with every kind of merchandise suited and intended for Southern consumption, and to [be] paid for in money produced by Southern slave industry—Southern merchants are expected to buy. They are treated as friends, customers and brothers by our merchants, as they always have been. Let us hope, then, that they will not be *voted down* as enemies, even impliedly, by the election here or a representative of that party which is energized along by the *conflict* doctrine.—If they are to be treated while here as friends, customers, brothers, let us vote them so after they have left us for their own peaceful homes and happy firesides. Let us throw the powerful arm of the ballot-box around them at a distance, as we would our own arms whilst sojourning here among us in the pursuit of business or pleasure. * * *

III

The Election of 1860

1. Augusta County

Staunton Spectator, "The Four Great Parties—Their Relative Position and Policy," July 31, 1860

The Spectator *reflects on the upcoming 1860 presidential election, attempting to explain for its readers what must happen for Abraham Lincoln to be defeated. The* Spectator, *a Whig Party newspaper, favored the election of the Constitutional Union candidate John Bell. Like most Virginians, however, the paper's editor wanted above all else to defeat Lincoln and the Republicans. People throughout Augusta County carefully considered the different ways the four-way presidential race could turn toward the South's advantage.*

The country now beholds the extraordinary spectacle of four great political parties striving for ascendancy in the Presidential contest.—There is the Republican, or Northern Sectional party, the Breckenridge, or Southern Sectional party, the Douglas, or Squatter Sovereignty party, and the Constitutional Union party. The policy of the first two named—whatever may be the intention of their supporters—necessarily leads to disunion. Neither of them has the order of nationality about it. They represent only the extreme opinion of their representative sections, and the success of either would be the triumph of one section over the other. The result would be to strain to the utmost, if not to break, the cords, which bring the Union together.

The Douglas party represents the small modicum of nationality which yet belongs to the Democracy. In Virginia it has its strength in the Tenth Legion and other districts most devoted to the Union, whilst in the secession, fire-eating districts, it is powerless. Objectionable as this party is, it is far more acceptable to the conservative sentiment of the country than either of the sectional parties, because it does not threaten the integrity of the Union.

The only purely national party now before the people is the Constitutional Union party.—It presents itself under the auspices of a Convention composed of distinguished men—men known to the whole country—and with candidates entitled to the confidence of the whole country. Bell and Everett are statesmen of mature experience, tried patriotism, and acknowledged ability. Amidst all the excitement of sectional strife, neither of them has been led into the expression or advocacy of extreme opinions or measures.—They have been emphatically men of moderation. Prudence, a wise discretion, and a catholic nationality, have characterized all their public conduct. The crisis demands the services of men of their stamp. The country now has more the need of the rein than the spur. The temper of the public mind is explosive. We require men who, by wisdom and conciliation, will calm down and smooth the popular excitement, and restore harmony and the spirit of concord to the nation. The divisions in public sentiment are such as to render it extremely doubtful whether there will be an election of the President by the people. Judging from the past, the Republican party is likely to have a plurality of the electoral vote, though in common with all men of national sentiments, we most earnestly hope that it will not rise into a majority.—The danger, however, as matters now stand, is from that quarter. It behooves all national Union-loving men, therefore, to consider maturely, the best means of arresting such a dire calamity as the election of a sectional Black Republican President. To this end, every arrangement for co-operation should be made by other organisations, which can be effected without an abandonment of fundamental principles.

Let us then proceed to consider what is the true policy of the conservative men of the Union:

The Republican and the Breckenridge or Secession parties, being both, as already stated, essentially sectional, and tending to the

same end—DISUNION—but by different means—it is manifest
that neither of the parties claiming to be national and Union-loving
can unite or co-operate with either of them. It would be like
mingling oil and water. It would involve an abandonment of the
cardinal principles of their national organizations. Between the
SECTIONAL and the NATIONAL parties there is an impassable
gulf—as wide as that which separated Lazarus and Dives.

But between the Douglas and Bell parties, there is no such in-
separable barrier. True they differ—differ widely on many important questions; but these are administrative questions, which are
entirely subordinate to the greater question of the permanency of
the Union. In view of the strong bond of sympathy between them,
arising out of a common devotion to the Union, these parties may
well afford to adjourn all functional questions for future adjudica-
tion, and address themselves earnestly, energetically, and patrioti-
cally to the preservation of the organism of our political system.
There is no vital antagonism between them, and no good reason
why they should not act together in the extraordinary emergency
that has arisen.

It must be obvious to every friend of Douglas that he cannot be
elected President by the Electoral Colleges. He has great strength
in the North-western States and in some of the Eastern and Middle States, but in the South he is powerless. His most sanguine supporters, therefore, can hardly suppose that he will carry a majority
of the whole number of electoral votes. The determined and relentless hostility of the Seceders, headed by Breckenridge, aided by
the Democratic Senators, and backed by Buchanan and his horde
of officials, precludes the possibility of his obtaining a majority.

His only hope, then, is in defeating the election of Lincoln by the
people, and going before the House of Representatives as one of
the three highest candidates. Lincoln will certainly be one of those
three. It is almost equally sure that Bell will be another. The only
question is, then, who shall be the third? The contest lies between
Douglas and Breckenridge—every vote cast *for Breckenridge* is substantially cast against Douglas. It is a death grapple between them.
One or the other must go to the wall, and it is entirely within the
power of the friends of Douglas to decide who it shall be. We advise the friends of Douglas to have a clear perception of this view

of the case, and for that purpose we will submit a practical illustration of it. Douglas certainly has no chance of carrying Delaware, Maryland, Virginia, North Carolina, Georgia, Florida, Tennessee, Kentucky, Missouri, Alabama, Mississippi, or Louisiana.—The Seceders are stronger than he is in many of these States, and almost as strong in others?—What then is his policy in regard to those States? If he should be soft enough to go into convention with the Seceders, is it not obvious that he would be in effect giving those States to his rival? This would be the consummation of folly—it would be suicide! Douglas holds the balance of power in most of those states. He can decide how they shall be thrown in between Breckenridge and Bell, and his friends should have the sagacity to see that every vote taken from Breckenridge adds to the relative strength of Douglas. It is to be hoped that they will perceive this palpable truth, and act accordingly. Douglas understands his game perfectly, and hence we shall see that Forney, professing to speak by authority, scorns and spits upon all chattering proposals of the Breckenridge men for a bargain. He knows that the embrace of the Seceders is death to him.

But let us look at the question in another aspect. Suppose we are in error in regard to the inherent and independent strength of the Bell ticket. Suppose that Breckenridge has more strength than Bell, would this enure to the benefit of Douglas? Certainly not. If he is to go before the House of Representatives it is clearly to his interests that Breckenridge should not be there to compete with him and divide the Democratic vote. It would be much better for him to have Lincoln and Bell as his competitors, because as against them he can unite the whole Democratic vote.

View the matter, then, as we may, it is clearly the policy of the friends of Douglas to see that the votes of the Southern States are cast for Bell, and to accomplish that object they should, if necessary, even vote for the Bell ticket.—We lay it down as a self-evident proposition that every man who desires to see Douglas have a fair chance in the House must use every effort to squeeze Breckenridge out!

Patriotism, too, prompts the adoption of the same course which policy dictates. Douglas himself, in his speech at Washington, denounced the Secession nomination of Breckenridge at Baltimore as a disunion ticket. Secession from [the] party is a prelude to secession from the confederacy. Believing this, it is the duty of every patriot to frown indignantly on every measure that tends to alienate one part of the country from the other, or to suggest even a suspicion that this Union can be dissolved. Believing this, Douglas and his friends cannot, without a sacrifice of principle and public duty, give their aid, either directly or indirectly, to the election of the Yancey Rhett candidate. * * *

* * * We say, then, to friends of Douglas, make a gallant fight wherever you can. Carry for him as many States as you can. But wherever, as in Virginia, for example, you cannot carry the State *for* Douglas, take especial care that it shall not be cast *against* him, by being given to Breckenridge. Use your power to rebuke party treason and secession, and to frustrate the ignoble purpose of Buchanan and his crew to trample you and your favorite under their feet!

Having thus given our views of the policy of the friends of Douglas, it only remains for us to say a word or two as to the course which should be pursued by the Constitutional Union party in the North.

Our primary objective is the defeat of the Sectional Republican candidate. Every other consideration should be secondary to that. As practical men, we should aim to achieve the greatest good to the country, and where that is not attainable, we should aim at the second best thing. We should strive to carry for Bell every State that we have a reasonable prospect of carrying; but where that cannot be done, we should throw our weight in the scale of Douglas as the most national and the least objectionable of the other candidates. By this interchange of support between the friends of Douglas and Bell, Lincoln can easily be defeated, and the election carried to the House where the choice must fall on Bell or Douglas. Wherever we are the strongest, as in the Southern States, Massachusetts, Rhode Island, Connecticut and New Jersey, the Douglas men should come to our aid. Whilst in Maine, New Hampshire, New York, Michigan, Illinois, Indiana, Ohio, and the other Northwestern States, our weight should be thrown in the scales of Douglas.

In regard to Pennsylvania, it may be doubtful which is the stronger, Bell or Douglas. Such being the case, it would be fair to make a division of the electoral ticket, and thus ensure the defeat of Lincoln.

It seems to us that the policy thus indicated, is the only one by which Lincoln can be defeated. * * *

John H. Cochran to His Mother, October 8, 1860

John Cochran writes to his mother in Augusta County about the upcoming presidential election. A zealous partisan of the Democrats and supporter of John C. Breckinridge in the 1860 election, Cochran explains his position on the election and his willingness to leave the Union if Breckinridge is not elected. Many whites in the South shared Cochran's fears that the rights of Southern people and states—by which they almost always meant the right to own and sell slaves— were imperiled by the political advantage that could come to the North as a consequence of that region's rapidly expanding population.

Richmond Oct 8th 1860

Dear Mother

Your letter was received this evening and I take this opportunity of answering it. I am glad to hear that Franks opinions upon political principles are undergoing a change and hope that by the time he has a vote that like his brother he will be an orthodox democrat.

As to the party to which I belong being disunionists it is a charge that cannot be substantiated and I defy anyone to prove by our platform of principles or by the record of either of our candidates that we are.

There are men in the party (of which I am one) who seeing that without a vigorous effort we will be wrecked upon that shoal to which we have been slowly but surely been drifting for years—I mean slavish *submission* to a mear numerical majority. We hold to the principle among others that this government is not solely the government of a majority but that the minority have rights that *must* be respected. To preserve these rights the constitution was framed which puts such checks and restraints upon the dominant power as the framers in their far seeing wisdom thought necessary.

But it is said that at this late day we have suddenly waked up to the idea that we were not getting our rights in the Union and that the leaders of the party were disposed to ruin the country for the sake of reopening the slave trade. The last of these charges is a rediculous absurdity and could only been hatched in the brain of some unscroupulous opponent of the true States Rights Democracy.

Now as to the other question we have been battling against abolitionism in some form or other for many years. The abolition of slavery has been agitated in congress ever since 1790 first came petitions in that year for the abolition of the slave trade. Then petitions in 1805 for the exclusion of slave property from the teritories. Then in 1817 petitions against the slave trade between the middle and southern states. Then in 1831 petitions for the abolition of slavery in the District of Columbia. In 1836 Calhoun declared that the agitation of this question "would sunder the Union." "It was agitation here that they feared" James Buchannan showed that the moment it was abolished in the District that this Union would be dissolved. In 37 the contest grew hot in the house of representitives and there for the first time John Bell proved himself a disunionist by helping to keep open an agitation which Statesmen like Calhoun had declared would break up the Union.

From that time foarth he has acted with the abolition party sometimes openly at other times he failed to vote on either side— at others he deemed it prudent to represent his constituents.

Now on the other hand the party to which I am attached have always been consistently opposed to all such measures. We (speaking of the Democracy) have opposed the agitation of this subject in the halls of Congress. We have denied the right to petition upon the subject because slaves were propperty under the Constitution. (Though Botts in his late speech here took the ground that they were not) and could not be confiscated.

We have procured a decission of the Supreme Court in our favour (Dred Scott case). Speaking of the power of Congress in the teritories Judge Chief Justice Taney uses these very words. "The only power confered is the power coupled with the duty to protect of guarding and protecting the owner in his rights." Out of the nine judges of the court seven concured in this decission. And yet when we incorporate this in our creed and demand that Congress shall exercise this protecting power we are branded as traitors by the very party who were loudest in their professions of loyalty to the South a few short months ago. The party which declares that they go for the enforcement of the laws. Yet when we ask to have this power which the higest tribunal in the country has declared is legal enforced cries out that we want to break up the Union—and that we are a set of traitors who ought all of us to be hung.

We have been driven to the wall at last. As a last resort we stand upon the Virginia and Kentucky resilutions of 98 and 99. By them we have determined to stand or fall. Holding up the Constitution we have asked to have the rights it secures us given to us in the Union. If we have theme we are the last people who would wish to dissolve the Union. On the other hand we have determined that if it is necessary that we should go out of the Union for the purpose of maintaining these rights that we will do it. It is an alternitive which we do not seak but as a free people we will not submit to having our rights taken from us by that greatest of all tyrants a numerical majority. We will have no more men like Bell to compromise our rights away—compromise but invites aggression. For one I am like Harry Hotspur "upon a matter of right I will cavil to the ninth part of a hair." Upon the election of Lincoln which the opposition I fear are making but too sure—some if not all of the Cotton states will leave the Union if they are allowed to leave peacibly the other slave states will not be slow in following where interest points. If the Federal power attempts to coerce them into the Union again the border states will not be slow to make common cause with their more southern sisters. So that in any event we will have a *United* South. * * *

* * * Baylors proposiston to fuse with the Douglass faction fell like a bomb among us and I confess I among others was afraid a fusion upon that basis would be acceeded to. Thank Heaven that danger is past and that our [illegible word] electoral ticket remains

untarnished with the name of a single man who holds to the hericies or follows the fortunes of that desperate political gambler Stephen Arnold Douglass. * * *

* * * I suppose you are about as tired as I am by this time so I will close. Hoping that all are well

I remeain your affectionate son.

J.H. Cochran

Staunton Spectator, "Are You Ready?" October 23, 1860

Only two weeks away from the election, the Spectator *exhorts the people of Augusta to vote for John Bell as the only candidate with "a chance of defeating Lincoln." Although it continued to promote its own party and candidate, the newspaper hoped to entice others to vote for John Bell by urging people to place the preservation of the Union above their own particular partisan preferences. Even though Lincoln appeared nearly impossible to defeat by October, many people in Augusta continued to seek political alliances that might prevent the Republicans from winning the presidency.*

In two weeks from this day the people of the United States will be called upon to decide the most important election that has ever been held in this country. The very existence of the Government, it may be, is dependent upon the result of this election. The great and important issue is union or disunion. Will we remain a united, free, prosperous and happy people, or shall we be involved in all the evils of anarchy and discord, and all the indescribable horrors of civil war and fratricidal strife? This is a time when more considerations of party should be lost sight of entirely, and when every one should look alone to the preservation of our government, and the salvation of the Union, the only guarantee of our liberties. The man who, in this fearful crisis of our country's fate, is controlled by mere partizan considerations, is a traitor to his country. When the Government is not threatened, and when the Union is not imperilled, when we are concerned alone about the best mode of administering the Government, and differ only about the measures of policy, it is well enough then to be controlled to some extent by party preferences, and even blind party prejudice can be tolerated, if not excused, but when the Government is in danger and the Union is trembling upon the brink of ruin, it is time to turn a deaf ear to the syren [*sic*] voice of party and obey the solemn injunctions of patriotic duty. At this time our country calls and her voice should be obeyed. We concur with the *Frederick (Md.) Examiner* that the issue is Union or disunion.—Other issues may be interpolated and magnified, but they are of inferior consequence; the great and real issue is, the preservation of our form of free government, or the evils of Civil Discord, the danger of Anarchy and the prospect of States dissevered, discordant and belligerent, as the alternative.

In this fearful crisis, every lover of his country is expected to do his duty, as becomes a free-man. Fellow-citizens, are you prepared for the responsibility? Gird on the armor of patriotism, carefully survey the field, be ready, and may He who has hitherto guarded and guided us in every step by which we have advanced to the dignity of a great, powerful and enlightened nation, preserve us as a united people!

"Eternal vigilance is the price of liberty." See to it, therefore, that apathy or neglect afford no occasion for vain regrets and remorse. Let every man go to the polls, and forgetting party distinctions, repudiating the behests of party leaders, and burying by-gone political animosities for a season, vote with an eye single to the preservation of the Union, the maintenance of the Constitution and the Enforcement of the laws.

The enemies of the Constitution, whose fanaticism threatens evil and danger, are one in sentiment and purpose. The intoxication of prospective success excites their zeal beyond the restraints of prudence. The opposition is divided; its strength is frittered away in unprofitable contentions upon abstract propositions, and fostered prejudices. If the Union be dissolved, how can the factionists hope to decide their petty quarrels; where will the demagogues then be; how shall the right, they now profess to struggle for, be longer guaranteed them?

The time has come to meet the impending crisis in a manly, decided and Constitutional manner. It is clear that the friends of the Union must make common cause and rally under the leaders who can and will save the Union, restore peace and mutual trust, and crush out sectionalism. Who can do it? Can Douglas and Johnson achieve the repose the country so much needs? They may be many times stronger in the popular and electoral vote than their rival Southern faction; yet every one knows, they are impotent against Lincoln and in no possible event can either of them be elected to the Presidential office. Can Breckinridge and Lane accomplish more? Mr. Breckinridge is practically out of the fight; his friends know he stands no earthly chance, and that his continued candidacy only gives "aid and comfort" to Lincoln. Granting all the strength his most zealous friends claim for him, what can these avail? Absolutely nothing, except to weaken and divide the strength of the Union nominees! The calculation of Mr. Lane's election by the Senate is too remote and uncertain to authorize his course thus far. The ONLY candidates, who STAND A CHANCE of DEFEATING Lincoln and Hamlin, are BELL and EVERETT; the contest lies between Bell and Lincoln, and the duty of every conservative citizen is plain and urgent. The Union must and shall be preserved; Lincoln must and will be defeated, and the way to do both is by giving a united and cordial support to Bell.

The struggle is no child's play; it will be fierce and arduous. "Work, work," Conservatives, your country calls. From this hour to the close of the polls on election day, be active energetic and diligent. Reason with your neighbors, see that every voter goes to the polls.

Lucas P. Thompson to John H. McCue, November 1, 1860

Lucas Thompson, a member of the Whig Party, writes to his friend John McCue about the near certainty of Lincoln's election and his hope that Virginia will avoid secession. Like so many in Augusta County, Thompson believed that secession would produce even more dire consequences for Virginia than Lincoln's election.

Staunton Nov 1. 1860

Dear Sir

I enclose you an [illegible word] of appeal in the case of Dickinson vs. Page: As to the election our prospects are gloomy enough; almost every person I see has despaired of defeating the Black Republican Lincoln. My Motto is Nil desperandium. I am Still hopeful of the election of Bell & Everitt or some one of the antirepublican tickets, and if the worst comes to the worst and Lincoln is elected their will be neither Secession or disunion. Such a consequence would be of a piece with the Madness & folly of committing suicide for fear of dying. Let us wait for an overt act (which I verily believe will not be committed by Lincoln or his allies) and cling to our glorious union as long as possible consistently with honor safety & liberty, for in disunion I can foresee woes innumerable, no remedy for our grievances but rather as aggravation of them all, in short the greatest calamity that could befall not only the U S but the cause of free government throughout the world. We shall have a grand whig rally here tomorrow. Baldwin & Stuart will address the mass meeting.

Very respectfully
yr fr & obt st.
Lucas P. Thompson

Staunton Spectator, "Though Lincoln is elected, there is no danger," November 13, 1860

In the aftermath of Lincoln's election, the Staunton Spectator *attempts to calm its readers by reminding them that the Republicans now control only the presidency, and the Democrat-dominated Congress and Supreme Court could easily hold the executive branch in check. In seeking to persuade people that Lincoln would be unable to challenge Southern institutions, the paper hoped to keep Virginia from seceding from the Union. The* Spectator *shared the opinion of many in the county that secession would imperil Virginia slavery.*

It is with deep pain that we announce the triumph of a Northern Sectional party. We have labored earnestly to prevent that result, and supported the only ticket which carried the flag around which all the conservative strength of the country could rally without sacrifice of principle. The ticket we supported bore aloft a *national* banner around which conservatives North and South should have rallied with the view of preventing the success of sectionalism North or South. Our efforts were unsuccessful, though applied in the right direction, and sectionalism has triumphed over nationality.—Though we are mortified at the success of the Black Republicans in the Presidential election, yet we are rejoiced to know that the elections for Congressmen have resulted in giving us a very safe and decided majority against the Republicans in Congress. The success of the Republicans in the Presidential election is but a barren victory, and its fruits, like the apples of the Dead Sea, will turn to ashes upon their lips. They will have the Executive, but no other branch of the Government, and will, consequently, be impotent for mischief—they will not have the power to do any harm, however much disposed they may be to do so. We have the Senate, the House of Representatives and the Supreme Court in our favor, either one of which would of itself be a sufficient protection to our rights. As we have all three there can, by no possibility, be any danger that our rights can be violated. No law can reach the President for his signature without first having passed *both* Houses of Congress, and we know that as at present composed no bill violative of our rights can pass *either House*. So that we are perfectly safe. The President cannot even make an appointment without the consent of the Senate, so that we have nothing to dread in that respect. If we remain united we have nothing to fear from the Black Republicans, because, as before stated, we have both Houses of Congress and the Supreme Court in our favor. The danger is in secession. If several of the Southern States secede, they will leave us in a minority in Congress, where we now have a safe majority. This may be the reason why some of the Southern States are in such a hurry to secede. They think that if they secede and leave us at the mercy of a Black Republican majority in Congress, that we will secede likewise. This is the way in which they expect to drag us into a like destiny with them. They will secede when we have a safe majority and there can be no danger, that we may be left in a minority where danger will threaten, in the confident belief that we will then secede and unite our fortunes with theirs. To secede when there can be no danger would be adding cowardice to treason. To give up when we have the game in our own hands would be cowardly, foolish and criminal. South Carolina, and other States disposed to secede, should remember that comity due to neighboring States should restrain them from taking action without consulting the wishes and interests of other States, particularly such as Virginia which is more deeply interested than all the Cotton States combined. As no man has a right to destroy even his own property when by so doing he will endanger that of his neighbor, so no State has the right to secede when that act will involve other States in the common ruin. Virginia has interests independent of the Cotton States, and she should take care of them in spite of the action of those States.

2. Franklin County

Simon Cameron to Abraham Lincoln, August 1, 1860

Simon Cameron, a Franklin County resident who would become Abraham Lincoln's first secretary of war, writes to congratulate Lincoln on his nomination for president by the Republican Party. Cameron assures Lincoln of delivering Pennsylvania—a possible swing state in the election and critical to the party's success—for the Republicans. As presidential candidates during the period did almost no campaigning themselves, Lincoln relied on men like Cameron who operated the party organizations in each state to rally supporters to the polls.

Harrisburg. Aug. 1. 1860.

My dear Sir,
   I should have written you sooner, with the view to congratulate
you, upon the cordiality with which your nomination has been responded to throughout the country and the abundant assurances of
final success heard from all quarters, but have waited until, I had
seen enough of my friends in different parts of our own state to
form a positive opinion of the election here, in Pennsylvania.
   I can now do so and am glad to say that you will get the state beyond the shadow of a doubt. Your friends need give themselves no
trouble about us; and may occupy their time in making Illinois &
Indiana safe. We need no help here, *of any kind*. The state is for you,
and we all have faith in your good intentions to stand by her interests as they are connected with her coal and now beyond which we
have no desires.
   My young friend, Mr. Lesley told me you had shown him your
notes of speeches made in 1844, on the subject of protection, and
his account of them gratifies all of us, very much.
   We shall elect our Gov. M Curtin, by a handsome majority, but
by no means as large a one as you will get in Nov.
   I only regret that our opponents are not united for we would
have beaten their great man Douglas with all there forces concentrated, and would [illegible words] a context [illegible word] when
they will unite on him or [illegible word] other single candidate. His
friends and those of Breckenridge, are now more bitter against
each other than they are against us and I fear that after the elections they will try to ascribe their defeat & our victory solely to their
divisions. We will try to keep this [illegible word] from them by
making your majority a very large one.
   I regret that Pennsylv. is safe.—as much so as Massachusetts or
Michigan, and I hope our friends in other states will give all their
attention to Illinois & Indiana. Your friends here will be responsible
for Pennsylvania.

Very truly yr friend
S. C.

Franklin Repository, "The Victory," November 14, 1860

The Repository, *like all Republican newspapers, revels in the news of the election of Abraham Lincoln as the first Republican president. Covering many of the central concerns of the Republican Party in this celebratory article, the newspaper predicts that Lincoln's administration will provide new opportunities for white laborers throughout the country.*

The battle has been fought and the victory won! The spirit of the people rose with the fierceness of the contest!—The loud, wild, angry war-whoop of disunion did not frighten the brave sons of liberty! The more terrible appeared the foe, the more valliant became the army of the free! No struggle, since the formation of our Government, was fraught with such important principles! A long list of abuses, frauds, peculations and crimes filled up the measure of the party in power. Bankruptcy, as a necessary consequence of the ruinous policy of the dominant party, covered the land with its sable pall since the inauguration of the existing Dynasty. Idleness, want and starvation, the necessary adjuncts of a depression of the industrial interests of any nation, were obtruding their unwelcome form into the dwellings of our working people. Endurance ceased to be a virtue, and resistance became an absolute duty. The times required decisive action; the people rose in their might and applied the proper remedy.

After the 4th of March, 1861, another administration, another class of men will take hold of the helm of the old ship of state. They will begin with a clean sheet; no foul blots mar the pages of their record. No party ever was more loyal to the whole country—more devoted to the best interests of all classes of society, than is the Republican party. The poor man, desirous of employment, has the prospect of work in the Tariff policy of our party—which seeks to foster every branch of American industry against ruinous foreign competition. He who wants a home for himself and little ones, who has no means to procure one, is cheered with the expectation of the speedy passage of a Free Homestead bill—knowing that "honest old Abe" will never veto such a measure. All who desire the beautiful prairies of the far West preserved sacred from the polluting foot-prints of a slave, will feel their hearts bounding with joy as they read, not only in the public prints of the day, but in the sparkling eyes of Freedom's honest devotees, the glad news of the Victory of liberty over oppression; of truth and justice over falsehood and cruelty.

Franklin Repository, "A Prophecy Fulfilled," November 14, 1860

The Repository *asserts that Abraham Lincoln received numerous votes in several Southern districts, despite the fact that the position of the Republicans on slavery had been misrepresented in the South. Republican newspapers like the* Repository *hoped the party would be able to establish a base of support in the South among the non-slaveholding whites who made up 75 percent of the region's population in 1860. Lincoln, however, failed to draw any significant support in the South. He did best in Missouri (where he drew about 10 percent of the vote), but failed to garner almost any votes in the rest of the South (where he was not even on the ballot in nine states).*

* * * No candidate for the Presidency, we believe, ever before received such tremendous majorities of the popular vote as has the old Rail-splitter of Illinois—"honest Abe Lincoln." His vote in the Free States especially, is overwhelming—crushing—and if the Republican party had been permitted to canvass the Southern States, and thus have been able to disabuse the public mind as to its true intention and policy, Mr. Lincoln would have carried the Electoral Vote of many of them too. But the minds of the Southern people have been poisoned against the Republican party and its leaders, so much so indeed, that a hearing was not only not granted, but it was as much as a man's life was worth to even intimate, in a Southern community, that he favored the election of a Republican. Locofoco Demagoges, North and South, have persisted in stigmatizing

the Republican party as "sectionalists," "abolitionists," "nigger-worshippers," and as "enemies of the South," who would, if suc-cessful, liberate the Southern Slaves. To such an extent was these foul-mouthed misrepresentations indulged in, that the people of the South, hearing nothing else, believed the statements to be true, and thus were educated to regard every Northern man, and especially a Republican, as a friend of John Brown of Harper's Ferry notoriety, and a bitter enemy of their domestic peace and tranquility. The whole course of the Locofoco party, in this respect, has been an out-rage—a *libel* upon the rights of free speech and a free press.

But we are gratified to announce the fact, that in the face and teeth of these slanders, the returns show that we have a consider-able party South of Mason and Dixon's line. Lincoln leads the col-umn in the city of St. Louis, in a Slave State, polling 8,962 votes, beside a very respectable vote through the State. He polled over 800 votes in two counties in Western Virginia and 600 in the city of Wheeling. He also polled 268 votes in Newport, Kentucky. 100 in Louisville, and more than 1000 in Baltimore, besides a considerable vote in Washington. In the State of Delaware, Abraham Lincoln runs second best. The *Wilmington State Journal*, which is quite jubi-lant over the result, contains returns which are nearly complete, and which foot up for Breckinridge 6,147; Lincoln, 3,751; Bell, 3,272 and Douglas 992. Besides this, George P. Fisher, who sympa-thyzes with the Republicans in all their leading ideas—the non-Extension of Slavery, Free Homesteads, Protection to American Industry, &c.—is elected to Congress from little Delaware.

In view of the John Brown raid, which so terrified the South, and the infamous falsehoods and misrepresentations promulgated by the Locofoco press and leaders, North and South, we think the foregoing presents a very encouraging picture. And after Abraham has taken hold of the helm of the Ship of State and navigated her for a year or two, by that time the fears, of our afrightened and timid Southern brethren will have become allayed—their shattered nerves will have become settled and calm, and they will then be in a position to look back coolly, perhaps blushingly, upon the ridicu-lous figure they have displayed before a laughing world. Then they will be in a condition to listen to reason, and we confidently expect such a re-action in Southern public sentiment that the next

Republican candidate for President will sweep the South just as Lincoln has now the North, and that he will be carried to the White House, with, if possible, more proudly "flying colors" than are those of our newly elected Chief Magistrate, Abraham Lincoln.

For the present, however, we would say, soothingly, to the South—"Do thyself no harm"—the bugaboos won't hurt you.

Valley Spirit, "The Election," November 14, 1860

The Valley Spirit, *a Democratic paper, expresses its distaste for Lincoln's election, sympathizes with Southern fears of a Republican president, and predicts the secession of multiple parts of the country. Most Democrats in the North shared the* Spirit's *fears of what Lincoln's election might mean for the nation, though most also hoped that a political compromise between the Republicans and the South could prevent secession and civil war.*

The election is over and so far as the grand result is concerned there is no longer any suspense. The North has rolled up a decisive majority for ABRAHAM LINCOLN as President, and HANIBAL HAMLIN as Vice President of the Nation. It is the first time in the history of the country that its national head has been elected by a purely sectional vote. What the result of this sectional triumph will be it is not difficult to conjecture. Fifteen States are without a President—they took no part in his election, and refuse their consent to come under an administration founded upon a sentiment hostile to their social system. A contemporary remarks—"It remains for the fifteen slave States to say whether the Union shall continue, or whether by secession this confederacy of thirty-three States shall be reduced to eighteen. That occurring, it will then have to be determined whether the Middle States will consent to remain in association with the New England States, and whether the empire of the Northwest will remain as it is, or set up for itself. Let disintegration once begin, and no man can tell where it will stop."

While we fear the worst results to the nation from the election of LINCOLN we still trust that the threatened calamity may be averted—that He who holds the destiny of nations in His hands and whose high prerogative it is to change curses into blessings and to extract good from evil may turn aside the danger in our way, and our glorious union still remain—

"Giant aggregate of nations;
Glorious whole of glorious parts,
Unto endless generations
Live united, hands and hearts!
Be it storm or summer weather,
Peaceful calm or battle jar,
Stand in bounteous strength together,
Sister States, as now ye are."

Valley Spirit, "The Secession Movement," November 21, 1860

The Valley Spirit *argues that the South has just cause for "war-like prepara-tions" in the wake of Lincoln's election, although the paper also warns that Southerners will lose Northern sympathy if they try to nullify federal laws. The* Spirit's *editor, like many Democrat editors in the North, believed that the Re-publican press was trying to drive the South from the Union and that secession could still be avoided if heated political rhetoric among Republicans would cease.*

We present in the columns of the *Spirit*, this week, copious ex-tracts from our exchanges, all over the country, in relation to the se-cession movement in the South. We give the news on both sides as we find it. While one portion of the Southern people appear de-termined to set up for themselves, another portion, evidently the minority, tell us the disunion sentiment is rapidly losing ground and that the "great panic" will subside without "firing a shot." Our readers can peruse the extracts and judge for themselves how portentous are the dangers which threaten the Union.

That the South has just ground for complaint, and much danger to apprehend from a sectional administration of the Government, cannot be doubted or denied; but we do not believe that secession from the Union is the best remedy to right her wrongs. We put in no protest against her war-like preparations, we do not object to her arming her citizens, we have no fault to find with her for placing herself in a complete state of defense ready for any emergency that may arise requiring her to protect her honor, safety or property. That course is all right—that is patriotic. Thus far the South has now advanced and if she maintains her stand there she will find plenty of "aid and comfort" in the North. It is certainly much to her credit that amidst all the excitement and turmoil which prevails among her populace not a single act of resistance to the laws of the United States has yet been committed. While this is her position, and so long as she maintains this attitude, she will not only command the admiration of the North but will find no lack of willing hands and sympathising hearts to assist her in repelling any and every aggression that may be essayed against her constitutional rights. If the South, however, has made up her mind that we are bad neighbors and is determined to cut loose from us and nullify the laws of the land, without a good and sufficient cause to show for it, she may place herself beyond the pale of sympathy or support from any quarter and will have to depend on her own resources to "carry the war into Africa."

While we have no hesitancy in asserting that there is a strong feeling among the masses in the North in favor of the South, and no disposition to meddle with her affairs, we would not at the same time desire to conceal the fact that a portion—and a very large and influential portion too—of the northern people would readily plunge the country into civil war if they thought they could thereby inflict injury on the slave-owner. The tone of the Republican press, pretty generally, indicate this state of feeling. Their deep unmitigated hatred of the slave-holder is the moving spring of their policy—not because they desire the freedom or happiness of the slave—that is words without meaning to them—but because the Southern States are strongly Democratic in sentiment they would drive them out of the Union. The language of irritation and menace which the North is so fond of applying to the South is not very well calculated to allay excitement and restore good feeling between us and our Southern brethren. If the North would act in good faith towards the South and not set the bad example of nullifying the plain provisions of the Constitution and the laws of Congress this trouble would not now exist and peace, confidence and prosperity would be restored to the country. The blame lies at the door of the North—let us act righteously towards the South and we will bear nothing more of Secession or Nullification.

Alexander K. McClure to Edward McPherson, December 14, 1860

Alexander McClure, a prominent Republican and newspaper editor in Franklin County, writes to Edward McPherson, the Republican U.S. Congressman for Franklin and Adams counties, about the difficulties of compromise between the North and the South. For McClure, as for many Republicans, it appeared impossible for the party to compromise its opposition to the expansion of slavery into the western territories. McClure also recognized that Southerners felt just as strongly that slavery must be allowed to spread west, and he despaired of finding a compromise that would prevent secession and avoid war.

Chambersburg Dec 14th

D Sir

Yours from of the 10th was duly recd. & read with pleasure

However impracticable may be the Southern leader at Washington & in the discontented States, it is manifest that the righteous, firm & temperate position of the Republicans generally is telling upon the Southern people.

I do not see myself how the matter is to be compromised. The difficulty may be adjusted & the adjustment termed a compromise; but it must in fact be a surrender on one side or the other. How is the right to hold slaves in *transit* to be compromised? How is a Slave Cide to be compromised? The North can never consent to the universal dominion of Slavery in this nation and nothing less will satisfy the South; and indeed nothing less will ensure the perpetuation of Slavery. The restoration of the Missouri Compromise line & its extension to the Pacific, would grate very harshly upon the connections of the Northern people. It would be no concession to the North, for it would make no territory free that could by any possibility be slave; while it would inevitably force Slavery into Southern California, New Mexico, & would be followed by the annexation of Cuba & the absorption of another slice of Mexico. Rest assured that if the North concedes its present forces, the South will ever here after have the preponderance in the Senate & practically the supreme [illegible word] of the government. Our present victory would be fruitless save to disgrace us as a party in our establishment & in the eyes of the civilized world.

What is to be done I can scarcely suggest. I know what should be done. The North should enforce the laws at home and also enforce the supremacy of the laws with all insurgent States; but as a party we are divided, & I am not hopeful of a happy & creditable solution of the difficulty. * * *

* * * I see that a paper is circulating among the Penn Members enjoy Cameron for a Cabinet appointment. I trust our delegation will not add to the already dangerous force of that man. He can't go into the Cabinet. For the rebellion will be terrible wherever it seems to be possible, & the party would not survive his rule a single year.

Will you be home during the holidays? If so perhaps we may meet at Harrisburg about New Year. Write me often

Very Truly Yours
AK McClure

IV
Secession

1. Augusta County

John D. Imboden to John H. McCue, December 3, 1860

John Imboden, a prominent Augusta lawyer and Whig, writes to his friend John McCue to explain his views on secession. Although he favored the secession of Virginia, Imboden did not believe that Virginia would be justified in leaving the Union unless Lincoln committed an act of aggression against the South, worrying that slaveholders—such as himself—would otherwise be hard-pressed to convince non-slaveholders to support the cause.

Staunton
Dec 3. 1860

Dear John,

My apology for delaying an answer so long to your letter in the old place of business. I have never been more engaged in my life than Since my return from Ky. I read your letter with interest. We are not really so far apart as you suppose. I understand that you are a "Union man"—So am I—You would resist Republicanism—so would I—We neither think V*a* ought to secede—or rather revolt *just* now. You think S. Carolina ought to go out now, I think not—and here is the only point of difference between us, so far as I can see. That the entire South will speedily have to leave the Confederacy under the present Constitution I entertain no doubt whatever, but I dont think S. C. has put the issue upon a defensible ground—the mere election of a President under the Forms of law &c. Hence you have a *divided* South. My idea is this—regard Lincoln's election as another step towards that sectional domination to which we never will submit if it be attained, and so regarding it, let us go to work to *prepare* for resistance when *actual cause* arises. Then you would be prepared for any contingency. Then you would have a *united* South. But to break up the Government for the mere loss of an election is not regarded by thousands as justifiable. It is regarded as a mere pretext on the part of disunionists *per se* to precipitate a revolution. You can't make the great mass of the people—especially the non slaveholder's understand the political philosophy of our government, and the nice principles on which the Secessionists are now attempting to act. And there is great danger of creating a party with sympathies for the incoming administration, here in our midst. The non slaveholder will fight for his section as long as the slaveholder if you can convince him that *his* political rights are really threatened, as *a citizen*. But he is not willing to leave his family & offer his life in a struggle which he believes is a mere contest between politicians for the spoils of office—and while he believes that the successful party ought to have the opportunity to develop its policy. Therefore I am opposed to immediate action. I am for preparation now—defence when the equality of my State is actually denied.

If I had my way now, I would fight the Republicans thus—I would say to Lincoln "You have been elected by the vote of only about one third of the people of the U. States. Your party is revolutionary in its organization, tendencies & aims. No man of your party ought to fill any national office if it can be prevented. We—the conservative 2/3rds of the American people still control the Senate & H. of Reps. of the U. States. We will use our power in those bodies to protect ourselves. We understand your party aims at the subjugation of 15 States & you as their head are expected to further their objects. We therefore declare war upon you & your party as you have declared war upon us. You shall have no tools of yours in office to aid you in your unholy work. The Senate must confirm all your appointments to office before they are valid. Now Sir! no man of your party is fit for *any* office, because his political opinions are destructive of American liberty. The Senate therefore will refuse—as they ought to do, being the reps. of the Sovereignty of the States which you seek to assail—to confirm to office any man who votes for you. We offer you the range of all other parties from which to select your Cabinet, your ministers, Post Masters, Collectors, Attorneys, Judges &c and we will confirm no others." If this ground was firmly taken & maintained, Lincoln would be utterly powerless. It would soon be understood that not *he*, but the *Senate* was the real appointive power, and then no man need hesitate about taking office under his administration for he would hold it, not from Lincoln but from the Senate. The President would have a Cabinet to watch him & control him. It may be said such a course would be revolutionary—perhaps it would—but it would be under & within the Constitution. And I would go further if he refused to submit to this control. I would defeat all appropriations of money for *all* purposes whatever & thus dissolve the government into its original elements. This would disband the army, destroy the navy, break up the P. Office & Judiciary, and leave each State as it was before the Constitution was adopted, Sovereign & free. All this I would do & do speedily, rather than leave this government in existence & organized to do us all the harm in their power in the event of our revolt now. Hence I think S.C. &c [illegible word] to go off now till these various modes of resistance have been tried. These are mere hints on the various points mentioned. I have not time to amplify them. But I fear revolution is upon us. I expect Civil War before the 1st of June. I am ready for it, if it comes but it will be awful in its consequences to the whole country. I shall be ruined by it. Instead of leaving my children as I had hoped well provided for they will be left, as I began life, poor, with the wide world before them. But while I cant help looking at such consequences, I would face them all, lose all, even life before I would submit to be less than the political equal of any man who treads American soil. I am afraid the die is cast, and that no power on earth can avert the impending ruin of anarchy & bloodshed. But I forbear dwelling longer on this theme. If I can get the time, I will one of these nights write you my views in full. * * *

* * * We are all well. Mollie sends love to Coz Liz. We often speak of you & wish we could see you more frequently.

Yours truly
J D Imboden

Staunton Spectator, "To the People of Augusta County," January 22, 1861

Alexander H. H. Stuart writes an open letter to the people of Augusta County, urging them to resist secession. A leading Whig in the county, Stuart represented Augusta in the Virginia General Assembly and would later be elected as a Unionist to the Virginia secession convention. In his letter, Stuart stressed the hardships—particularly economic—that he believed Augusta would endure if Virginia decided to leave the Union. Stuart was the most prominent of the Unionists in the county who sought to convince their neighbors and friends that secession would imperil the future of Augusta County, including slavery.

Fellow Citizens:—Ten days of the session of the General Assembly have passed away, and little has yet been done toward the adjustment of the controversies which unhappily distract our country. Knowing the anxiety which all true patriots must feel in regard to the condition of public affairs, I am impelled by a sense of representative duty, to give you such information, and such words of counsel, as seem to me appropriate to the occasion.

Since the first day of the session, Richmond has been the scene of unexampled excitement.—The disunionists from all parts of the State have been here full force, and have sought to bring every influence to bear to precipitate Virginia into secession and civil war. It will be for the people to determine, whether their efforts shall be crowned with success. It behooves them to be vigilant, if they value the peace of the country, and desire to escape the burthens of Military service and grinding taxation. If secession takes place, in my judgment, civil war is inevitable, and the people must expect their taxes to be doubled, if not quadrupled. State bonds are now selling, in New York, at a discount of twenty-five per cent, and it is idle to talk of borrowing money. It must be raised, and raised in millions of dollars, by taxation. The newspapers inform us, that in South Carolina, negroes are, at this early stage of their struggle, taxed sixteen dollars per head, and that the government has resorted to forced loans from the Banks and property holders. One case is mentioned, in which a merchant, with a capital of $40,000, was compelled to loan to the State $8,000.

Sooner or later, the burthen must fall on the landholders. Slaves, stocks, bonds and other personal property, may be sold and removed, but the land must remain, to bear the brunt of taxation. It is proper that you should understand this, that you may vote intelligently on the questions which will soon be submitted for your decision at the polls.

I do not propose, in this brief letter, to enter into any elaborate discussion of the doctrine of secession, or to point out all the disastrous consequences that would flow from it. It will suffice to say, that it is a doctrine of New England origin. It had its birth among the Federalists of that section of the Union, during the war of 1812, and was nurtured in the celebrated Hartford Convention. In 1814, it was denounced by such Republicans as Spencer Roane, and Thos. Ritchie, as treason. While I do not endorse this strong language to its full extent, in my judgement, it is at war with the whole theory of our institutions, and is subversive of every principle of popular government.

The favorite scheme of many of the leading politicians is, to break up the Union, with a view to re-construct it. Their plan is, to form a Southern Confederacy. I am unalterably opposed to both of these propositions; I believe that either would be the source of incalculable evil. In my opinion, there is no natural antagonism between the Northern and Southern States. On the contrary, each is necessary to the other. They are the complements of each other, and together constitute the most perfect social, industrial and political systems, that the world has ever seen. Each is indispensable to the welfare of the other. They minister to each others' interests and necessities. The South produces what the North wants, but cannot produce; and the North furnishes what the South needs, but cannot supply for itself. The diversity of productions, and systems of labor, should therefore be a bond of Union instead of a source of Discord. The present condition of antagonism and alienation is unnatural. It is not the legitimate result of any conflict of the social and industrial systems of the two sections, but is the work of those "DESIGNING MEN," both North and South, against whom Washington so impressively warned us in his farewell address.

It is true that the Northern States, under the lead of such men, have been guilty of gross outrages on the rights of the South—outrages which would justify the most energetic measures of retaliation, but I have not been able to persuade myself that a dissolution of the Union furnishes the appropriate means of redress. I believe that all our rights can be secured, and all our wrongs most effectually redressed in the Union, and under the Constitution. Secession, instead of being a remedy, would be an aggravation of them all. I have not been able to perceive how we could add to the security of our slave property by surrendering the guarantees of the Constitution, and substantially bringing down the Canada frontier to the borders of Virginia. It would lead to emancipation and probably to emancipation in blood. Nor can I see how we would *secure* our rights in the territories by *abandoning* them. I am equally at a loss to understand how we will establish any of our demands against the Northern States on a firmer basis, by severing our connection with them, and thereby from us, the million and a half of friends we had in those States at the last election.

My view of the true policy of Virginia is, that she should remain in the Union until all Constitutional means of obtaining redress for the past and security for the future, shall have proved fruitless. I do not think the time has come for an appeal to the arbitrament of arms.

Should the Union be dissolved peaceably, and a Southern Confederacy be formed, it is clear that the policy of the new government will be shaped by the Cotton States. Free trade and direct taxation for the support of the Federal Government, will be the cardinal features of that policy, on your interests.

The expense of sustaining the present government of the U. S., ranges from sixty to eighty millions of dollars per annum. This amount is raised by duties on foreign goods, imported into the country. Those persons who purchase foreign goods, pay the tax, as an element in the price of the goods, while those who buy no foreign goods, pay none of the tax. The tax is therefore *voluntary*, if paid. But under the system of free trade and direct taxation, the tax would be *involuntary*. No election would be left to the people to pay it or not, as they might think proper. It would be levied, like the State tax, by assessment on the property of the country. Assuming that the cost of maintaining the Southern Confederated Government would be but one half the amount expended by the present government of the U. S., the contributive portion of Virginia would approximate five millions of dollars. You will readily comprehend how heavily it would bear upon the people to pay this large amount, in addition to the present State taxes, out of their hard earnings.

The postal system in Virginia now costs the general government $263,389 more than all the receipts from it. The cost of carrying and distributing the mails, in the Southern States, exceeds the revenues derived from postages in those States, by $3,510,648. If the Union is dissolved this expense must be provided for by direct taxation, or the people must dispense with the facilities afforded by their mails.

Should war follow the dissolution, the consequences must be of the most frightful character. Brother would be arrayed against brother, and the whole land would be drenched with blood. The border country would be ravaged and laid waste with fire and sword. Firesides and fields would be desolated by invading armies, and the wail of the widow and the orphan would be heard in all our valleys! Real estate would be depreciated more than 50 per cent; business in all its departments would be paralyzed; credit destroyed; personal property of all kinds impressed for public use; our slaves incited to insurrection; and ruin and desolation would overwhelm the whole country.* * *

* * * Fellow Citizens! the issue is in your hands! A heavy responsibility rests on you!

May the Great Disposer of events so guide your conduct that peace and happiness may be restored to our distracted country, and that the Union which we have been taught to regard as the Palladium of our liberties, shall be established on a firm foundation and rendered perpetual.

Very respectfully,
Your fellow citizen,
ALEX. H. H. STUART.

George W. Imboden to John McCue, February 12, 1861

George Imboden writes to his friend, John McCue, about the resistance in Virginia to secession and his own desire for the state to leave the Union. In an election held on February 4, 1861, voters in Augusta selected three delegates to represent them at Virginia's secession convention. Although people in the county overwhelmingly chose Unionists—rejecting secessionist candidates such as Imboden's brother, John—secessionists like George Imboden remained convinced that Virginia should leave the Union.

Staunton
Feby 12*h* 1861

Dear John

Your draft on J D. Imboden came to hand through the Valley Bank and John was out of town, and to save *protest* I paid it, and I have drawn on you at 30 days which I hope you will *accept payable at the Bank in Howardsville. or some other Bank and enclose Back to me.* as I can not draw directly on you through the Bank, [illegible word] accepting the draft *payable* at *some* Bank.

I have no news of interest to write. We are all well, and John's Family are well. John takes his defeat like *all other* defeated candidates. Who wished to have their name placed on the *Book* of *fame,* or *declaration* of *independence.* Of course I mean nothing personal!

I think V*a* has turned fool, but my opinion is contrary to the opinion of the *people* and I will awate the arbitrament of time to prove who is right! I can in a few lines tell you where I stand, I am in favor of a united South, first last and all the time, whether right or wrong I go with the South. I am anti-disunion and anti coercion, but the union is dissolved and what's the use to shut our eyes to the fact, if we cannot reconstruct let's all go together peacibly if we can, forcibly if we must. for we have but one and the same destiny, one and the same interest, then what's the use to deny the true state of the case, and fool & cheat the people by singing hozanahs to the union when there is no union! I am called a *fire eater disunionist* &c

&c, but I dont care what they call me, I am going to say what I think and believe, and let consequences take care of themselves.

Hoping you are well
I remain
Yours Truly
G. W. Imboden

J. D. Imboden to John McCue, February 24, 1861

John Imboden, disheartened by his failed bid to represent Augusta at the Virginia secession convention, writes to John McCue about the Unionist sentiment in the state. Convinced that most Virginians wanted to remain in the Union, Imboden declared that he would leave the state if the Old Dominion accepted a compromise with the Republicans. During the secession crisis, numerous attempts were made at compromise measures that would appease both Southerners and Republicans—and thereby avoid war. Kentucky Senator John Crittenden's proposal to extend the Missouri Compromise line through the western territories all the way to the Pacific Ocean was the most popular of these, although none were ever adopted.

Staunton
Feby 24/61

Dear John.

Your letter asking me to meet you in Richmond this week was recd. yesterdy. I am sorry I cannot do so, but as I returned from Richmond on Thursday I cannot go back again so soon. * * *

* * * I wish I could be with you in R. You will soon be disgusted with the submission feeling that pervades the body of the Convention. Gov. Wise is the only real living embodiment of the true spirit which should animate Virginia at this time. I told him in R. the other day that I delegated him to represent *me* on the floor of that body, as I have no immediate representative there. John we are

going to have fearful times here in Virginia. I am afraid we shall have a war amongst ourselves. I have made up my mind that if Va submits to the dishonor of standing by and seeing war made in the Seceded states, I will leave Va. I am persuaded that a majority of our people here are ready for that. I am not and never will be. We must have *immediately* the constitutional guarantees of the Crittenden plan *at least* or go with the South. If these are refused, and Va *submit*, I never will. I shall go to Florida or Louisiana, take my family & cast my lot there for life. I will *write* to Gov. Wise whilst you are in R. Mary writes in love to you and yours. She is a red hot Southern Confederacy woman.

Yours truly
J D Imboden

John Baldwin,
Secession Convention Speech,
March 21, 1861

John Baldwin, a Democrat and one of three men elected to represent Augusta at the Virginia secession convention, gives a speech on the convention floor about the causes of the current sectional crisis. Acknowledging the "subject of African slavery" as the root cause of the crisis, Baldwin defended the institution as "a blessing alike to the master and the slave." Baldwin—along with the other representatives of Augusta, Alexander H. H. Stuart and George Baylor—defended slavery while also continuing to resist secession throughout the convention.

* * * I claim for her [Augusta County] the proud position of being the Queen county of this great Commonwealth, in point of population, and of wealth; in point of varied production and pursuit, in every particular that goes to constitute a great people. She is represented in the great popular branch of the General Assembly by three delegates, and by an equal number on this floor speaking the voice of the largest constituent body in the State. In the

Senate of Virginia she speaks by her own Senator, representing
there a county which stands first, aye, sir, first, upon the list in point
of wealth and contribution to the common government. Situated at
the centre of the State, connected with both East and West by the
great lines of travel and improvement, and with the great Valley,
midway of which she stands, she is connected with each and all by
every tie, social and industrial, that can bind communities together.
She occupies a position in the great heart of the Old Dominion,
and I claim that he who represents her people is entitled to speak
for a representative county of this Commonwealth.

Sir, in behalf of such a county as this, I desire to be heard; not
merely for the reasons that I have stated, but because she is identified with every interest and every institution that is recognized as of
value in Virginia; and in regard to them all occupies what I might
call a great central, conservative position.

If anywhere in Virginia there are extremes of opinion on the
one hand or on the other, if there are extremes of prejudice in one
quarter or another, Augusta county and her people know nothing
of them. They stand central in point of geographical position; central in point of sympathy, interest and association; ready to engage
in a conservative yet earnest consultation, about whatever concerns
the rights, the interests, or the honor of the Commonwealth.

Well, sir, what is the great cause that has assembled this august
body here to-day? What is it that has already divided and distracted
our people and that threatens to overthrow completely the great
fabric of this government of ours? What is the moving cause so far
as Virginia is concerned? Understand me, I wish to consider these
questions from a Virginia standpoint. I wish to confine myself in
their consideration to their effect upon Virginia's rights, Virginia's
interests and Virginia's honor. I say, then, that viewed from that
standpoint, there is but one single subject of complaint which Virginia has to make against the government under which we live; a
complaint made by the whole South, and that is on the subject of
African slavery. Why, sir, what is the position of Virginia on other
subjects? What is the position of this Commonwealth in regard to
all the great principles of government, in regard to all the great
measures of administration which have been in progress since our
government was first inaugurated? It is the pride and boast of our

people that on all the great questions of administrative policy, on the great doctrines of constitutional construction, Virginia has from the beginning given tone and direction to the opinion and the policy of this nation; that from its earliest foundation, with very rare and brief exceptions, the administration of this great government of ours has been, if not in the hands of Virginia's own sons, in the hands of men of Virginia's own selection whose principles, whose opinions, and whose policy have been time and again approved and ratified by the people of Virginia. Not only in the Executive department has this been true, but over and over again, year after year, we have been informed that the legislative policy has been shaped by the principles which have been taught by the sages of Virginia, and that judicial department of the Government has had its principles impressed upon it by Virginia; and thus, as to all the departments of this Government, in all its administration—in all its dealings with the great affairs of State, we have Virginia standing this day estopped from denying that the Government has been administered to her satisfaction.

But, sir, the great cause of complaint now is the slavery agitation, and the questions growing out of it. If there is any other cause of complaint which has been influential in any quarter, to bring about the crisis which is now upon us; if any State or any people have made the troubles growing out of this question, a pretext for agitation instead of a cause of honest complaint, Virginia can have no sympathy whatever, in any such feeling, in any such policy, in any such attempt. It is the slavery question. Is it not so? We have heard, for days past, the great issues before the country discussed by able and eloquent gentlemen upon this floor—and I ask this Committee if any man has yet been heard, in all the recounted injuries that we are alleged to have suffered from the administration of the Government—if he has heard, in the long list of apprehended wrongs in the future, the slightest reference to anything else, to any other ground of complaint, except this subject of slavery? Thus we have it confessed, upon all hands, that in the main—with this one exception—this great government of ours, from its origin down to the present time, in its administration, in all the departments that concern the industry, the energy, the business of thirty millions of people, has been conducted upon the principles and in a manner satisfactory to the people of Virginia. Put down that admission before we proceed to consider the grievances alleged to grow out of the slavery agitation. * * *

* * * Sir, in regard to the question of slavery, I hold views which were regarded at one time as peculiar, but I am gratified to know that they are becoming, day by day, the opinions of all kinds and conditions of men in this Commonwealth. I have always held the same opinions, from my earliest recollection, on this subject; I have had to undergo no change, such as was described in his own case, by the gentleman from Orange, and it may be owing to the fact that I have none of the fierce zeal of the new convert, that I am unable to follow him in his violent measures for summary redress. I have always entertained the opinion that African slavery, as it exists in Virginia, is a right and a good thing—on every ground, moral, social, religious, political and economical—a blessing alike to the master and the slave—a blessing to the non-slaveholder and the slaveholder. I entertain these views and opinions now. Sir, I am not one of those who look forward with expectation or desire, to its extinction at any time or in any place. I am not one of those who look with any sort of sympathy upon attempts to restrict it to any particular locality, but, so far as I am concerned, if it can be done by fair, legitimate and honest expansion and extension, I have no objection that this mild, beneficent and patriarchal institution may cover the whole earth as the waters cover the great deep. * * *

* * * Let us come then to the consideration of the grievances of Virginia growing out of the institution of slavery. Having by consent narrowed the inquiry down to the question of slavery, let us now treat it more closely and more exactly. I undertake then to say, that upon the slavery question the mouth of Virginia is stopped as thoroughly and as completely to charge misconduct on the part of the Federal Government, as upon any of the other great subjects of administration in this country. Aye, sir, I go further, and undertake to say that Virginia is estopped more completely, more thoroughly to charge anything against the Federal Government in relation to slavery, than she is upon any other subject; because if there is any matter in the whole round of administration in regard to which it has been the pride and boast of the politicians and statesmen of Virginia to claim the ascendancy, aye, the undivided ascendancy of

Virginia ideas and Virginia principles in the administration of the General Government, it is this question of African slavery and its accompaniments. * * *

Staunton Spectator, "Policy of the Border States," April 2, 1861

The Spectator *argues that because the state is so close to the border with the North, secession would pose a far greater danger to Virginia than it would for states in the lower South, such as Mississippi or Alabama. Many people in Augusta believed that Virginia's position along the border meant that protecting slavery in the state depended on remaining in the Union, where they enjoyed a federal fugitive slave law that required Northern communities to return runaways to their owners in Virginia.*

Having steadfastly adhered to the doctrine that civil war, or danger of constant collision between the Border, Free and Slave States, could only be averted by a peaceful settlement *in the Union* of our present troubles, and that it was really the interest of the Border Slave States to maintain their present relations with the Free States on our border, and with the whole Union if possible, we have deduced therefrom a difference between our condition and that of the Gulf States. Nothing that has occurred, therefore, has served to change or even shake the conviction, that we have interests in the Union that are paramount—interests that the Cotton States have not; and that therefore we should not rashly imperil them through any fancied identity of interest with the States that have left us for weal or for woe, to work out our own destiny as best we may. We have maintained that it is neither our interest to go with them, nor really essential to our interest that we should. We are glad, therefore, to find so respectable a journal in one of the seceded States, as the Milledgeville (Geo.) *Recorder*, supporting the views we have advocated. In the issue of that journal of the 12th inst., we find the case thus strongly stated, as follows: "If the line of the Southern

Confederacy touched that of the Free States, there being to law or treaty for the rendition of fugitives from labor between *foreign Powers*, the mischief would be such, practically, that a collision of arms would be unavoidable, unless the Slave States receded altogether from the claims on which they insisted while in the Union, of having their property returned to them under the plain behest of the Constitution and the acts of Congress to carry it into effect. In the simple matter of convenience and expediency, therefore, we believe that the Border States will be of more advantage in their present position to the Southern Confederacy, a wall of defence against Northern aggression, than if they were to become members of it, with all their frontier exposed to fanatical hatred and pillage. We should then have to try an experiment which otherwise we might be under the necessity of making with the Free States, and which no amount of wisdom or valor may contemplate with indifference. If slaves from the Border States are stolen or enticed away by the abolitionists, the game would become vastly interesting in the absence of any stipulations recognizing slaves as *property*, which we have reason to believe could never be obtained. Outrage would follow outrage in rapid succession, and on a scale of such magnitude that war would be the only mode of redress."

Ought not this candid avowal, from a source entitled to credit, induce the people of the Border Slave States to make every effort *compatible with their honor* (and we would not have them do more) to avert the catastrophe, before they rush into the vortex of secession? This word, with us, has a deeper signification than it can have in the Gulf States. We trust our people will do nothing rashly.

Staunton Vindicator, "The Alternative— North or South," April 12, 1861

The Vindicator *argues that with the lower South already out of the Union, slavery will ultimately be doomed in Virginia if the state remains in the United States. With seven slave states no longer sending representatives to the U.S. Congress, many people in Virginia began to worry that there would be little to stop the Republicans from passing any anti-slavery legislation they pleased. Indeed, by mid-April 1861 the secession of the lower South and the failure of compromise measures had prompted many in the county to reconsider the benefits of Unionism and the possible repercussions of remaining in the United States.*

A dissolution of the Union on the slave line, it is contended, would destroy the institution in Virginia. We do not think so. But admit it did. In that case, the slaves would be gradually removed South, and the change would not so seriously affect the private fortunes of individuals, or the general prosperity of the State.

Suppose, however, Virginia should become a Border State of the Northern Confederacy. How then? Could we hope abolitionism would be more considerate of our interests? Assuredly not. Fanaticism never relents. Then what would be our condition? With six hundred thousand Negroes amongst us, denied all outlet, and rendered worthless and uncontrollable, a nuisance and a pest, not only their whole value as property would be annihilated, but Virginia herself, ere long, would cease to be a house for the decent, industrious white man. Her lands and houses would rapidly depreciate, a degraded race of negroes and mixed bloods would huddle into the deserted homes of her people, and a desolation and ruin spread out around them, like that which, under British emancipation, has blasted the most fruitless isles of the Indies.

What son of Virginia can hesitate as to his duty, when such a choice is presented to him? Nay, is it not an insult to our manhood to speak of it as a choice? War is an evil, but not the worst. Life itself has limits to its value. And he must be a dastard indeed who will not defend his friends and his home.

Clinton Hatcher to Mary Anna Sibert, May 29, 1861

Clinton Hatcher writes to his friend, Mary Sibert, in Augusta County about the mobilization for war, his enthusiasm for secession, and his recent success in convincing his parents to allow him to enlist in the new Confederate army. Once

Virginia seceded, hundreds of young men like Hatcher bolted at the chance to sign up for the new regiments being formed in the South. By August 1861, over 1,500 men had enlisted in Augusta County for the Confederacy.

Maplegrove
May 29th 1861

Miss Mary:

Your very *very* welcome letter came to hand on the evening of the day before yesterday and deserves my heartiest thanks. * * *

* * * I have at last succeeded in getting Ma's consent to my joining the army and my name is down on the roll of a rifle company which will organise tomorrow and will probably be in camp by the first of next week. I am beginning to feel "as savage as a meat axe" and am afraid before I am in the army long, if I am not shot I will get to eating Yankee stake for breakfast.

I must confes I do not think your reasoning on the subject of my going to war, entirely logical. I think now that Virginia is invaded it is becoming that every true Virginian should shoulder his rifle and march to the rescue. I should have enlisted sooner but disliked to go without the consent of my Parents and now that they have very reluctantly consented I am preparing to hurry on as fast as possible.

I had the pleasure of casting the first vote of my life last Thursday and was happy to give it in so good a cause as that of ratifying the ordinance of Secession. Our county gave 902 majority in favour of the Ordinance. We have several abolitionists here round us but I can't get any one to help me hang them. I wish I could.

Is Chum dead, or has he enlisted in the army? I have only received one short note from him since I came home and if he is not dead he had better be before I see him again.

I spent about four or five hours at Harper's Ferry yesterday. It is almost impossible to find any one you want to see. I tried to find the Augusta Rifles Capt. Grinman, but could not. I had to enquire of about fifty persons before I could even find out where the Cadets were stationed.

You need not have the slightest apprehension of my being disappointed in your letters; if they are any thing like the one which I am making a desperate attempt to answer, I would consider myself an ugly fellow with dreadfully poor taste if I did not appreciate them.

You ask me what I think of Carlisle. I think about as well of him as of Scott; he is worse than Seward because a Virginian and a thousand times worse than Lincoln because poor fellow he don't know any better. Nature has not been unusually bountiful to him with regard to brains. By the way the Republicans attempted another of their base strategems in Alexandria. I heard from my cousin a day or two since, who was in the army there he said that on the morning the city was taken the ships which brought the troops down sent a boat on shore with a flag of truce and gave them until nine O'clock to evacuate the city promising not to enter the place until that time then as soon as the messenger returned they commenced landing and attempted to surprise our troops and take them prisoners. But fortunately they were on the alert and all of them escaped except one Fairfax company. Such another cowardly and direct breach of faith is not recorded in the history of civilised nations. * * *

* * * By the time you write again I shall probably be in camp in Leesburg so please direct to that place. And write me another *long* letter very soon. I hope you will. I am conscious of not being exceedingly deserving but hope you will be accommodating nevertheless.

I am most truly,
Your sincere friend,
Clinton

2. Franklin County

Franklin Repository, "Value of the Union," November 14, 1860

Reflecting its Republican affiliation, the Repository *argues that the founders of the American Republic abhorred slavery and that the Union was established to*

*preserve liberty throughout the United States. By exaggerating the anti-slavery
pedigree of men like George Washington, the paper hoped to connect the aims of
the Republican Party with those of the founding generation and to argue that no
portion of the country could secede without endangering the liberty of every state.*

If, without being guilty of sacrilege, an American citizen can
treat upon so sacred a theme as the value of the Union, then do we
propose to examine that subject. We have no desire, whatever, to
speak lightly of holy things; to undervalue so important a matter as
the Union of the American States. We believe the bonds which
hold together the various parts of our great confederacy to be in-
dissoluble—the noise, confusion and bluster of hot-blooded, weak-
headed partisans to the contrary notwithstanding. We know that
foolish men, in the warm regions of our country, have threatened
to tear down the temple of Liberty, from turrut to foundation, if the
powers of the Union were not diverted from their original design;
if the strong arm of the Union was not brought to bear in a way
and manner entirely repulsive to the finer feelings of our nature,
and in direct opposition to the plan laid down by the founders of
the Republic; but we have no fears about boasting cowards doing
themselves or others any injury.

The reader of American history is familiar with the fact that the
Union between the States was formed by our fathers for higher and
nobler purposes than the establishment or perpetuation of human
bondage or the degradation of any portion of our fellow beings.
The wise, patriotic, honest men who laid the foundation of the
present form of government, which resulted in the erection of
the Union, began by declaring certain truths to be self-evident.
They, unhesitatingly, admitted the right of all men to life, liberty
and the pursuit of happiness. They, having felt the galling chains
of oppression and wrong, felt the misfortunes of the down-trodden
children of sorrow, and were not ashamed or afraid to express,
in manly language, the holy truths which possessed their very souls.

It is regretted that mad-caps in any portion of the Union are allowed to raise their impious voices against the last experiment of
man at self-government; for if this fails, there is nothing left to humanity but the old obsolete dogma—the divine right of monarchs

to govern, by their wills, the masses of mankind. If those who talk so lightly of the confederation of the States would consider what it cost to establish freedom in this country, they would scarcely think, much less speak, of destroying so priceless boon, so precious a blessing. He is, certainly, a black-hearted traitor who can trample upon the holy compact, cemented as it was by the heart's blood of the greatest, the purest, the bravest men this country, if not the world, ever saw; who considers of no value that blood which was spilled in securing liberty, out of which sprang the Union, for mutual protection and defense.

To read the papers published in the one section of the Union, and to listen to, or read the speeches of their politicians—would-be statesmen—one, unacquainted with the facts, might be led to believe that our fathers had uttered the hellish thought which proceeded from the wicked heart of Roger B. Taney—That one portion of God's creatures had no rights that another portion of his equally dependant beings were bound to respect. A stranger to the sentiments of the great and good men who endured the hardships of the Revolution might suppose that they, like our modern lawmakers, were intent upon building up a great slaveocracy; that they too considered slavery, as do the hot-spurs of our day, to be the highest type of civilization; but an examination of their record will satisfy any man that they deplored slavery as a great, a crying evil.

An examination of the "American Archives," a collection of the writings and debates of the revolutionary patriots, will satisfy the earnest enquirer that there was some other cause for forming the Union than the building up and spreading of slavery, that there were other and higher motives for forming a confederation of the various divisions of our country; for uniting in one the different governments of a common people, than the nationalizing of perpetual servitude. No person ever denounced American slavery in plainer English than did Thomas Jefferson—one of the bright stars in that brilliant galaxy. No person deplored the institution more than did George Washington—the father of his country. No man of them all can be found who did not declare slavery to be an evil, temporary in its character, which would soon be entirely eradicated.

Every Colony—now State—held its convention (in Virginia, and many others, the people of each County held their Conventions) in which strong resolutions were passed. Among the action of these conventions, whether held by a County or a Colony, is to be found unerring indications of the utter abhorrance of slavery to the people of the earlier and purer days of our history—the days that tried men's souls. They struck at the root of the evil. Their voice was unanimous against the accursed Slave Trade; against the horrors of the middle passage, and they battled manfully for its complete, its eternal suppression. The reasons given by them for discontinuing the Slave Trade, are worthy of consideration. They declared that "the filling up of the land with slaves prevented its settlement by mechanics, manufactures and other useful citizens." If their descendants were as honest as were they, the truthfulness of this proposition would everywhere be admitted.

During the War of Independence the colonies hastened to the assistance of each other. They saw, early in the struggle, that they were compelled to make a common cause of the quarrel; that when the army of Great Britain made an attack upon the North, the troops of the South must hurry to the assistance of their neighbors; and when the enemy pounced upon the South, the yeomanry-soldiers of the North must fly to the relief of their brethern—consequently there followed the desire to unite in one every division of the land. The value of the Union *then* was the result of the war; the victory of right over might; the establishing of freedom on the ruins of despotism.

The value of the Union *now* is full equal to what it was *then*. If liberty was the result of union, it can only be retained by union. Although the injury to ninety-nine hundredths of the people might not be so great if the other hundreth should withdraw from the Union as to that fraction itself, yet the disruption could not take place without seriously affecting the flow of good feeling which for so many years permeated every portion of our body politic. Therefore, as nothing but good flows from an undivided Union, and as we are unable to look into the future, and cannot tell what evils may follow a disrupting of the ties that bind us together, we had better be content with what we have, than fly to evils of which we know nothing. We should all consider the Union of too much value to *talk* about destroying it.

John Berryhill to Simon Cameron,
January 11, 1861

*John Berryhill writes to Simon Cameron, a Republican senator from Franklin
County and future secretary of war in Abraham Lincoln's cabinet, about his
views on the secession crisis. Berryhill—like most Northerners—was appalled
at the idea of secession, and he suggested that the middle portion of the country
consider forming its own separate nation if compromise measures failed to prevent the disunion of the United States.*

Chambersburg
Jany 11. 1861
Hon. Simon Cameron

Dear Sir,

I have been here for several Weeks and have been watching the
general course of events, by reading the Philada Enquirer, Press, &
New York Tribune & occasionally the Herald, & I can assure you
Crittendon's course is the most proper and popular at this time, and
if you cant compromise, so as to retain Virginia, Maryland Tennessee Kentucky and Missouri in the Union, Then let the Southern
Fire eaters and rabid abolitionists and uncompromising *shall I say*,
Black Republicans go their own way to distruction for that will be
their distruction & I fear of the whole country, but before this let
the Middle Portion of the Republic go for a separate, Independant,
& free country or Join Canida & come under Queen Victoria and
secure us life liberty equality & protection, Our Country must have
a larger Millitary force and Scott & Anderson, to wield the helm of
State, no more temporizing with Trators & disunionist. King of
your house, used the right language, to Davis & these lackeys should
be expeled. Traitors, setting there accepting pay and compensation
to dismember the union it is disgraceful and I might say horrible
when the consequences are taken into account, I hope still for
peace & my voices for this still, but the over ruling power of the
conservatives—I have as you know always been a Whig & a Jackson Man, but now I feel, looking at Hickman Stephens & other

Republicans, like joining the Democrats, the [illegible word] Stripe—Douglas is rather too versatile to be trusted * * *

with sentiment of high regard I am your friend &c
John Berryhill

Valley Spirit, "An Abolition Despotism to be Established by the Sword," February 27, 1861

The Spirit *adamantly opposes Lincoln's incoming administration, accusing the Republicans of attempting to inaugurate a sectional war by not taking active steps to diffuse Southern fears. During the secession winter many Northern Democrats—and Democratic newspapers like the* Spirit—*blamed the Republicans for the secession crisis and openly sympathized with the complaints of white Southerners.*

The bill of Mr. Stanton, of Ohio, authorizing the President to accept the services of volunteers, is but a part of the war policy which the Republican party is pursuing. The design is to invest the incoming Administration with every function and attribute of military power, so that the anti-slavery programme may carve its way and enforce its triumph by the sword. Despotism has been defined—a union of the purse and sword. As if to effectuate this definition in the person of Mr. Lincoln, the Black Republicans are engaged in hurrying money and force bills through Congress. If they succeed, when Mr. Lincoln comes into power, he will, through a super serviceable Congress, find himself ready to begin his projected war, that is if he can raise the troops and the money voted. Fortunately, curses cling to sin, and often paralyze it in its hour of anticipated triumph. To vote money is one thing—to raise it another. We have abundant reason to suppose that capitalists will refuse money which is designed to be used in the prosecution of a civil war. As for volunteers, there will be few, we opined for such service. Volunteers have to be paid as well as regulars, and without money they cannot be paid. They may be promised plunder, but they will have to fight hard for all the plunder they get in the South. There are few large cities there to be sacked. Besides, such as they are will have to be captured before they can be pillaged. Houses may be burned and fields may be laid waste—but negroes, although property there, would, if carried off, be unproductive here. The volunteer would get a plenty of bullets but find scarcity of plunder. They would, in the language of Mr. Corwin, be "welcomed with bloody hands to hospitable graves." But is it not unlikely that they would have to do some fighting here before marching South.

The generous and gallant old tar, Commodore Stockton, is reported to have said in his speech before the Peace Conference, that—"for every regiment that would be raised in the North to coerce the South, another would spring up in the same North to oppose the first." This sentiment of the noble Commodore is fast becoming the popular sentiment here, for all patriots and all reflecting men are convinced that a Black Republican sectional war will forever destroy the Union and place it beyond the possibility of re-constructing, and they regard with horror and will oppose to the last the reckless men who would inaugurate such a war.

To see with what horror those movements in Congress, that even squint at such a war, are regarded by all save the blind and infatuated Republicans, we have only to glance at the debate that took place on Tuesday on Mr. Stanton's bill.

Said Mr. John Cochrane, of New York—"Pass this bill when you may, it will indeed be the *mourning* hour for the country."

Mr. Burnett, of Kentucky, said—"*You are attempting to involve the country in war.*"

Mr. Boteler, of Virginia, said—"*There is no more efficient mode to break up the Union[.]*"

Mr. Cox, Ohio, said—"*While the Peace Congress is here, I regard this as a disunion measure.*"

Mr. Sickles, of New York, said—"*The people of the North will regard this measure as substituting coercion for justice, and the abandonment of conciliation for war.*"

The Republicans are seemingly acting with steady and consistent reference to the permanent dissolution of the Union. The border slave States make the preservation of the public peace and the careful abstinence from all measures tending to bring on collision the condition of their remaining in the Union long enough to test the willingness of the free States to render them a constitutional adjustment; and the Republicans, in utter disregard of that condition, and of the obvious and inevitable consequences of such conduct, are, with unexampled energy and despatch, hurrying war bills through Congress.—Their policy seems to be to make war in order to create peace, a paradox as senseless as it is dangerous. They seem to be endeavoring to drive the border States from all conference by outing off all hope of agreement, and act really as if their object was not to arrest, but to promote secession; not to save, but to destroy the Union; not to give the blessings of peace, but the curses of war.

Having driven off seven States, they are endeavoring to drive off eight more, and then after driving them off they are resolved to crush them under the armed heels of their Abolition soldiers. They ask the Northern Democrats and conservatives to unite with them in this, so as to make the whole North an *Abolition* unit. They impudently ask men, who have always *voted against* them, to *fight for them* and thus establish, what to them is of all things the most abhorrent, an Abolition despotism.

Valley Spirit, "Ready, Aim, Fire," April 24, 1861

In the aftermath of the firing on Fort Sumter in South Carolina, and the subsequent secession of Virginia with several other border slave states, the Spirit *accuses Southerners of treason and exhorts its readers to defend the Union. Once the war began, many in the North abandoned any sympathy they previously held for Southern complaints against Lincoln and transformed themselves into ardent supporters of the Union war effort.*

Every man in the community should set his house in order and be ready to meet any event, and assume any duty, that may be required of him in the present struggle to maintain the Constitution and Laws of his country.—The danger is at hand, even at our very doors, and before everything we hold near and dear as patriots is snatched from us we should take the stand that will encourage the timid and cheer on the brave. A formidable band of traitors have broken up the Union and made war against the government. While we considered them friends we battled for their rights *in the Union,* but when they determine to break up the Union and array themselves as enemies against us, *we are their enemies.* They are no longer of our household but enemies up in arms against us. Let us then be up and doing and crush the monster before it crushes us. Let us be watchful on every side and allow no man to slumber at his post while the flag of his country is in danger. Let the watch-word of all be—"READY, AIM, FIRE."

Diary of Reverend Abraham Essick, April 30, 1861

Abraham Essick, a preacher raised in Franklin County, recorded his thoughts on the outbreak of the Civil War and Virginia's decision to secede. Essick noted how the secession of states like Virginia, combined with the outbreak of hostilities at Fort Sumter, galvanized sentiments in the North, which he believed would prompt large numbers of men to volunteer for the Union war effort. Franklin County produced many soldiers for the Union, although fewer signed up during the first few months of the war than did in Augusta County for the Confederacy.

Winter has gone and spring has come again, the gayest and loveliest of the seasons. How pleasant it is to walk forth in the green meadows or on the sunny side of the flower-decked hills! The orchard regales our senses with its fragrant blossoms, the groves and the meadows are clothing themselves in living green, the singing of birds has come, and all nature is joyous with new life. But alas, the din of war, and clash of arms are distracting our once happy land. The sectional strife, arising chiefly from the unfortunate contest

about slavery, has culminated, and the result is a civil war between the north and the south. The attack of the secessionists on
Fort Sumter has aroused such indignation in the loyal people of
the free states that they are unanimous in favor of chastising the
offenders. Active preparations for war are going on throughout
the whole land. The President (Lincoln) has made a requisition
upon the states for 75000 men, and will soon call for more. In the
present state of feeling any number will be at his service.

V

Fighting in the Armies

1. Augusta County

James R. McCutchan to Rachel Ann McCutchan, September 22, 1861

James McCutchan writes to his sister, Rachel McCutchan, about his boredom with life in a Confederate camp. Throughout the war, soldiers spent most of their time in camp whiling away weeks—and sometimes months—of inactivity. When not drilling and preparing for campaigns, soldiers occupied themselves as best they could by writing letters, reading newspapers, and playing games.

Camp Near Fairfax C.H.
Sunday Sept. 22nd, 1861

My Very dear Rate

I promised to write to you when I came back to camp & I will endeavor to do it this evening, as I havent any thing else to do. I havent felt a bit like writing letters since I came back. I havent written but 4 since I saw you—I got back safe, though I had a heep of trouble with the things I brought down. I had 1500 lb for different ones in the comp'y & it is no little trouble to take care of *so many things*. I found the boys generaly well at their encampment near Centreville. We left there last Monday & we are *now 3/4 mile* from Fairfax C.H. Our encampment here is a very pretty as well as convenient one, but I can't like it myself, but there is no place on this side of the Blue Ridge that I do like. It is a beautiful country here, but somehow or other it hasn't the charms for one that the mountains & hills of Western Virginia has.

There is a fight going on down at Alexandria this evening. The canons have been firing ever since I commenced this letter. Boom after boom of the heavy old guns strikes upon my ear—it stirs up my soul & makes me feel like going to the aid of my fellow soldiers. There is canonading going on most half the time across the line between the two armies, though there is not much mischief done by it. I am looking for one of these skirmishes to bring on a general engagement & I hope how soon it may. It will never be ended except by fighting & the sooner we do it the better. I despise inaction, I want to be doing something, something that my mind or hands can be employed at. Some people accuse me of laziness but I'll venture the assertion that there is not one in Beauregards army that despises this thing of doing nothing worse than I do. I love something that employs my mind & energies. This dismal routine of drilling at little going on guard occasionly & *cooking* day after day & week after week just kills one.

The army is still increasing here. I have no idea how many are between the Junction Alexandria now now. Not many less than 200,000 I suppose. Nothing is to be seen but soldiers, waggons; encampments & military bustle and confusion, nothing to change the monotony of the same; from morning till night & from day to day is all the same. How long will it continue so God only knows. Here I am now cut off from my friends and from all that is dear to one from society & enjoyment of every kind. How often I think of the past when I was free as the little birds that sing their songs among the branches. I didn't know how to appreciate home, friendship, society, pleasure or any thing else then but now when I am cut off from all these blessings I can see & feel the need of them. Here I never see the face of a woman. * * * I have often heard it said that man when taken away from female society will become like a brute, & I am forced by experience to acknowledge it to be true. I believe, too, to take a woman away from the society of men that in a short time she would be no better.

Well it is night now. I quit writing & eat my supper, & just as I got done eating orders came for us to prepare a days rations & be ready to march by six o'clock tomorrow morning. We are going on picket down in this side of Alexandria. I expect we will have a hot time down there. We have to stay 5 days in sight of the enemies picket & they are continualy firing across at one another. I didn't intend to finish this letter till morning but I wont have time then. John Wade is sick & he asked me this evening to stay here with him. I will stay if the Cpt. will let one I want to go along with the boys down there but I will do anything for John that I can. Mr Craig is still living, but no better, he is just living & no more. I don't think he can possibly get well if I don't go tomorr I will write some more if I go I wont have time to write any more for 5 days. Give my love to all. Kiss the children & write to me soon. Direct to Fairfax Station in care of Cpt. H.J. Williams Com D. 5 regmt Va vol.

Don't let any body see my letters, if they want to know what is in them read it to them, the part you want them to hear.

Yours as ever
James R. McCutchan

Jedediah Hotchkiss to Sara A. Hotchkiss, March 30, 1862

Jedediah Hotchkiss, a school teacher in Augusta County before the war, writes to his wife Sara about recent military developments and his appointment as mapmaker for General Thomas "Stonewall" Jackson. Hotchkiss's detailed maps proved invaluable to Jackson and Robert E. Lee throughout the war. At the time of this letter, Jackson was on his 1862 Valley campaign, where he used Hotchkiss's maps to out-maneuver Federal troops in the Shenandoah Valley.

Mt. Jackson Va.
March 30th 1862

My Dr. Wife:

I have just recd. your brief note saying that Nelly is out of danger—I am truly thankful that a merciful God has spared us the sad affliction of depriving us of our first born—praised be his name that has granted it. I have written to you that I am now on Engineer duty again, and have a good place, though no rank as yet, simply Act. Top. Eng. on Gen. Jackson's staff, have a wagon assigned me for my transportation & a good driver, and can get along without much exposure, though I shall have to ride about considerable reconnoitering the country. I have a very nice chief of Eng. Lieut. Boswell—belonging to the regular corps, he is a fine fellow, & I suppose we will form a mess together. Yesterday I was down in front of the army though Ashby's Cavalry was far in the advance— Ashby is a gallant fellow and always keeps the enemy at bay. I saw Mason a few days ago, he is looking finely—says he considers himself a poor man now—so may of their slaves have run away, and their fine farm in Fauquier has fallen into the hands of the enemy—he has raised 240 cavalry and will be made a Major I suppose. Yesterday the order came from the Gov. to draft all the militia into the Volunteer companies now in the field, so as to make 1000 men in each regiment, with 10 companies, and now there is much uproar among the militia, this will throw all the officers into the ranks as privates—I am sorry for some of them, for they are good men, but it will be a fine thing for some of them for they will thus learn what the duties of a soldier are. I am glad that I have made my escape from the militia before this proclamation, for I had labored very hard to get them fixed up & had got them so supplied by strenuous efforts that they were very well satisfied, and expressed great regret at parting with me &c &c, & I should have been very sorry to have to take part in disbanding them—especially as they wish to stay as they are. Gen. Jackson regrets that this order has been issued, as he was more than pleased with the way in which the militia of Augusta has conducted itself. Yesterday was very raw & cold and last night it rained & sleeted The militia were the only troops that had any tents, all the others having been sent back to Harrisonburg, and the poor fellows suffered much—Today it is raining too and the trees a completely crusted over with ice—I am keeping a sort of Sunday, abstaining from work—The work of last Sunday turned out so disastrously to us that that I suppose we shall try and keep more Sunday hereafter—tho' it is almost impossible to keep the day as it should be there are so many contingencies to provide for—but of the four great battles of this war that have been fought on Sunday, the attacking party has lost the day.

I hear with regret that Gen. Ed. Johnson has been ordered back from Alleghany and is to come here, leaving the Alleghny line entirely undefended and I fear the enemy will soon come to Augusta—We hear that the enemy has fallen back to Alexandria from Manassas, it is supposed to aid in an attack on Fredericksburg. I wish you would write often as you can—I hope you will all get along well. I may come home after some maps—the only way I can possibly get off—My love to all May God bless you. Have you got your sugar yet—Write to Mt. Jackson—to me as Act. Top. Eng. of Gen J's staff—

Your Aff husband
Jed. Hotchkiss

Jedediah Hotchkiss to Nelly Hotchkiss, December 17, 1862

Jedediah Hotchkiss writes to his oldest daughter, Nelly, about the Battle of Fredericksburg, illustrating it for her with a map he drew of the fighting. Union forces under General Joseph Hooker suffered terrible casualties at Fredericksburg after assaulting entrenched Confederate positions. Soldiers on the front lines, like Hotchkiss, often attempted to convey through their letters the horrific experience of battle to their families back home.

Moss Neck, Caroline Co., Va.
Dec. 17th, 1862

My Dear Little Nelly

I promised to write you a letter, when I was at home, so I will take a few minutes this evening and make my promise good. I left home Sunday, you know, and went to New Hope that day, the next day I went across the Blue Ridge Mountain and the next day went on to Orange Court House and then travelled nearly all day

Moss Neck, Caroline Co. Va.
Dec. 17th. 1862

My Dear Little Nelly.

I promised to write you a letter, when I was at home, so I will take a few minutes this evening and comply with make my promise good. I left home Sunday, you know, and went to New Hope that day, the next day I went across the Blue Ridge Mountain and the next day went on to Orange Court House and then travelled nearly all day through the woods, and where the road is sandy, and then got to where the army was the next day, on the Mattapony River. If you look in the large Atlas, in Virginia, you will find four rivers, the Mat, the Ta, the Po and the Ny and they all come together and make the Mat-ta-po-ny river, near which we had our camp, among the long-leaved pine trees, the evergreen holly bushes with prickles on the edges of the leaves; and the Sweet Gum trees that look as though they were winged, or rather the little limbs look so, for the bark projects on each side and causes

the winged appearance I spoke of. We had a cold
snow storm while we were at Guinea Station
near the Mattapony river, but our cloth houses
were very comfortable, for we had a stove, with the
pipe sticking out of the door, or the slit in the sides
of the tent, that serves for a door. Not far from our
tent ran a pretty stream of water, with a bottom of
white sand and white and yellow quartz pebbles, that
look very prettily through the clear water. You never
saw such fences as they have here, they call them wattled fences — they throw up a ridge of dirt, leaving a
ditch on one side, then they drive a row of stakes, nearly
six inches apart, along the top of the ridge, and then
they get long, slender cedar limbs and weave them in
among the stakes, like the splints of a basket, and so
make a tight fence 3 or 4 feet high. Nearly all the fences here are wattled ones — and then they have cedar
trees growing up by the sides of the fences, and we sometimes go a long ways through two rows of pretty ever-green
trees. The country here is very flat, with a good many
swamps, but no very high hills, and a great many pine
forests — where the trees are all pines, and very thick. I
saw a very pretty grave yard the other day, made by planting

cedar trees in a ring and they had grown up thick & had come together at the top and the limbs had been kept cut off on the inside, and there was a place where you could go in, and when in it was like a green house, shaped like half an egg, and the ground on the inside was thickly covered with myrtle, and there were several graves with nice marble slabs — on the outside it looked like one big tree. I must now tell you about a battle we had last Saturday, the 13th of Dec., and I will make a little map for you to look at and see how the armies were located when they fought. Look at the map I have made for you. The roads are put down red lines, our troops in black lines and the Yankees in blue ones

Our army was on the hills in front of the Mine and Telegraph Roads, mostly in the woods, and we had cannons where you see a black line with a dot on each side. The enemy came across the river on pontoon, or boat bridges made so — ~~~~ of boats fastened in the streams with planks laid across them, at Fredericksburg and at the mouth of Deep Run, and they came up into the flat where the short blue lines are & they had cannons where I have made short blue lines with dots beside them — When they came up towards the woods where our men were we fired a great many thousand guns at them and they fired at us, and so we did for a long time, and we at last drove them back, having killed a large number of them and wounded many more — We had a good many killed and wounded too, but not as many as they did, for we were protected by the woods — Now they have gone away across the river, and we must thank the good Lord that he enabled us to whip them and drive them away, for they would come and destroy us and our country if they could.

We are now on a neck of land in a big bend of the river, called Moss neck — there is a great deal of pretty moss growing here.

I am glad you say so many good lessons, as your Ma tells me — be a good girl and learn all you can — help your Ma and be kind to everybody and always good-natured and be sure to love God and do right. Kiss your sister Anna for Pa — So good night, my daughter. From your Pa — Jed. Hotchkiss through the woods, and where the road is sandy, and then got to where the army was the next day, on the Mattapony River. * * * I must now tell you about a battle we had last Saturday, the 13th of Dec., and I will make a little map for you to look at and see how the armies were located when they fought. Look at the map I have made for you. The roads are put down in red lines, our troops in black lines and the Yankees in blue ones.

[Jedediah Hotchkiss sketched a map of the battle.]

Our army was on the hills in front of the Mine and Telegraph Roads, mostly in the woods, and we had cannons where you see a black line with a dot on each side. The enemy came across the river on pontoon, or boat bridges, made so—[small drawing of a pontoon bridge] of boats fastened in the stream with planks laid across them, at Fredericksburg and at the mouth of Deep Run, and they came up into the flat where the short blue lines are & they had cannons where I have made short blue lines with dots beside them— when they came up towards the woods where our men were we fired a great many thousand guns at them and they fired at us, and so we did for a long time, and we at last drove them back, having killed a large number of them and wounded many more—We had a good many killed and wounded too, but not as many as they did, for we were protected by the woods—Now they have gone away across the river, and we must thank the good Lord that he enabled us to whip them and drive them away, for they would come and destroy us and our country if they could.

We are now on a neck of land in a big bend of the river, called Moss Neck—there is a great deal of pretty moss growing here.

I am glad you say so many good lessons, as your Ma tells me—be a good girl and learn all you can—help your Ma and be kind to every body and always good-natured and be sure to love God and do right. Kiss your sister Anna for Pa—

So good night, my daughter—

From Your Pa—
Jed. Hotchkiss

Report of Col. J. H. S. Funk,
5th Va. Infantry, August 18, 1863,
on the Battle of Gettysburg

Col. J. H. S. Funk files his report on the actions of the 5th Virginia Infantry, an Augusta County unit, during the Battle of Gettysburg. Funk details the movements of his men over the course of the battle, including the desperate fighting that forced the 5th Virginia to expend all its ammunition, and reports the regiment's losses. After engagements, officers were typically required to file reports on the actions of their men, providing a detailed account of the battle as experienced by a particular unit.

Lieutenant C. S. Arnall
August 18, 1863

In conformity to a circular from brigade headquarters, I have the honor of submitting the following report of the engagement at Gettysburg:

On the morning of July 1, my regiment left camp near Fayetteville with the brigade. We crossed South Mountain, and marched in the direction of Gettysburg, where Gen. Heth's division had engaged the enemy. Reached Gettysburg near dark, passing through a portion of the town, and following the York and Gettysburg Railroad nearly 2 miles, then filing to the right, where we were thrown in line of battle with the brigade on the extreme left of the division, northeast of the town, my regiment being in the center of the brigade.

On the morning of the 2d, we were aroused early by our skirmishers firing. We remained in this position until late in the afternoon, when, after changing our position several times, moved in direction of Wolf's Mountain (or Red Hill), where the enemy had taken refuge.

About 2 a. m. of the 3d, we were placed in position in rear of Steuart's brigade. At dawn we moved up to some breastworks, behind which lay Steuart's brigade, who were then skirmishing with the enemy. Remained here an hour or more; then ordered by Gen.

Walker to the right, to relieve the Fourth Virginia, which had exhausted their ammunition. Advancing to the top of the hill in front of the enemy's works, we were engaged for over two hours. After having exhausted our ammunition, and used the cartridges of the killed and wounded, were relieved by Daniel's brigade. The brigade was then reformed. Moving to the right some 400 yards, relieved Gen. Nicholls' brigade, where we were hotly engaged for some three-quarters of an hour, under a murderous and enfilading fire.

The line on the left began to give way, which was soon followed by the whole line. Falling back some 300 yards, reformed, and took position on the right of Jones' brigade, where we remained skirmishing with the enemy until 1 a. m. the 4th, when we fell back, and took position on the hills 1 mile westward of the town, the enemy being in too crippled a condition to follow.

It is gratifying to state that the coolness, bravery, and determination displayed by both officers and men during this engagement have not been equaled by them on any of the hard-fought fields which have been marked by their dead. Their efforts not being crowned with the usual success, they retired stubbornly from the field, manifesting a willingness to hurl themselves upon the foe again, if so ordered.

I regret the loss of Lieut. Jacob [H.] Keifer, who fell, mortally wounded. He was a gallant and efficient officer. His loss is felt throughout the command.

Color-Sergeant Speck deserves mentioning for his gallantry throughout the engagement. The casualties were 3 killed, 42 wounded, and 11 missing.

Respectfully submitted.
J. H. S. FUNK
Col. Fifth Virginia Infantry.

Jesse Rolston, Jr., to Mary Rolston, September 5, 1863

Jesse Rolston writes to his wife Mary, complaining that he has received few letters from her, and asserts that the North will never be able to defeat the South. Soldiers on the front lines frequently complained that they did not receive letters from home often enough—a result, in part, of the difficulty of forwarding letters to an army on the move. Many Confederates, both at home and in the army, shared Rolston's steadfast conviction that the South would emerge victorious from the long struggle.

Camp Mt. Pisga
September 5th 1863

Deare companion

I received your letter dated August the 27th last eavening. it put me out of sorts to heare that you have not heard or got no letter since i hav bin in this camp. i have ritten some 7 letters to you since the first day of august. i think it long between your letters. i have received some 3 or 4 that was dated in august from you. i cant tell why mine dont go to you. it haint because i dont start them but i trust that they will come to hand yet. it must be the falt of the mail some whare or how i dont no which. if the paret is with calf and her is not it may be that it would be best to beef her tho i leave that with you to judge. it will suit me the way you think or doo best. you want to no what i think of the war. i think it is a hard war but i dont think that it can last a great while longer tho it may last longer than i think. they is a good deal of confusion amongst some of the soaldiers in some of the brigades. it is moastly of the noth carolineans. some virginians they say that the South is whiped but i don't think that and i don't think that the yankeys will ever subjugate the south by fiting. for my part i can't say how long it will last but i still hoap and trust god will soon see fit to put a stop to this horabel war. we have had a great revival of religion in our brigade and still a going on yet. * * *

* * * I must come to close by informing you that i am well and i hoap and trust to god that this will find you and all of the family injoying the same blessing of health which God has bin so kind to bless me with.

As Mr. Hanna is a waiting on me i send my love you and all

Jesse Rolston

Jedediah Hotchkiss to Sara A. Hotchkiss, November 8, 1864

Jedediah Hotchkiss writes to his wife, Sara, near the end of the war on various topics, including the probable reelection of Abraham Lincoln in the North and the proposed arming of slaves for the Confederacy. At the time of this letter, Hotchkiss was with General Jubal Early in the Shenandoah Valley, engaged in an unsuccessful attempt to drive Union forces under General Philip Sheridan out of communities like Augusta County.

Hd. Qrs. V. D. New Market Va.
Wednesday Nov. 8th 1864

My Dearest One:

We are off again tomorrow, I suppose, for "down the Valley" again, as it is reported that the Yankees have left Cedar Creek & we must go to see where they have gone & keep watch of them that they do not slip off to Richmond & so bring an undue force against Mas. Robert—We are all in a good humor at the idea, poor creatures that we are, we soon get tired of the quiet & monotony of "camp life" & long for the "storm & bustle & hurricane of war." Heaven grant that we may meet with no disaster & that we may not have to fight another battle this fall & sadden many a hearthstone with the *inevitable* news. I was talking with Mr. Lacy today & he says he can but think as I do, that in the good Providence of God this year will end this long & cruel war—I do not see that any good can come to us from this Yankee election & yet I long to know how it has gone—to know if the majority of the people have approved the course of "Old Abe" for the last four years & desire a continuance of the same—I do not think there will be a *real* election, so many have been sent from the army & from government employ to use the influence, patronage & means of corruption at their disposal that they will carry the election by *fraud*, if no other way—One of the Consuls of the "Hessian States" from New York has been here for a few days—he left there three weeks ago—he says there are many Southern sympathizers there, but they are so closely watched that they do not dare to express their sentiments—he also says that the frauds practiced on foreigners to entrap them into service are almost beyond belief. I send you the paper today containing the President's Message—he broaches some "new doctrines"—the country is much divided in regard to the proper employement of the slaves—I think the soldiers are opposed to arming them—they want them used as wagoners &c but are unwilling to see arms put into their hands—the President handles the subject cautiously as though treading on uncertain ground. I wrote you that I was very busy, am really tired I have been working so closely, & am glad to ride again & have field duty—then it has turned warmer today & the air is inviting—I suppose we shall now have "Indian Summer" I have not heard from Mr. Euritt so I suppose he got off as he desired, else he would have let me know as he agreed. Our men have been much improved by the course of discipline they have undergone & are in better "trim" than at any previous time during the campaign, I hope much from them. Gen. Early has issued orders in regard to the keeping of the Sabbath, getting liquor &c which have had a fine effect; the men have been kept in camp & drilled most of the time, then so many have come back from hospitals &c and filled up our depleted ranks—& so I might go on—"hopeful as usual" you will say. I hope William has been of *some* use to you, though of not much—for I fear he was out of the way—during my absence he got hold of liquor and got a taste of the accursed stuff & has used every effort to obtain it since—I shall take him in hand after he returns—I gave him money to pay his way up & back, but I fear he spent it—yet I can stop him & will do so—I shall try now to get some of the things you want—hope William will come tomorrow & bring letter—I have had a pair of shoes made for myself by one of the Engineer Company—I got some 7 yds. of linsey from Cumberland—that is, it is on the way—I want my cape lining completed & you may have the balance—I may let you have it all—

I hope Nelly and Anne are making good progress in their studies & are good & dutiful children—fearing God & obeying their Mother. I must write to Nelly—I shall expect her to be able to make me a loaf of bread when I next come home—when I shall be in her debt somehow—& Anne shall not be forgotten if she shows progress according to her years—Also remember me to Mary—I hope she does well—Write soon—Goodbye & God bless you

Your aff husband
Jed. Hotchkiss

I enclose you Twenty Dollars—

2. Franklin County

Alex Cressler to Henry A. Bitner, May 21, 1861

Alex Cressler writes to his friend, Henry Bitner, about Union regiments being formed in Franklin County—which had recently been reviewed in Chambersburg by Pennsylvania Governor Andrew Curtin—and rumors of Confederate troops headed north. Reflecting the heady confidence felt by both sides at the start of the war, Cressler predicted certain Northern victory. Close friends and young men at the outbreak of the war, neither Bitner nor Cressler enlisted in the Union armies, each remaining in the county as school teachers.

Chambersburg
May 21st 1861

Dear Henry
    Yours of yesterday was received in due time and being fully digested I embrace this privilege of writing to you again. I was sorry

to hear of your disappointment on Saturday last, and can only measure your feelings by imagining what mine would have been under corresponding circumstances. Saturday was a day of interest and satisfaction to me having never seen the like before, when I cast my eyes along the line, which was formed along the one side of the street, with arms presented and beheld the field of bayonets elevated above the heads of thousands, and the Governor of the Commonwealth of Pennsylvania, which is the Keystone of the Arch, moving steadily and silently along that line, with his penetrating eye firmly fixed upon them, and his countenance remaining unmoved and apparently speaking of the condition of the Country and the object for which so many sons of labor had been called together, I was led to exclaim, "who can tell what a day may bring forth." From a person who came from Williamsport Md. yesterday we learned that two Regiments of Secessionists had come there and by yesterday's Tribune, that the plan is to come on through until they reach Philadelphia, in order to get provisions, should they attempt to carry out that design, we will have a bloody time here, and you may be sure the men here will give them a breakfast job at any rate, and I hope Shippensburg and the Pines will, by the time they reach you, have their 10 O'clock peace ready for them and see that every man gets his portion due. This is to much to trifle about, as it may be their design, however I am not yet uneasy, but should they come it may be that I might never see you again let come what will, I expect to be prepared for the worst that can happen to me. The citizens of Chambrg. are calm, and do not apprehend an attack from the rebels from the South. I have not in my imagination marked out the plan by which the present troubles may be settled, but find that the opinion of some is that war is the only remedy. if such be true then the Northern boys must go to the work, and what could be more cheering to the hearts of freeman such as we are, than to see that the whole north will move to the work, as one mighty machine none of the parts being wanting, but all complete, and all of which have been tried in the days of '76, and found to be as true a steel, and since the fall of Sumpter it has been greatly strengthened and now is the Greatest Structure, and most complete machine under the Canopy of Heaven, and when it begins to move forward upon the foe, stretching from the Atlantic to the Pacific,—every part reveling in grandeur and might, not being driven by steam, but the hearts blood of million, and the smiles of Heaven, although moving slowly, its tread will be the surer, and long before it reaches Cape Sable, *secession* will be crushed out of existence, and like a mighty cloud, it will rain Union sentiments on every farm and plantation south of Mason's and Dixon's Line. Let us start the ball rolling, and send secession to the place from whence it came, you will now allow me to tell you a little anecdote, which I heard a few days ago Mr.—A said "that it has often been his wonder what the D—l tempted people to sin for that their sin could not make him any better," when Mr.—B said, "Don't you know that he is a secessionist—that he was the first to seceed from Heaven, and consequently the father of secession,"— more truth than joke— * * * write soon if it is not to much trouble, I sometimes think that I am imposing on your time to ask you to write but I cant help it no person else will write and I am very glad to hear from the pines.

Yours Forever
Alex. Cressler

Report of Capt. Emanuel D. Roath, 107th Pa. Infantry, August 15, 1863, on the Battle of Gettysburg

Capt. Emanuel Roath reports on the actions of the 107th Pennsylvania Infantry, a Franklin County regiment, at the Battle of Gettysburg. The 107th came under heavy fire throughout the battle, losing several men killed and wounded in vicious fighting on Little Round Top and Cemetery Hill.

Captain Byron Porter
Rappahannock, Va.
August 15, 1863

Capt.

I have the honor to submit the following report, as per orders from brigade headquarters, from June 28 to July 22, inclusive, viz:

The following is the report of Lieut. Col. J. MacThomson, of the One hundred and seventh Pennsylvania Volunteers, during the action of July 1, at Gettysburg, he being in command up to that time, viz:

July 1.—After the engagement, we fell back to the left of Cemetery Hill, and threw up strong breastworks, which we occupied until next morning.

July 2.—During the forenoon we were relieved by the Third Division, Second Corps, and taken a few hundred yards in the rear to support a battery. We lay on our arms until about 6.30 p. m., when we were marched to the left, toward the Round Top, under a heavy and effective fire, to assist in driving the rebel hordes back in the famous charge of the second day of the fight. After the charge, we marched back to near the cemetery, and were ordered to lay in rear of a stone fence, being a protection for the men from the enemy's sharpshooters in our front.

Our casualties during the second day were 1 commissioned officer and several men wounded. Our strength was about 78 guns and 12 commissioned officers.

July 3.—At 4.30 a. m. we were posted in the rear of Cemetery Hill, in support of the batteries stationed on that point, remaining in that position until 1.30 p. m., when the enemy opened upon us with a heavy and furious artillery fire. Our division was moved to the right of Cemetery Hill, at the same time lying under two direct fires of the enemy's sharpshooters and one battery. The strife became terrific and the artillery firing terrible. At this crisis our services were required to support the batteries, when the regiment was marched with others along the crest or brow of the hill in rear of the batteries, through the most deadly fire ever man passed through, it appearing as though every portion of the atmosphere contained a deadly missile.

After our services were no longer needed to support the batteries, the division to which my regiment was attached was moved to the left of Cemetery Hill, to participate in crowning our arms with the glorious victory achieved that day.

My strength was about 72 guns and 11 commissioned officers. Casualties, 2 commissioned officers wounded; 1 private killed and several slightly wounded. The day being very hot, 3 of my men were carried insensible from the field on account of the intense heat.

After resting a few hours, we sent out a line of skirmishers to the front, and threw up breastworks to protect the men in our position, where we remained for the night.

July 4.—We lay all day in the position of the previous night and strengthened it; did some skirmishing with the enemy's sharpshooters; had no casualties.

It is proper here for me to state that the officers and men displayed great gallantry and determination throughout all the engagements of the previous days, and are entitled to the praise and gratitude of a free and loyal people.

Respectfully submitted. I am, captain, with much respect, your most obedient servant,

E. D. ROATH
Capt., Comdg.
One hundred and seventh Pa. Vols.

Jacob Christy to Mary Jane Demus, May 13, 1864

Jacob Christy—one of 45 black men from Franklin County who enlisted in the first black Union regiment, the 54th Massachusetts—writes to his sister, Mary Demus, about his experiences and frustrations as a black soldier. Christy is proud to be fighting for black freedom, but remains frustrated that he receives less pay than a white soldier. The U.S. government paid black soldiers $10 each month (compared to $13 for a white soldier) until 1864, when all U.S. soldiers began receiving equal pay regardless of race.

Morris Island South Carolina
May the 13th 1864

Dear Sister

I take my pen in hand to inform to you that I am Well and I hope these few lines may find you the same We are all well at preasant And are geting along verry well I received your letter and was verry glad to hear from you All once more We have now Come back to Morris Island Again the gun boats are still fighting with the rebels thay capture one of the rebels boats While we we was at Florada The rebels blowed up two of our boats with torpetos And since we come back to Morris Island We was one picket one night And the rebels was throwing Shell and thay was apeice of shell struck standley Johnson A kill him

our men are at richmon fighting away thay wont pay mor they wont let us home And so the men all says that thay will wate tell the last of this month and if thay dont pay us we will get Troublesum on their hand if we cant get our rights we will die trying for them We have been fighting as brave as ever thay was any soldiers fought I know if every regiment that are out and have been out would have dun as well as we have the war would be over I du really think that its God will that this ware Shall not end till the Colord people get thier rights it goes verry hard for the White people to think of it But by gods will and powr thay will have thier rights us that are liveing know may not live to see it I shall die a trying for our rights so that other that are born hereaffter may live and enjoy a happy life

We all keep our health verry well David is well he is cooking now Samuel and Joseph and George Demas are all well and thay all cend their love to you and father and Elizeberth

I wish when you rite that you would let me know wither the letters that I cend without postage stamps cost anything to get them out of offerce or not now I will bring my letter to a close

rite soon Direct to Compy J 54 Mass vols Morris Island South Carolina by way of Hilton Head

Jacob E. Christy

Jacob Christy to Mary Jane Demus,
August 10, 1864

Jacob Christy, a black soldier from Chambersburg, writes to his sister Mary about the recent Confederate raid of Chambersburg, the treatment of black prisoners of war by the rebels, and the unequal pay of African American soldiers. On July 30, 1864, Confederate troops seized Chambersburg and burned it to the ground after locals refused to pay a ransom. Soldiers like Christy learned about the raid through newspapers and wrote to loved ones, hoping their homes and families had been spared.

Morris Island South Carolina
August the 10th 1864

Dear Sister

I take this preasant time of informing a few lines to you that I am well at preasant hopeing these few lines may find you the same I receive your kind letter and was verry glad to hear from you all that you was well and was geting along so well and was verry glad to hear That the Rebels had not disturb you or none of the rest yet but I seen in the paper that the rebels had come to Chambersburg and burnt it but i hope that thay did not due any damage to you father And Elizebeth I think that thay was a pretty set men in Chambersburg that would let two hundred rebels come and burn the place for I am a soldier myself and I know what fighting is the compy that I belong to has 80 sume men in it and I know that we can Wipe the best 200 rebels that thay can fetch to us or let us get where thay are Samuel and Joseph is well and cend their love to you and Elizabeth And to father I seen David to day and he is well and cend his love to you and the rest George and all the rest of the boys are well it is verry warm here but we have verry easy now nothing to due but picket duty And were we are we can see the rebels every days and hear them hollow but the river is between is thay was a rebels boat came down to our fleet with a flag of truce it came from Charlston to exchange prisners and thay sade that thay had sume prisner out our regiment thay had the list of three men out our compy but thay did not fetch them along with them but still I was verry glad to hear that thay had not killed them thay been a great deal talk of them killing all the collard soldiers that thay catch

We due not serpose to fight much now any more for we have not been pade anything since we have been in the feild thay have offed to pay us but did not want to give us as much as white soldeirs and so we wont or wouldant take any

I think we will get home before verry long yet and when you rite I wish you let me know What harm the rebels his dun my love to you and father and Elizebeth and all inquireing frends is roll call and I must clothe good night untell again pleas to rite soon and Direct your letter to Compy J 54 Massachuettes regiment volentears Morris Island S.C. via of Hilton Head

Jacob Christy

Sylvester McElheney to Harriet McElheney, December 14, 1864

Sylvester McElheney describes for his wife, Harriet, a raid that he recently participated in and the execution of several deserters from his regiment. Executions for desertion occurred on both sides throughout the war, serving as a means for maintaining discipline and order in the ranks. Raids against civilian populations, however, were more common in the later years of the war. McElheney considers his raid into rebel territory for supplies to be just retribution for the July 1864 Confederate burning of Chambersburg, Pennsylvania.

Camp in front of PetersBurg
Wenesday December the 14th 1864

Kind and respected Wife

I take the oppertunity this evening of in forming you that I am well at presant. I receved your letter on Satterday the tenth and was glad to heare from you and that you was all well. I would have answered your letter sooner but we have not been in camp since

Friday evening about six oclock only a little while on Monday morning and last night we came in to camp again about Eight oclock but we dont know how long we will stay We have been out on a rade. We started on friday evening at about six oclock and marched about two miles and encamped for that night and the next day it comenced to sleet and rain when we was putting up our tents and it sleeted the whole night and rained part of the next day. I tell you that we had a rough time of it we was encamped in a field and it was nothing but mud. Well now before I go any further about our rade I must let you know what I seen that day. It was satterday the day I received your letter. There was two men had deserted our Army and went to the rebles and took up arms against us and they were captuer sometime ago and on satterday they were both hung between one and two oclock. They were marched in front a regiment and a bras band and [illegible word] their cofins carried alongside of them. There cofins was set down along side of the gallos and they were marched up on the platform with two officers and a preacher. The officers talked to theme awhile and then the preacher prayed for them and then the officers put the bandage on there eyes and the rope around there neck. I tell you that it was not many seconds to they were dead. You had better beleave it was a pretty hard site. Well now I will leave that subject and go on with our rade. So we started that evening about four o'clock and marched the whole night through the mud halfway up our boot legs and after we got through our picket line our Regiment was ahead and then we was halted and ordered to load our guns and then the two front Companys was ordered to go ahead that was Co A and Co F and we marched on to five oclock on Sunday morning and then we encamped on the bank of the Nottoway river. We did not cross the river but the sixth corps had crossed the river sometime before and that day about 10 oclock they commenced coming back. The first that come was the pioneers on the waggons with the pontoon bridges and then a lot of cattle that they had captured and then the cavelry. There was a pretty long string of them. I was standing on the bank of the river and I seen John Boggs and he said that your brother got wounded. He did not say that he was bad or not. I seen severall of the boys that I new. They were all well and in good spirits. There was some of them had geese and chickens tied to their sadles. They had a little of everything with them. Well now I will give you the balance of our trip. We did not capture anything but some sheep. There was a flock in a field with them in it. You may know that our two companys went into them. We got all of them. Bill Sibert got one hind quartre and Phillip got the other one and then Jacob Shearer got at and cooked some of it for that was all we had to eat that and a little perched corn. We eat some of it and then we started back. It was about 3 oclock and then I only seen part of ther army. We could not see anything but horses and men. There was some of the Cavelry in front of us and they did put fire to all the buildings along the road and some of them was most splendid houses but they are paying them for burning Chambersburg. We came into our camp that night. It was about 2 oclock when we landed in camp. There was some of the boys did not get in that night at all. Phillip was one of them that did not get in and there was a good many others that did not make it in to camp that night but I made out to get in and night watch at that for my feet was most awful sore and the [illegible word] in my shoulder but them that did not get in to camp that night had it better than we had for we had to march right back in the morning again about 2 miles and they saved saved that and we encamped in the woods that morning and stayed there until yesterday evening to about 6 oclock and then we marched back to our camp. You had better believe that we slept good after we got our supper. There was some of the boys feet got that sore and some of them froze that they could not put on their shoes. My feet did get a little sore but I maid it to camp.

Well now if we stay here I will try and hunt him up and see how he is now. I have wrote once a week to you since I cam out and I want you to do the same and then I will know if you get them all or not. You sent me your likeness and little Annys. I did not get Marys I dont know if you sent it or not. So I think that I will bring letter to a close for this time and when you get this letter and reads it you may give it to Father and let him read it. So nothing more at presant but remains,

yours truly
Sylvester McElheney

David Demus to Mary Jane Demus, January 24, 1865

David Demus, a black soldier from Franklin in the 54th Massachusetts, writes to his wife Mary about his role as a soldier in the war. Demus argues that slavery "Was the Ruson of this ofel Rebelon" and asserts that without black troops fighting for the Union the war would continue for another ten years. During the course of the war, more than 179,000 African Americans enlisted for the Union cause, granting the United States a distinct advantage over the Confederacy in their ability to raise and maintain armies.

Morris iland south C
Jenawary the 24th/65

Dear
   i heave bean think Riteing you a few lines to inform you that i am Well at present and I hope Whean thes fu lines Reach you tha Ma find you injoing good healte i am going to state a solders letter But i hope that you Will Rite a sort letter to ansr this letter Wiy you Can see that i had Nothing to doow and i thot i Wod spnd the [illegible word] Day and Rit i hope Whean i get Back a gane Wiy i Will heave soming else to Dow on sundy fer i Cod injoing Mi Celf Biy tock to you and tell you What a soldurd life is and how tha heaft to get a long But i Can tell you that Whean a Man set dow and study a bout his daners that he hast to put thow But a Mi Dear Jest let Me say to you if it had Not a bean for the Culard trups Wiy this offel Ware Wod last fer ten years to Cum but Now it Wis plane to see that if We all had a stade at hom Wiy What Wod a becum of us Culard peapel We Can say Now how Can say tha dun Wiy us Culard Men Was the Ruson of this ofel Rebelon Was averry Now i Can tell u that i heave sow som hard times but With all i Can say that i heave got out safe so fer and Withe all the peapele say that i am a lukey Man but still i hope that i May stay out of the Cumeny but i heave bean out of the Cumeny for all Most too years and if god spears Me to stay out a bout fortten Munth Wiy i Can Com Cum home safe but if i live to get home Wiy i thot that i Can stay

at hom a What a happy time We Will heave a happy Day and a happy Nighte to gether But i hoppe that you and I Ma live to get together a gane a What a happy time We Will heave and i think that We Will Never part a gane a Mi Dear whean you Rite to Me wiy Whean i get yor letter Wiy i jest heaft to go and look at yor Dear and lovely face and then i Will lok at yor Dear lovely face and then i think a What a folhelsch Boy i Was to leave you behind and Cum a Way so far Whean i Cant see you a tall but Whean i think of the pleaser that We Will heave at When i Dow get hom i think that i make oup From all the last thee years But Whean i get hom Wiy i Can tock a Mile fer to mak up fer all but still i ant the only Man but i think that tha Will be a grate Meny of as Meny Relist a gane for 5th years but i dont think that unkel sam has got Muny a nuf to Relisnt Me a gane but still if you think i had better tey in the army Wiy i ant a going to Dow it fer i think i heave bean out long a Nauf now to see the day

David A. Demus

Charles Smith to Anthony W. McDermott, April 15, 1865

Charles Smith writes to his commanding officer for permission to visit his family and make arrangements for their housing and security. Smith had resided in Augusta County until the war broke out, when he moved his family to Franklin County in Pennsylvania. After the burning of Chambersburg, Smith joined the Union army but was unable to provide a new permanent home for his family to replace the one destroyed by the Confederates. Now that the war was over, Smith hoped he would be granted leave by the army so he could help his family rebuild.

Lieut. Anthony W. McDermott
Adjt. 69th Pa. Vet. Vols. Camp 69th Pa. Vet. Vols. April 15th, 1865

Adjutant,
   I would hereby make application to you for a leave of absence for the space of Twenty days in order to visit my family at Chambersburg, Pa. and make provision for their comfort and happiness.

I would state that four Years ago I was a citizen of the State of Virginia, and was obliged on account of my Union sentiments to leave my home which was in Augusta County. I took with me my family and settled in Chambersburg, Penna. of which place I was a resident until it was burned by McCauslin. I was then compelled to find a home for my family, and through the kindness of one of the citizens, I received permission to occupy a portion of his house for my family, until I should have been able to make other arrangements. The period allowed me for such occupancy expired upon the 1st inst. and I am exceedingly anxious to visit Chambersburg and provide suitable accommodations and a home for my wife and family. I have no one capable of acting for me in my absence from home, hence my urgency in the matter.

In October 1864 I entered the service as Asst. Sg'n. of this Regiment, and although there were many matters requiring my personal attention at home, I felt a delicacy in making application for a leave of absence from the fact that I had been in the service for so short a period of time. I have thought however that the present was an opportune moment, when my services might be spared for the period asked for, and my application meet with approval.

Requesting that this application be forwarded to the proper authority, I am

Very Respectfully Yours
Charles J. Smith
Asst. Sgn. 69 Pa. Vet. Vols.

VI

The Home Front

1. Augusta County

Mary A. Smiley to Thomas M. Smiley, April 26, 1861

Mary Smiley writes to her brother, Thomas, who is serving in the Confederate army. In addition to recounting for Thomas recent events in Augusta, such as the formation of a home guard to defend against slave uprisings, Mary implores her brother to write home more often and in greater detail. People at home were as anxious as soldiers to receive letters from their loved ones, always hoping for word that their family and friends on the front lines were well.

Friday night, 10 o'clock
April 26th 1861

My Dear Brother

As we are getting your other uniform ready to send I will write a little and send it in your bundle for we do not know where to direct to, and I suppose you will be certain to get it If the weather is as warm where you are as it has been here for the past few days you will certainly need something lighter than your winter uniform We have received two letters from you one Wednesday and one to day and I tell you we (as well as others) were about as anxious to hear from you as we could well be only Thomas they were entirely to short Ma wants you to write the occurences of every day, if possible, and then when you get enough to send it home. It appears like there has been a stop put to buisness of every kind there is very little doing except what is obliged to be done that is farming. Pa has been ploughing this week. it sets very hard with him. Runnels is still about he has joined a vollunteer company at Brownsburg. The Brownsburg troop passed this evening on their way home I guess there would be a great many persons glad this evening. I wish we could be surprised in the same way. Providence congregation looked sadder last Sabbath than it has done for many a long day. There has been a Home Guard formed around here and I suppose it is needed for some of the negroes are not to be trusted even around here and then they are backed by some of the mean white folks There is one of the Sensabough that there has been a talk of taking to jail and they have a son of Davies Kerrs in jail. We are all well and have been since you left and we want you to be very careful of your health do not expose yourself rashly if you get your clothes wet try and dry them and above all dont sleep on wet clothes if it is possible to have them dry for as you know it is so very much more injurious to health than when you are taking exercise We would like very much to know what sort of a life you lead in camp What have you to eat and have you plenty of it. great fears are entertained that you will suffer for food so many soldiers and where will bread come from to feed them Who cooks for you or do you have to do it yourselves and how are you camped, in houses in tents or in the open air with the sky for your covering. I would like very much to know who your messmates are. How is cousin John Berry getting along has he got his spirits raised yet or is he still down. I reckon you live in excitement I hope you dont have to live on its so near the city. If you want any thing write for it and if we have an opportunity we will send it.

Farewell dear brother do yor duty as a soldier and as a man and if I never see you again may we meet above.

from your sister
Mary A Smiley

P.S. Write often and tell me when you received this and where to direct to so that we can write. *Mary*

Staunton Spectator, "Our Enemies," April 8, 1862

The Spectator *ranks and lists the various enemies of the Confederacy, condemning "our home enemies" as worse than the Union armies. Though most whites in the county supported the Confederacy, some in Augusta spoke out against the war while others attempted to take advantage of the shortages created by the conflict in order to make a profit. The* Spectator, *among others in the county, denounced all those who did not actively support the Confederate war effort.*

The Confederate States have three distinct classes of enemies, which the Memphis Appeal forcibly describes as follows. We think our home enemies are worse and more detestable than the Yankees themselves:—

1. The Government and people of the United States are our enemies. But they are open enemies. They meet us upon the field with arms in their hands, and make war upon us. They shoot down our soldiers, burn our houses, destroy our property, and steal our negroes. We know where to find and how to deal with such an enemy.

2. The second class of enemies are the croakers—the long-faced men of faint hearts and weak nerves, who go up and down the country, seeking to impart their own despondency and cowardice to all with whom they come in contact.—Everything goes wrong, according to these Dismal Jemmies. The government is weak and negligent; our officers are lacking in skill; and the army is destitute of courage. If the government has done its duty, this or that thing would not have happened. If the officers had possessed a grain of foresight, they could have held this or that position against the enemy. Nothing is done right, according to these gentry, and everything goes wrong.

The enemy will certainly overrun the country; the Confederate government will fail; and we will all go to perdition together. If they only had charge of affairs, how smoothly and successfully everything would move. Arms would be procured immediately; an army would be improvised in the twinkling of an eye; and the enemy—

McClellan, Buell, Halleck, and all—would be driven out of the country the first pleasant day that came. Napoleon would still be the "little corporal" by the side of these wonderful warriors—the mighty men of valor.—Weak of purpose, faint of heart, and cowardly in spirit, they would destroy the confidence of every body else and abandon every thing to the Federals. We would suggest to have petticoats put upon these miserable creatures, and curls hung about their craven foreheads, but for the insult we should thereby offer to our brave women.

   3. The speculators and extortioners constitute the third class of enemies. These characters operate upon the necessities of the country.—They are interested in the war, insomuch as it enables them to make money. Beyond this, they care but little who wins or who loses.—They set no fixed price upon what they have to sell. Their price is all they can get. The purchaser may be a poor man, a needy woman, a destitute soldier, or the widow of some brave fellow who has fallen in battle with his feet to the foe. Still, if the extortioner can grind out of her five dollars per bushel for salt, he takes it; if ten dollars, he takes it; if a thousand dollars, still he would take it. As between him and a Lincolnite, we have infinitely more respect for the latter. The one is an open enemy, and meets you on the field; the other is a secret foe who takes advantage of your necessities, and seeks to undermine the cause by oppressing the people and sapping the foundations of our strength.

Diary of Nancy Emerson, July 4, 1862; January 8, 1863

Nancy Emerson records in her diary her thoughts on life on the home front in Augusta County. Although born in Massachusetts, Emerson had long lived in Augusta with her brother, a Presbyterian preacher in the county who owned two slaves in 1860, at the time of the outbreak of the war. Emerson described experiences and emotions shared by many Confederates who remained at home, such as her belief that Richmond would never fall to Union armies and her visceral reaction to the Emancipation Proclamation and Federal attempts to end Southern slavery.

July 4, 1862

What are the people in Yankeedom thinking of today? Perhaps however they have not got the truth yet & are still hugging the delusion that Richmond will soon be theirs. McC[lellan] will get up a battle of falsehoods as usual, but truth will out sometime, & how astounding when it comes. Pity, pity, that the Northern people should have been made the dupes of such a set of knaves. I seldom think of it without remembering the lying spirit which was permitted to take posession of Ahab's prophets, that he might be persuaded to go to R— & fall. This judgment from God has fallen upon the North because of their declension from him. Its effects, it is true, have come upon us, & more heavily thus far than upon them, but the end is not yet. We too have cause for deep humiliation, but we shall achieve our independence, & if guided aright, shall fulfill a high destiny & be far more prosperous than ever before. Never for one moment since this struggle commenced, has my mind wavered as to the final result.

January 8, 1863

The first of Jan has come & gone, & Lincoln's proclamation has brought no desolation. What awful disappointment will be experienced by our friends the abolitionists. Never was a more quiet and orderly Christmas & New Years. Even Sister C. who is so [illegible word] timid, *forgot* to be afraid! I do not forget it, but a little circumstance may show how much I was terrified. Bro. L. having been to Charlottesville, Cousin S went to S. for him, & did not get home till late. I sat up for them, and having occasion to visit my chambers, went repeatedly in the dark, & near midnight. Indeed, never since have I been in this state have I felt any reluctance to visiting any part of the house in the dark either here or in Highland. This whole agitation about slavery which has prevailed at the S. these years, is the most monstrous humbug ever got up since the flood. I am if possible a thousand times better satisfied of the propriety of slavery than I was before the war. I believe this violent abolition spirit grows out of attempting to be wise above what is written, & it shows itself out where it is carried out, by leading those possessed with it to throw away the bible. It is my full belief that the infatuation which has precipitated the North into this war, is a judgment from God upon them for their deep declension from him manifested among other ways by their fanaticism and every other ism. The fear of the Lord had so nearly ford where the land, as there is reason to fear & therefore this whirlwind had suffered to burst upon them. It has spent much of its force upon *us* thus far, but if this is the end of the matter, I have miscalculated this eclipse altogether. Both nations may have to make a long sojurn in the wilderness before they reach the land of Canaan.

Staunton Spectator, "The Spirit of the Boys," May 24, 1864

The Spectator *reports that the presence of a regiment of black Union soldiers in Winchester, to the north of Augusta County, has spurred "thirty boys" from the area to volunteer for service in the Confederate armies. Few sights infuriated Confederates as greatly as that of armed African Americans fighting for the United States. Over the course of the war, the Confederacy mobilized more than 80 percent of its eligible white men for their armies, periodically expanding the age of eligibility to include both younger and older recruits.*

We are credibly informed that within the past three months not less than thirty boys, between the ages of sixteen and eighteen, have come out from Winchester, and are now not boys, but fighting men in the ranks of our army. The impulse to this movement received additional strength from the appearance of a negro regiment which occupied the town some weeks ago, the greater portion having joined the army since that time. Such indignation and disgust seized the community, that, not only the boys, but the children, were roused and only wanted years and strength to have placed themselves by the side of their brothers only a few days older.

These boys are now fighting as willing and ardent soldiers to re-
claim their homes and firesides, outraged and desecrated by the
presence of such a foe. May they reap such success as their courage
and manliness deserve. This, no doubt, is more or less the case
throughout the border wherever these black regiments have made
their appearance. Verily, our enemies have served us many a good
turn since the commencement of this war. From the generous acts
of Mr. Banks, our Commissary General, who has strewn his favors
with a lavish hand all over Virginia and Louisiana, to the negro
proclamations of Mr. Lincoln, we derive no other feelings than
those of the most unalloyed satisfaction. * * *

Staunton Vindicator, "Apologetic," July 8, 1864

The Vindicator *apologizes to its readers for being unable to publish recent issues of its newspaper, explaining that the occupation of Staunton in May 1864
by Union General David Hunter—including the subsequent vandalism of the*
Vindicator's *press—made normal business impossible. Hunter's troops, who
had been sent by Union commander Ulysses S. Grant to subdue the Shenandoah
Valley, damaged many homes and businesses in Augusta and neighboring counties.*

Our last paper made its appearance on May 27th, 1864, and we
were preparing as usual to issue on the next week and were nearly
ready when the advance of Gen. Hunter to Harrisonburg rendered
it necessary that all who could be serviceable in repelling the invaders should go forth to meet them. Together with the citizens of
town and county my printers were called to arms and consequently
the publication of the paper on June 3rd was impossible. Owing to
the misfortune of June 5th at Piedmont, Augusta, the enemy in
force occupied Staunton on the next day, Monday June 6th. They
proceeded to my office to destroy it, when to their amazement they
found the sole tenement in Washington Press, (the type having been

removed to a place of security on Saturday previous to the battle of Piedmont,) which they damaged, as they thought, beyond repair. The repairing of the press occupied but a short time, but the movement of the reserves with the forces of Gen. Breckinridge, and their participation in the rapid and fatiguing pursuit of the robber Hunter and his plundering incendiaries, prevented the return of my hands until the latter part of last week, thereby rendering the publication of my paper at an earlier date impossible. We have not, as far as the office is concerned, suffered a very material loss, a few hundred dollars covering the amount. However, we regret exceedingly the annoyance the delay has occasioned our readers and hope to be able to make ample amends by a regular issue hereafter.

To the people of the county and valley we tender our earnest, fellow-feeling sympathy, (our house like theirs being plundered by the vandals,) for the losses they have sustained.

To our readers we have only to say that we hope they will appreciate the difficulties under which we labored and promise should the vandals ever come this way again, that, with a few hours notice, we will place our office beyond the power of their fiendish malice to destroy and thus preserve it for the convenience of our people, no matter what may be the desire of the enemy to the contrary.

To many of our people, who have heretofore not been connected with us as subscribers or readers, but who have congratulated us upon rescuing our office from destruction, and expressed their gratification on account of its being preserved, we return our most heartfelt thanks and hope by a steady adherence to the course marked out at the commencement of our editorial career, to retain their kind wishes, at least, so long as we are connected with the editorial fraternity.

To the enemies of our country, the vile Yankees, we desire, in closing to say that what they have done to us, in common with our neighbors, has not varied the tone of our feeling towards them one iota. We have always hated them and what we have seen (or felt), of them in their late raid through our valley could not possibly have lowered them in our estimation, but has served simply to prove conclusively to us that we were not wrong in the estimate we placed upon them many years ago. They have injured us permanently to some extent, but they have not accomplished their purpose. The

Vindicator will make its regular appearance in spite of their attempts to annihilate it and will continue to speak its true sentiments of the Yankee fiends who rule the hour at Washington and their worthy emissaries, who, faithful to their masters, shun the glare of Southern muskets, but vauntingly advance upon and plunder the widowed hearth and fatherless home.

Diary of Nancy Emerson, July 9–13, 1864

Nancy Emerson records the recent incursion of Union troops into Augusta County. During the last year of the war, two separate U.S. forces swept through the Shenandoah Valley—the first commanded by General David Hunter, the second by General Philip Sheridan—each destroying many of the fields and farms in the county that supplied food to the Confederate armies. For Emerson, as for civilians on both sides, encountering enemy troops was one of the most terrifying experiences of the war.

July 9, 1864

* * * Our friends at the North have probably been thinking some about us of late, hearing that the Yankees have taken Staunton, though *what* they have thought is beyond my power to divine, ignorant as we are of each others feelings. Sister C. & I very often talk of them, wonder how they fare & what they think of us, whether they set us down for incorrigible rebels against "the best government in the world," always winding up however by arguing that we do not & cannot believe they favor this unjust & abominable war, though such strange things happen these days that nothing ought to astonish us.

But I commenced with the intention of telling a story about some Yankee raiders. We have often had alarms about their coming but have been preserved by a kind Providence until this season. Not long since, they favored us with two visits (on June 9 & 10th) which will not soon be forgotten in these parts. The first day, they came in from the West, across the mountain. A party of 40 or 50 perhaps, came riding up, dismounted & rushed in. "Have you got any whiskey" said they, "got any flour? got any bacon?" with plenty of oaths "Come on boys," says one, "we'll find it all" With that, they pushed rudely by Sister C. who was terribly alarmed, & had been from the first news of their coming, & spread themselves nearly all over the house. Finding their way to a fine barrel of flour which a neighbor had given us, they proceeded to fill their sacks & pillow cases, scattering a large percent on the floor, till it was nearly exhausted. The last one told us, on our remonstrating, to hide the rest.

Some went upstairs, opened every trunk & drawer & tossed things upside down or on the floor, even my nice bonnets, pretending to be looking for arms. They stole Cousin Samuel's gold sleeve buttons & pin (a present to him) his best shirt, a good coat, & pair of shoes. The shoes, it being nearly impossible to get shoes these days, he afterwards persuaded the fellow to *sell* him back for an Ohio ten dollar note, as good as gold to him. He could with a much better appetite doubtless have knocked him down, but there was no choice in the matter.

We did not say anything to provoke them, but did not disguise our sentiments. They went peeping under the beds, looking for rebels as they said. Baxter told them there were no rebels here (meaning rebel soldiers) Cate spoke & said We are all rebels. Ellen spoke & said "Yes Baxter, I am a rebel." The Yankee looked up from her drawer, which he was searching just then, & said "That's right." Cate then said, "I am a rebel too & I *glory* in it." When Sister C. remonstrated with them about taking the shoes, asking them why they injured innocent persons who had taken no part in the war, one of them replied, "You need not tell me that, I know all the people along here have sons in the army." She then pointed to B & said "That is my only son." Ellen then said, "I have no brothers in the army, I wish from my heart I had." He then said, "Now Sis, I don't wish you had brothers in the army. I wouldn't like to kill one of your brothers. I got some corn here," (pointing to his plunder) An officer rode up after the rest had gone having the appearance of a gentleman, & asked civilly if he could get some flour. Sister C. telling him how they had stripped us of nearly every thing they could find, said he could go & see what they had left, & help himself. He said no, he never had searched a house & never would, & it was a shame they should do so.

That night they camped away a mile or two from us, extending along the road two or three miles, & got a fine supper from the farms around them. Sister C. was afraid to undress, but lay down quite exhausted two or three hours in the night. Ellen kept watch the first part of the night, & Cousin S. the last. E soon called to him, "I hear footsteps." He went out & saw some coming up the road with a torch. Thinking they might be coming to burn the house, he came to our door, saying we had better have something ready to throw around us if we should be called out for any reason taking care not to alarm us. But our fears were groundless. They started off in the night for Staunton where there were several thousand of them. Our visitors belonged to Averill's command.

July 13, 1864

They told us that Crook's men were a great deal worse than they, & that was true, but they were bad enough & worse at some other places than with us. At one of our neighbors, Mr. H they took every thing they had to eat, all the pillow cases & sheets but what were on the beds, & the towels & some of the ladies stockings. One of them made up a bundle of ladies clothing to take, but his comrade shamed him out of it. They then poured out their molasses, scattered their preserves & sugar & other things about the floor, & mixed them all together & destroyed things generally. The ladies there are very amiable & genteel in their appearance which makes it the more strange. Their visitors as well as ours however had taken a drop too much. This gentleman had kept some things for sale of late, had a quantity of tobacco & some other things on hand, all which they took to the amount of several thousand dollars.

At another neighbors, they took all of their meat (some 30 pieces of bacon) & nearly everything else they had to eat, all their horses (4) & persuaded off their two negro men. One of these was afterwards seen by one of our men crying to come back, but was watched so closely that he could not escape. No wonder he cried. He has been twice on the brink of the grave with pneumonia, & was nursed by his mistress as tenderly as if he had been a brother,

& she was always kind to him, his master also. He will not find such treatment anywhere else.

The Yankees (I give them this appellation be cause every body else does) took off all the negro men & boys they could, as well as all the horses, told the women they would take *them* next time they came. Many sent their horses to the woods. Some of these were found & captured. People here do their farming with horses instead of oxen, & it is an immense loss to have them & the servants swept off to such an extent, just as harvest is about to begin too. Many sent off their servants in one direction & another, some of whom were overtaken & captured & others escaped.

The lady before mentioned has told me since that no tongue can tell her feelings the day the Yankees were there. In the first place, they fired on her little son & another boy several times, as they sat on the fence watching their approach, & afterwards pretended that they took them for confederate soldiers from their being dressed in gray. Then her husband & oldest son were hid in the bushes in the garden, & she was in momentary fear of their being discovered & fired upon. The men & boys always kept out of the way, as they were sometimes taken off, & did not know what treatment they might receive, & thus the women were left to shift for themselves as best they could. Another of our neighbors was fired upon several times until he either dropped or lay down, it was not known which. They said it was because he ran, but he was passing between their pickets & ours, who were firing at each other, & was obliged to run. We heard of the circumstance, & were very uneasy, but he providentially escaped injury. They always fire upon those who run from them.

Staunton Vindicator, "Bad Eggs and Things," September 9, 1864

The editor of the Vindicator *suggests that the newspaper's readers should consider turning to less common sources of food—such as rats, frogs, and snails—*

given the current hard state of affairs. Union armies had laid waste much of the Shenandoah Valley during the preceding year, destroying crops and livestock throughout Augusta. With winter approaching, people in the county had to consider how they would feed themselves.

A great many people are unhappy if they can't have beefsteak for dinner, or lament the failure of the vegetables this season. We pity the helplessness of such poor creatures. The earth, the air, the waters abound in materials for food. Almost anything that you can crack is good to eat. Since the refreshing rains, with an ingenious friend of ours, we have been gathering mushrooms. He is a person of exceedingly active appetite, and is ever ready to lend us his experience in the preparation of a breakfast. With prejudices against what we had vulgally associated with the agaric muscarius, or devil's snuff box, and which we ascertained from our friend was a fungus putting up from decayed vegetables, or decomposing animal matter—we have found the champignon a most delightful article of food—a rare and notable delicacy. Care only must be taken in the selection, the rules for which may be found in Miss Leslie's familiar Cookery Book. The Agaric Campestri, or common mushroom, is found out on the commons, in grassy lanes, in meadows, &c. It is cooked with milk, butter and crackers—seasoned with salt and pepper. Care is to be taken in the distinguishing between the good and the bad, as we have remarked, as the calling of the toad stool has the effect of killing you.

Among the most difficult articles of food to procure now are bread and salt; that these are not absolutely necessary, is proven by the fact that the Laplanders never taste either; they substitute animal oil and exercise.

Rats are another well known, but neglected source of commissary supplies. The Chinese have them in their markets, just as we have hares and partridges.

Frogs are said to be of exquisite flavor, and are numerous, almost any evening on Main street. An excellent article, akin to this, is *fried snails*. They are greatly relished in l'aria. Almost any well is full of them. (not fried.)

The young rook is eaten in England, and as we know of no difference between the rook, and the crow, we do not see why young crows may not be eaten, or, indeed, in war times, old crows.

For consumptive people, snakes are excellent: the recipe for making viper-broth may be found in the pharmacopoea.

This month of August is the season for locusts, and numbers may be gathered in any yard. Locusts and wild honey it may be remembered, were the food of a celebrated character, whose example we recall to our Baptist friends.

In China, the common earth worm is always in good dinners. They are, we believe, eaten either cooked or raw. Birds' nests would probably answer, though, of course, less delicate. The head of the ass is also greatly fancied by the chinese, as well as cats and dogs, (the latter already known to be numerous here from statistics already published).

The old Romans stuffed their pheasants with assafoetida, but this, we take it, is hard to get now. In his feast, in the manner of the ancients, Dr. Smollett speaks of a very pleasant dessert, which was a sort of jelly composed of a mixture of vinegar, pickle and honey, boiled to a proper consistence, and candied assafortida, called among the ancients the *laser Syriucum*, and esteemed so precious as to be sold to the weight of a silver penny.

The article commonly known as "bad eggs" is eaten with avidity in Cochin China, but we have an unconquerable aversion to it.

"A word to the wise is sufficient," we merely throw out these hints. Talk about starving the South.

Staunton Vindicator, "Sheridan's Raid," March 24, 1865

The Vindicator *provides its readers with the latest information about the movements of Union troops under the command of General Philip Sheridan. Ordered by Ulysses S. Grant to subdue the Shenandoah Valley and capture Confederate supply depots, Sheridan's troops marched relentlessly throughout the Valley during the fall of 1864 and early spring of 1865, destroying anything that could be of use to the rebels. Farms, businesses, and homes in Augusta and neighboring counties were razed by Sheridan's men.*

From the best information we can get we give the following statement of Sheridan's force and movement.

His force consists of two Divisions and one Brigade of Cavalry under the command of Genls Custer, Merritt and Devin, with four pieces of artillery, the whole numbering from seven to nine thousand men.

He broke camp at Winchester on Monday 27th Feb. and reached Staunton on Thursday morning and pushed on to Waynesboro, meeting and scattering Gen Early's small force at that place, capturing, it was supposed by persons who saw them pass through Staunton, about six or seven hundred prisoners, and pressed with his advance through Rockfish Gap to Greenwood that night. He entered Charlottesville Friday 3rd inst. about 2 P.M., the Mayor and Council having surrendered the town and received promise of protection. He remained at Charlottesville until Monday at 10 A.M., when he moved in two columns, on the Lynchburg and Scottsville roads, the first column leaving the Lynchburg road, moved in the direction of and struck James River at New market, thence this column moved down the Canal, preceded by the column from Scottsville, to Columbia, whence they diverged in the direction of the Va Central R R, which they struck at some point between Louisa C.H. and Beaver Dam, and it is supposed have made their way around our extreme left to Grant. They destroyed the bridges and depots, except at Charlottesville, on the Central Road from Staunton to Shadwell, tore up the track of the Charlottesville and Lynchburg R R about 8 miles from Charlottesville and destroyed the bridges and depots on the road as far as they proceeded. They burned the locks and otherwise damaged the canal from New Market to Columbia and it is supposed have destroyed the track of the Central Road at and for some distance beyond Beaver Dam. In many of these depots they destroyed considerable quantities of Government supplies.

In the country along their march they behaved with their characteristic vandalism, insulting women, stealing, plundering and burning.

Owing to the fact that our forces had been scattered at different points for the purpose of more easily securing a supply of forage, Sheridan was enabled to move over the whole line of his march, almost without an impediment. It is to be hoped that our forces may be kept more concentrated hereafter, to do which the Farmers of the Valley and adjacent counties east of the Blue Ridge, must be willing not only to furnish their tithe, but must spare all they can to supply the army, if they desire to save their property from the devastating tread of the Barbarian Yankees.

2. Franklin County

Valley Spirit, "Victory or Defeat," January 29, 1862

The Valley Spirit *warns its readers that the war will likely drag on longer than many originally thought, and exhorts people to continue to support the Union cause. Like many Democratic newspapers, the* Spirit *did not want the war to be fought for any other cause than the restoration of the Union, arguing that a war for emancipation would force the Confederates to fight on indefinitely.*

It is useless to attempt concealment or disguise of the fact that the American Republic is approaching the most solemn moment of its history. We all feel it, through the entire nation. The war which has now been nearly a year in progress, must before long assume a more bloody aspect than heretofore, and a half million of men, Americans—brothers, friends—must grasp each others' throats in the conflict. It cannot be many months longer before the dead of the war will be counted by scores of thousands, and the question which has been referred to the arbitrament of the sword, will be in process of settlement by the sword. * * *

* * * Never, until now, have the people appreciated the magnitude of the struggle. Unaccustomed to war, they were easily led to think it a matter of quick decision, a little skirmishing, perhaps one great battle, and then one side or the other was to abandon the contest. The present moment admits no such ideas. If the half million

men now called into the field are unable to accomplish their work, if the five hundred millions of money already in the war are not productive of success, it is very easy to say that we must raise more men and expend more money, but it is difficult now to foresee what result either increase will produce. If our present armies are defeated, the nations of the world will probably at once recognise our enemies as a nation, and we shall have double the work before us to do which we had when the war commenced.

It is, therefore, necessary for the national cause that, in the struggles about to take place, success should be assured. Let no man call for a hasty advance. Let no man blame the Commander-in-Chief for wise and prudent delays. Let every man reflect that the forces have been gathered, the means have been provided, and present success with these men and these means is the business of army and officers.

It is most emphatically the duty of every citizen, who has not gone to the war in person, to submit the management of the army to the President and the Commander-in-Chief. All agitation, all attempts to coerce them into particular plans of warfare, or particular lines of "military necessity," are but disturbing and annoying forces, tending to the injury of the great cause. We have undertaken war, we have raised our armies, and we have chosen our leaders. We owe it to them, and we owe it to our own good sense, and character for national prudence, to forbear all factious opposition to their military plans.

A few weeks or a few months will decide the first great campaign. We do not pause to consider what will be the results of defeat to the national cause. We prefer rather to look on what ought to be the results of victory. It is not remotely probable to-day that the Southern leaders or people would accept any settlement of the differences except on the absolute acknowledgement of their independence, and it is hardly probable that they would accept that without also having the slave States, including the District of Columbia, abandoned to their power. But the first great effect of victory in this campaign for us must be considered the final decision of the question of Union. If we are successful the South must abandon its extravagant ideas, and at once yield to the conviction that they are hopeless. We shall not have conquered the South, nor shall we have accomplished the subjugation of the rebellion by victories in Kentucky or on the Potomac. But we shall have settled forever the possibility of the division of the Union.

Then follows the effect on Southern minds. If the victorious armies were marching to the desolation of the Southern country, the abolition of slavery and the overthrow of the rights of States, the war would be one of endless duration. We see a remarkable feature of the contest in the fact that in South Carolina, where the people are a unit, they abandon their homes to our invading forces, and retire from our reach as we advance. This sight was hardly ever before witnessed in any war, among civilized nations. It is an indication of what we may expect as the results of victory where the enemy believe us to be invaders for ruin, instead of the armies of a constitutional government. When invasion is for punishment or for mere conquest, every house becomes a fort, every stream a defensible position, and the last intrenchment of the defenders must be reached and taken before the end of the contest is attained. God forbid that such be the course to which we are lead in victory by the principles of our war, or the cries with which we send our men to the field.

On the other hand, victory, accompanied as it will be under the present conservative management of Mr. Lincoln, with assurances of faith to the Constitution and its provisions, while it results in settling the question of the dissolution of the Union, may be followed by a speedy termination of the war, if the South is not wholly given over to madness. The Union sentiment, small though it be, may develop itself at once. The impossibility of independence must become manifest to all, and the question will then be asked how far the North designs conquest and interference with State sovereignty. That question, answered by the voice of the conservative masses at the North, East and West, may lead to a sudden revolution in the South, which will overthrow the leaders of the rebellion and restore the power of the Constitution. For such results every good man must earnestly hope. Victory to be followed by a long and desolating invasion can only be wished for by those who hate slavery and slaveholders more than they love the Union. It becomes the conservative men of the North to stand firm in their principles, and be ready to welcome the first voice of allegiance from the revolted States.

Valley Spirit, "Arrival from Dixie," June 18, 1862

The Valley Spirit *recounts a recent train of Confederate prisoners that passed through Chambersburg on its way to a prisoner-of-war camp. The newspaper's editor notes the contrast between the ragged appearance of the rebels—asserting that the Confederate army must be degenerating—and the opinion of the prisoners that the South was winning the war.*

On Sunday last about four hundred rebel prisoners passed through this place, on a special train, their destination being Camp Curtin, near Harrisburg. They were guarded by three companies of Wisconsin and Indiana troops. The prisoners were very poorly clad and presented a very unsoldierly appearance. To judge by the appearance of these men one would say that "Secesh was pretty well played out." How it is possible to hold an army together in such a degraded state is more than a northern mind can understand. Our three month's men made a great ado about their equipment but had they seen these rebel soldiers they would have been forever content with "Curtin's Commissariat." During the short time the train stopped here our citizens talked freely with the prisoners and as a general thing received respectful answers to all questions. They are certainly the most deluded set of men we ever heard talk. They profess to believe that they have gained all the battles, captured more arms and prisoners, and have had the best of the war in every respect. Their own looks was a poor corroboration of their assertions, for a more completely used up lot of men could not be found in any army in the world. If the balance of the Southern army are like these they are hardly "foemen worthy of our steel." No one could look upon these wretched creatures with any other feeling than that of pity, and in the very large crowd assembled around the cars we noticed but few attempts to taunt or insult them, and these exceptions were by persons of no account in the community, and who never possessed much reputation for sense or decency. The prisoners themselves seemed to feel that they were receiving better treatment than they deserved and it may, perhaps, convince them that "Northern barbarism" is still a more refined article than "Southern chivalry." These prisoners were taken by Gen. Fremont who, report says, has about a thousand more of the same sort to send this way as soon as transportation can be obtained.

Valley Spirit, "The President's Proclamation," October 1, 1862

The editor of the Valley Spirit *expresses his deep disapproval of Lincoln's Emancipation Proclamation. Issued immediately after the Union victory at the Battle of Antietam, the proclamation proved highly controversial in the North. Many Northerners, particularly Democrats, deplored the idea of fighting for anything other than the restoration of the Union. Some feared that the proclamation would unite the South even more tightly, while others believed the president did not have the authority to issue such an order.*

The great agony of the radicals is over. They clamored for a proclamation until they succeeded. They besieged the President on all sides, and waged an incessant war upon him for months, until at last he succumbed to the "pressure" and issued a proclamation proclaiming unconditional freedom to all the slaves in the seceded States after the first day of January next. Where the President pretends to find his authority for issuing such a proclamation, he does not deign to inform us. This new policy is to be the great panacea for all our ills, and is to kill the rebellion at one blow. We shall soon see the fruits of the policy and know from practical experience, what abolition philosophy is worth. In the meantime we must be permitted to hold the same views we have ever held on this subject, until we are convinced to the contrary by practical results.

The conservative men of the country have been greatly disappointed in this action of the President. They had been persuaded that he was a man of honest intentions and desired to do what was best for his country. They hoped, even sometimes against hope, that he would eventually see the true ground of his position, discard the mad counsels and revolutionary teachings of the radical men of his party, plant himself firmly upon the pillars of the Constitution, and make an earnest effort to save the country. They caught at every exhibition of conservatism in the President to strengthen this opinion, and were prompt in commending and endorsing every act of his tending to strengthen and promote the great cause in which the country is engaged, where the abolitionists who are now in ecstacies over his recent proclamation, either treated him with silent contempt or broke out in open murmurs of discontent and opposition. Yet in the face of these facts the President has given way to their clamor, and thrown himself, body and soul, into the hands of the radical abolition faction, who have been seeking the ruin of the country for many years, and who have pronounced the Constitution a "league with death and a covenant with hell," and the honest and conservative masses of the free States and the loyal Union men of the Slave States, have been shamefully deceived, and the nation been made to bleed afresh at every pore through the weakness and imbecility of its chief executive officer.

A word as to the effect of this Proclamation. Practically it is not worth the paper it is written on. If the administration is unable to enforce the legitimate and Constitutional laws of the country, in the seceded States, how is this unconstitutional and foolish paper proclamation to be enforced? The President himself told the Chicago Delegation that it would be inoperative, and could not free a single slave. The proposition is too absurd for a moment's serious consideration.

But there is another aspect in which this subject is all important, that of its bearing upon the loyal Union men of the slave States. They have suffered long and much for the sacred cause of the Union in their respective States. They persistently denied the allegations of the Secessionists that this was war on the part of the Government for the abolition of Slavery. This was the great argument of the Secessionists by which they were enabled to carry the people with them. The Union men planted themselves upon the broad principles of the Constitution, and bravely contended for the old Union and the old flag, with danger and death oftentimes staring them in the face, trusting in the good faith of the administration to sustain them. How have they been sustained. Alas! how! President Lincoln, with one stroke of the pen, violates the plighted faith of the Government, and says to the whole southern people, that the Union men were wrong and the Secessionists were right. In no other way could Abraham Lincoln have done so much to strengthen and consolidate the rebellion. We have no doubt that Jefferson Davis would have given the last dollar in the Confederate Treasury to have just such a proclamation emanate from the President of the United States.

Diary of William Heyser: December 28–31, 1862; May 26, 1863; June 14, 18, 19, 1863; July 2, 1863; July 7, 1863

William Heyser writes in his diary about life on the Franklin County home front. Heyser, a prosperous shopkeeper, discussed escaped slaves who made their way into Franklin, the scene at the railroad depot when the bodies of slain soldiers returned to the county, and his thoughts on Northern politics. In June and July 1863, Heyser recorded the panic that gripped Chambersburg and Franklin County when Robert E. Lee's army passed through on its way to Gettysburg, and the aftermath of the battle.

December 28, 1862

Much work on our project, which seems to be going very well. Rev. Harbaugh has three colored boys in his class. Brought back from Virginia as contraband by our volunteers. They came here totally illiterate, now know their letters. Read well and cipher satisfactorily. One has been admitted into the church and the others promising. It was a pleasing sight to see these poor outcasts, far from their native soil pursuing the light of liberty. I hope they do not fall under the influence of many of the debased Africans now filling up our towns.

December 31, 1862

Snowing. We call a halt to our nearly finished work. I must leave for home, arriving there without accident about five p.m. Bodies of

John Oaks and Augustus Howser brought home for burial from Fredericksburg. A large concourse of people present at the depot.

The condition of our government more gloomy than ever. Nearly 70,000 of our soldiers slain, and we are in debt over 700 millions of dollars. We can see no end to this plundering of our resources.

Already the contractors of this war have emptied the treasury. Many of our soldiers going unpaid.

May 26, 1863

A young soldier, by the name of Henderson, one of our provost guards, was thrown from his horse last night and dragged to his death. It seems he and a friend were racing on the turnpike, he attempted to jump over a cow that was laying in his way, but at the critical moment rose up, throwing the young man's horse, which dragged him a short distance. He never rallied, and thus passed into eternity. He is of respectable parents living in Baltimore, who will be called to mourn over the death of a wayward son.

Talk of re-electing Lincoln for our next President. I do not feel his re-election is possible, after all his failures so far. He has not the ability of statesmanship to wield the destinies of our government. When this conflict is over, we will need a most able man to solve larger problems, than we have now—particularly those of the African race.

June 14, 1863

Clear and unpleasant. Reports of an engagement near Winchester. Our town in an uproar. Government property being loaded up and taken away. The drum calls for volunteers.

All the army stores have been packed up and sent to Philadelphia. Little attendance at church and Sabbath School. Much of the news is false we hear, but it serves to upset the people. We all feel Pennsylvania will be invaded. Many families are hiding their valuables, and preparing for the worst. Some preparing to leave town. Tonight we have many sleepless eyes, the houses all shut up tightly, but the inmates astir.

The stores are packing up their goods and sending them off, people are running to and fro. Cashier Messer Smith is sent off with the books of the bank and its valuables. The cars are crowded to utmost capacity. The colored people are flying in all directions. There is a complete state of confusion.

After twelve we got word the Rebels have entered Hagerstown. The stores are all closed, and the streets crowded with those that can't leave. I am urged to leave. As President of the bank, might be held responsible for its assets, which I doubt, anyhow I shall stay to defend my property best I can.

At 8 o'clock a number of contrabands entered our town, fleeing from Martinsburg with the Rebels not far behind. These were followed by a wagon train, many on three wheels, and less being dragged and pushed as fast as possible. The street is crowded with horses and wagons, all in the wildest state of confusion. Upon asking one of them as to their plight, said the Rebels are not far behind.

Suddenly about two hundred more wagons, horses, mules, and contrabands all came pouring down the street in full flight. Some of them holloring the Rebels are behind us. Such a sight I have never seen, or will never see again. The whole town is on the sidewalks screaming, crying, and running about. They know not where.

The road into town is almost impassable by the teamsters cutting loose their wagons and fleeing with their horses. This further jammed up our town, some of the horses fall in the streets from shere exhaustion. One soldier was killed by the fall. After the panic subdues, the teamsters that had cut loose their wagons went back for them. At twelve the excitement is beyond conception. I am again urged to leave. Mr. T. B. Kennedy sent me a message, feeling it was a good idea. I have consented against my will—packing up my valuable papers and at two, left with Mrs. Heyser in my buggy, for Carlisle, committing the house to William, Proctor my colored man, and girl. After I left they did not stay, but put off for the mountains. Had difficulty passing the wagon jam on the road and answering questions, arriving at Stoughstown about 6 in the evening, where I shall wait for news.

About midnight, awakened by the news that the Rebels were at Shippensburg. Dressing, we immediately left for Carlisle at midnight, being so dark and the roads jammed with wagons, made dangerous situation that I regretted leaving home in the first place.

However, thanks to Almighty Providence, we arrived safely in Carlisle about 4 o'clock in the morning. Tried to get more sleep, but impossible, excitement here is mounting.

We got a bite to eat, the horse fed, and left for Harrisburg. All along the way the news had preceded us, people out securing and leaving with their goods. Driving away their horses, and all shops shut up.

Stopped in Mechanicsburg, a prosperous, but now excited town, to learn of fortifications being made for Harrisburg. We were advised to stay here, but decided to press on. On approaching Harrisburg, I could see the fortifications with a large number of men working on them. The railroad cars were filled with troops on their way to Chambersburg with artillary.

We crossed the river without difficulty and found Harrisburg, in wildest confusion. Merchants shipping away their goods, families their furniture, and people fleeing in all directions. Almost laughable scenes some created.

Stopped at Harris's Hotel. See few females, mostly men moving furniture and stores, the streets are almost impassable. The excitement is greater than Chambersburg. All the records of the state have been removed under the expectation that Harrisburg will be burned. Our state is doing nothing to defend itself against invasion. Gov. Curtain seems to be paralized and unable to act. We need decisions badly, and can't expect them from Washington.

June 18, 1863

Warm. The Rebels have left Chambersburg taking with them about 250 colored people again into bondage. Gov. Curtain is presently very unpopular. Left Harrisburg for home about two o'clock, in the afternoon, by way of the turnpike. Traveling thru very beautiful and fertile countryside. Had tea in Carlisle, pressed on for Stoughs town to spend the night. Here we encountered many colored people fleeing the Rebels, as not all have left the area. These poor people are completely worn out, carrying their families on their backs. Saw some twenty from Chambersburg that I recognized. Some men from Shippensburg urged us to turn back, that danger was not past, but we decided to press on, even though the night was black, stormy, and the road dangerous. We were glad to see the lamps of Carlisle. Little did we know of the perils that had been in our way, Almighty Providence led us thru safely. It will be a journey my wife and I will never forget. I suggested she write a book about our adventurous journey. Weary and tired, we went to bed.

June 19, 1863

Pleasant, heavy rain thru the night. Much rumor—one knows not what to believe. All is still alarm. The stores are still all closed and business at a standstill. Unexpectedly met my man, Proctor, who had made for the mountains, worked his way to Newville from where he got to Carlisle. Of Fanny, our colored girl, he knew nothing.

The papers are now calling for McClelland's recall. Without him we cannot succeed.

Troops are coming in from neighboring states to support our few that we can bring some order to our situation. It is ridiculous that 800 Rebel troops can paralize the Southern portion of our state without opposition. This invasion had been expected for months, and totally ignored by our government.

July 2, 1863

Cloudy and very hot. The Rebels are leaving Chambersburg for Gettysburg. About 3 this morning, I was awakened by the rumbling of heavy wagons. There were about 60 of them, followed by a large body of troops, requiring about two hours to pass. They were quite jubilant in their passage thru town, pulling my bell at the door and hooting at me.

After their passage, all was quiet again, except squads of calvary passing to unite with their companies, all in the direction of Gettysburg. Somewhere near there is a heavy engagement. About ten, the town is vacant. The Rebels leaving their sick behind for us to nurse and care for. A few stragglers are to be seen, but the worst is over. We congratulate ourselves that we still have a roof over our heads. About 12, in the company of two other men, I walked out to my farm to assess the damage. Everywhere were holes cut in fences and grain trampled down by the exercises of the cavalry. I sustained a great amount of damage, nearly 4,000 men have encamped here. All of my fence gone, about 40 acres of oats and much damage to all other crops. My houses were all robbed of clothing and any kind of gear with which to work. The report was circulated that I was a Colonel in the Union Army and now made to pay greater than my neighbors. How unjust even your supposed friends can be. In passing over the fields and woods where they encamped, there is already a great stench.

I found two Rebels hiding on my farm and would have taken them back to town. They would have been willing prisoners to obtain their parole, but a large body of Stewarts' cavalry was passing near and I advised them to hide. One gave me his bayonet, which I brought back to town. Back home, more reports come in of a battle near Gettysburg. All night long, more troops pass thru town, their yelling is terrific. I keep indoors.

July 7, 1863

Much rain. The grain is in danger of spoiling. About 200 Rebel prisoners were brought in today. Many are deserting, Lee is making a desperate attempt to escape Mead's army. Our stores are reopening and cleaning up.

Gen. Couch's division is following the end of Lee's army thru Greenwood on what is called the Pine Stump Road. We are hoping Lee's army will be captured. If Mead allows him to escape, it will indeed be folly.

We hear the Rebel lose at Gettysburg 30,000 men, the Union 20,000. My sons, Jacob and William, just returned from the battlefield. It is a fearful sight. The fields full of dead, by all the roadsides dead are hardly covered by a thin layer of mud. Wreckage everywhere, the implements of war fast disappearing by souvenir seekers. Soon the cultivators plow will cover it all and put an end to military glory.

If Lee is allowed to escape this struggle will be prolonged. We hear of only skirmishes all along his route to the Potomac.

Franklin Repository, "Value of Government to the Poor," September 23, 1863

The Repository *argues that the war should be of the greatest concern to the poor whites of the North and South, as they stand to gain or lose the most by the conflict. Many Republicans, such as the editor of the* Repository, *saw the threads of class conflict woven into all aspects of the war. For so many Republicans, opposing slavery (and the disproportionate political power wielded by wealthy Southern slaveholders) was a fundamental part of their efforts to protect the interests of free white laborers.*

In the impending struggle between the friends of the government, and the opposition in the North, there is nothing sadder than to see the intense bitterness manifested by the last named party. * * * Already have their cunning appeals to party zeal and blind prejudice, their constant outcry about "oppressive taxation," the unconstitutionality of the draft and the "injustice of the conscription act to the poor" done too successfully their work. The poor have been excited against the rich, one laboring class against another, while riot and bloodshed such as would put to shame a heathen nation have followed as the legitimate consequences of such teaching. * * * From the same source too, we have denunciations of the policy of the government in freeing the slaves on the ground that they will take the place and lower the character of northern laborers. Did we hope to find any honesty in a press thus unscrupulous in the artifices they use to accomplish their ends, we should ask them to pause and consider what means they have of allaying the spirit they are thus conjuring up to their aid, should they be successful. * * * But we turn from those who seek in party triumph only their own gain, to the poor man himself, and ask him to consider a few facts. No one in the least acquainted with the antecedents of the rebellion which now distracts our land, will venture to claim that it has any democratic tendencies. It does not look down to the condition of the poor and weak and say, "it is for these that we have unsheathed the sword and thrown down the gage of battle." Among the many reasons gathered together to justify it, we have never yet seen the abject and disenfranchised condition of the poor whites in the South assigned as one. On the contrary this rebellion is notoriously a protest on the part of the South against the democratic tendencies of the North. The "Yankee idea of universal suffrage" and the dignity of labor are nowhere held in greater contempt than among the leaders of the slaveholders' rebellion; and were they to succeed, it would be the most fearful blow human liberty has received for many a long year. These facts are so well known that it seems almost commonplace to repeat them; but we ask him who has been led away by the delusion that he has no interest in this war, because he has no property, to ponder them a moment. The poor man is most vitally concerned at any time in the preservation of this government, but most especially when the attack against it comes from a party avowedly seeking its overthrow, that it may the more effectually enslave the laboring class. The war, then, that resists this, is emphatically the laboring man's war. It is the laboring man's flag, and the laboring man's government that are endangered; for nowhere else on the broad face of the earth, will he find his rights so secured, and himself so effectually guarded from oppression, as here in the free North. It is an utterly false conception that the excellency of government lies in the protection it gives to property, and that it is most valuable to him who possesses most wealth. Property is just as secure under the despotism of Austria as here; just as safe in aristocratic England as in republican America. In fact, an aristocracy is the rich man's government; it is made especially with regard to his wants. But we claim, as the distinguishing excellency of our government, the perfectness with which it secures the rights of all, high, low, rich and poor. While all those who love a common humanity are interested in its perpetuity, and the overthrow of this rebellion, the poor man is especially so. It matters little under what government the rich live; wealth, under any circumstance, must command influence and station. But it makes every difference to the poor man. * * * A party of men calling themselves democratic ask for their support. Democracy, the friend of slavery, the sworn ally of a proud aristocracy, proclaiming that the true theory of society is "capital should own labor!" The term in this case is a misnomer, and used only to deceive. We ask the laboring man then to reflect. We appeal to his reason, not his prejudices, and ask him to consider, whether in the ranks of those who are notorious for their sympathy with this rebellion, and avowed opposition to the war, who at this day are reckoned by the South as their best allies, and who, to gratify their lordly masters, are ready to re-fasten the fetters upon a thousand slaves, whether among these, or the ardent friends of the government and the democratic doctrines of "liberty and equality," will he find his truest and best friends?

Benjamin S. Schneck to Margaretta S. Keller, August 3, 1864

Benjamin Schneck writes to his sister, Margaretta, and her family about the recent invasion and burning of Chambersburg by rebel forces on July 30, 1864. Thousands of Union civilians, like Schneck, had been left homeless by the fires set by Confederates, and many residents of the town had to move into the homes of friends and relatives until they could rebuild.

Chambersburg
Aug. 3 1864

My dear Sister & Brother—

We are all safe, though homeless and with only some clothing left. Our stable is unharmed. We saved by far the smallest part of our clothing—I have a borrowed shirt, one straw hat, & so-on. My Library, even my Papers & Manuscripts (except my Deeds) all—all gone. The good prospect I had for one hour: of saving our house, kept us from saving furniture and clothing. Help there was none. I was on the roof, Rebecca & the girl carrying water up 3 steps, for everybody had enough to do for themselves for the firing began in different parts of town at one time. Some houses in each square were fired, and then the others caught. In some cases, money was offered to be taken (in out-of-the-way parts) by the men & the properties then saved. Except one house (the Misses Dennys 8 doors above and where we are now), every house down on both sides for 7 Squares, is gone. So with Main Street for nearly 1/2 mile, Queen Street, part of Washington, etc, Our Print Establ, *with all* (except the stereotype plates & Acct. Books) is in ruins. The Bank, *all* the stores, *all* the hotels, every shoe, clothing, and other stores (except in the outskirts some small grocery etc. shops) are all consumed. In *most* instances, little—in very many, *nothing*—was saved, not even a single change of clothing. But blessed be God, there are those who were spared, & their hearts & houses are open to the rest. Help in the way of provisions & clothing is coming in. None need to starve. But such a scene of Ruin! No imagination can conceive it. Gov. Curtin came up last evening and said to me: "The reality is fearfully beyond all my conceptions." He requested us to try & keep the people in heart, for many have left, & more do not know what to do here now. We have a little house out of town on one of my lots. The one half will be vacant soon & I suppose we will go in it—it has two little rooms below & two in the attic for small bedrooms—it is cottage style, 1 1/2 stories high. Further, I cannot say. But for the present, we must & will stay here.

I am hardly able to write. I thought I would write to you & the girls would be so good as to write for me to sister Sophia, Mary, Louisa & the rest. To Benjn I have just written. God bless you all, my dear ones. Rebecca has kept up well. If only we are preserved from future invasions. But this morning, there was news, that the enemy is at Williamsport & along the Potomac. Our force was repulsed there on Sunday. Petersburg has been recaptured by them, so far as it was lost. It looks dark for our country.

Some of the rebel officers & men that were here did not expect this vandalism, & they showed a good spirit—they did & would not fire any building & even helped people to carry out things out of their houses. They denounced the whole procedure as outrageous and wicked.

But I can no more.
The Lord be with you all.
Your Affectionate Brother & Uncle
B. S. Schneck

Valley Spirit, "Burning of Chambersburg," August 31, 1864

In its first article after the burning of Chambersburg, the Valley Spirit *details the events of that day and lays the blame for the destruction at the feet of the U.S. and Pennsylvania governments. Confederate General Jubal Early ordered John McCausland to march his troops into Chambersburg and extract a ransom or burn the town, which he did when they refused to pay. The Confederate assault on Chambersburg was, in part, a response to Union desecration of the Shenandoah Valley. While not entirely accurate, the* Spirit's *account of the burning represents how people in Chambersburg felt immediately after the town's destruction—the only Northern town burned by the Confederates.*

Where the Blame Belongs.

* * * To the stupidity of the War Department must we lay the destruction of Chambersburg. There is no use mincing terms about it. Let the blame be placed fairly and squarely where it belongs. The earnest appeals made time and again, by Gen. Couch, to the "powers that be" at Washington, to obtain and organize troops for the protection of Chambersburg against rebel raids cannot at this time be told. Gen. Couch is too correct a military man to publish them himself, even in his own defence, and the War Department Dare Not Do It. We know they were made and we know too that they were denied. * * *

* * * It will some day be made the subject of investigation, when the country is placed under better auspices, why the Shenandoah and Cumberland Valleys have been left as raging grounds to the rebels? * * * If such management, rather *mis*management of our military affairs, is not affording "aid and comfort to the enemy" then we know not in what direction to look for treason! "The border shall be protected" has been the promise since the war commenced. How it has [illegible word] fulfilled burnt towns and a plundered, homeless people can answer. Let us, however, suffer on patiently, and though our wrongs may be greater than we can bear, it must not drive us from our loyalty to our Government; it will not always be in bad hands; be of good heart, redress will surely come.

Force of the Enemy.

The rebel force detailed by Gen. Early for the destruction of Chambersburg, under written orders from that General to do the work effectually, numbered about 3000 mounted men, accompanied by six pieces of artillery. They reached the heights beyond the town, on the western turnpike, about 4 o'clock on Saturday morning, July 30th. * * * The force that entered the town on West Market street, by actual account, numbered 831, while 300 additional came in on the Wolffstown road. We have the authority of one of our most highly respectable citizens for this statement as to their numbers. * * *

Demand for Ransom.

No sooner had the rebels possession of the town than commenced the work of pillage. The men went howling through the streets for "whiskey" and "greenbacks," while their officers were industriously at work breaking open stores and dwellings and robbing citizens, wherever they met them, of their watches and pocketbooks. In the meantime McCausland had an eye to business and determined to drive a sharp bargain. He made a peremptory demand upon the town authorities for $500,000 in greenbacks or, if more convenient and agreeable, would take $100,000 in gold, or burn the town in ten minutes. It was very evident from the conduct of the men, from the moment they entered town, that it was a doomed place and would be destroyed under any circumstances. No attention was, therefore, paid to the demand and McCausland immediately fired the town as he would have done had every dollar of the ransom been paid down. Our citizens have the proud satisfaction of knowing, however ruinous their hopes, that they did not demean themselves by any offer to compromise, or conciliate in any way the freebooters by an attempt to negotiate with them. From the moment they entered the place they gave out that they were hellbent to burn the "d——d town" and they were suffered to carry out their hellish inclinations without making dupes of our citizens by extorting ransom from them when ransom would not have saved the town. Though we lost about everything else we saved at least our self-respect by having no voluntary intercourse with McCausland and his "hell-hounds."

Firing the Town.

They appeared to have adopted a systematically arranged plan for burning the town by firing in regular order from the center to the suburbs. The first house fired was a large unfinished building, belonging to Mr. Peter Brough, situated a few doors from the Diamond. It was full of combustible material, over which they poured coal-oil and applied the torch. It soon had the surrounding houses and the Arcade Buildings opposite in flames. The next place fired was the Grocery Store of Mr. Wm. Gelwicks of the Diamond and about the same time the Court House, and in ten minutes after flames were seen to issue from almost every house along Main and Market streets. No person can describe the scene of terror and confusion that ensued among the inhabitants. No warning was given the people to leave their homes and the first intimation they had that private dwellings would be burned was the smashing of their doors and having their houses filled with infuriated fiends, still more brutalized by whiskey, who would listen to no appeals, however pitiously made, for times to save some household goods and remove the sick and infirm. Their homes were fired over their heads in the midst, of their pleadings and they were left to get through the flames as best they could or perish in them. Many had the clothes burnt off their backs and their persons badly sacrificed in getting out of their burning homes. On leaving their dwellings women and children could be seen in the wildest terror running through the walls of fire on either side seeking an open space to escape the devouring flames, in many instances to be met by the merciless foe and robbed of the little they were struggling to save. In but few cases was anything saved except the scanty clothing on their backs.
* * *

The Future.

Everything has changed since the burning. Business is all conducted in little shops and shanties on the back streets, and in out of the way places. But a small assortment of goods are kept on hand and for these the highest prices are asked. Many of our citizens have removed to other places never to return. Others of our business men who remain have opened up in a small way in some unthought of place, or started some new branch of traffic that the necessities of the people seem to demand. One would scarcely suppose that so great a change could take place in a community in so short a time. Men seem in a degree reckless, they have lost all they possessed in the world, in an hours time, through no fault of theirs, and they appear determined to make it up by hook or by crook in the shortest possible time. Money seems plenty and "trust is played out" as may be noticed posted up in stores and shops. It is cash down for everything you get and everything you sell. People understand each others necessities and do not think of asking credit. As to the prospects of re-building the town they look exceedingly dark just now. But few have the means to rebuild and they are dubious about investing their money in property along the border while the war lasts. Those without means can do nothing but pile up their brick and let their lots take care of themselves until some appropriation is made for their relief. A few are already re-building—they are, perhaps, the wisest after all. The Legislature granted $100,000 to keep the people from starving and freezing this winter. Very charitable indeed! "Charity covereth a multitude of sins." The contributions from other places will not amount to much in the way of relieving the many wants of the people. The supply of provisions forwarded for a few weeks was liberal and relieved immediate wants. This aid has in a great measure stopped off and must soon cease altogether. The sufferers would return their grateful thanks to the good people of many towns in Pennsylvania for their substantial sympathy. A few things in the way of clothing and bedding have been sent in, but not enough to fit out twenty families when over three hundred are entirely destitute. How the people are to live this winter God only knows. Without stoves, coal, wood, bedding, furniture, clothing, flour, meat, in a word, all the necessities of life; and most of all without a roof to shelter them from the pelting of the storms. Our people will only realize what they have lost, and what hard times are, when cruel winter comes.

Valley Spirit, "Peace and Union," September 28, 1864

The Democratic Valley Spirit *argues that the war will never be won by following Republican policies. Northern Democrats were particularly displeased with the war's turn toward emancipation, and selected ex-General George B. McClellan as their 1864 candidate for president, promising to end the prosecution of the war for anything other than the restoration of the Union. Many Democrats, like the* Spirit's *editor, hoped the election of McClellan would bring the war to an end.*

The only true road to peace and Union, lies in a return on the part of the National Administration to the doctrines of the Critenden resolution passed by Congress at the commencement of the war, as declaratory of the ends and objects to be attained by it; namely, the return of the Seceded States to their allegiance to the Constitution and laws of the country. Since the passage of that resolution, by Congress, the party in power has diverted the war to other purposes, and now declares that the unconditional submission of the rebels can alone end it. Conditional submission *to what?* This is the great question all the time. The people of the rebel States have declared that they were fighting for independence but does any one believe that if they were assured that the government of the country would be administered in accordance with the Constitution as our fathers made it, so that it were rendered impossible to interfere with the reserved rights of the States, that they—the *people* of the South—would not soon throw their leaders overboard, and gladly to return to the shelter of the Union. It is in this view that, under the policy declared by Mr. Lincoln and his party, that they cannot have equal rights in the Union, that they are, as they say, fighting for independence. This is the very life and strength of the rebellion. They are required to submit to *something* they know not what, but not to the Constitution. It is this idea, pervading the whole South, that has enabled the rebel rulers to raise and keep up armies to fight against the Union; and so long as this idea is retained by the people of that section, and no effort is made on part of the government to disabuse their minds of the impression, the present sanguinary struggle may continue until mutual exhaustion compels a cessation of hostilities. When the rebel in arms is told that he must submit, he very naturally asks *to what?* If to a government which denies to him what the Constitution of the country guarantees, he indignantly spurns the act, but if it be unconditional submission to *the Constitution* which guarantees ample protection—protection as ample as he can gain by independence—the latent love in his heart for the old Union of his fathers, will revive in his breast and he will lay down his arms at once.

The time, in the history of this rebellion, when passion must give way to reason has arrived. Argument and conciliation must be used to convince these men in the South that they are wrong—madly, wickedly, desperately wrong. The false impressions created in the minds of the Southern people, by their ambitious and designing leaders, must be removed by a return to the first principles on which this war was waged.

The present Administration so far from acting on the policy which wisdom, right and justice dictates, and endeavoring to convince the Southern people, by its acts, of a determination to guarantee to them all their rights under the Constitution, has adopted a policy the very reverse. It has destroyed State lines and uprooted institutions founded in the laws and customs of their section, and punished them for obeying an irresistible force against which they had a right to ask its protection, and against which it had not the power to protect them. The Administration has by its confiscation acts, its emancipation proclamations and kindred measures, left the Southern people no other alternative but to fight on to the bitter end, and has added fuel to the flame of sectional hate; thus playing into the hands of the leaders of the rebellion; who, on their part, desire above all things, a permanent division of the Union. Had the true policy, the policy on which the war was conducted in its earlier stages, been adhered to, and their rights of property not been threatened by unconstitutional acts of Congress and executive proclamations freeing the negroes, these leaders would have been deserted by the mass of the Southern people, and ere this, we verily believe, would have returned to their allegiance. But it seems that the rulers to which Providence for some wise purpose of His own, has for a time committed the destinies of our country, do not desire that the Union shall be restored under the Constitution which for eighty years has given us peace, prosperity and safety. They desire a new Union and a new Constitution, under and by which, the black man shall become the [illegible word] of the white, and take a position in this land of ours clothed with all the rights and privileges which we believe cannot with safety to us, or profit to them, be conferred upon them. To this end they are sacrificing thousands of the bravest youths of our land and millions of money wrung from the hands of those "who earn their bread by the sweat of their brow" by a system of taxation that must ultimately become too heavy to be borne. To the misguided people of the South they say there can be no peace without your "unconditional submission." Unconditional submission *to what?* To the Constitution and laws of the country? No! but to the terms we shall dictate, the first of which is, the total abolition of slavery. This is their condition precedent even to entering upon negotiations with the rebels with a view to bringing the war to a close. Under this condition there can be no peace without the utter subjugation and extermination of the Southern people.

On the other hand how do the Democracy propose to bring about the restoration of the Union and the return of peace to this distracted land? With them *"the Union is the one condition of peace"* and the only one. In the words of their noble standard bearer:

"So soon as it is clear, or even probable, that our present adversaries are ready for peace upon the basis of the Union, we should exhaust all the resources of statesmanship practiced by civilized nations, and taught by the traditions of the American people, consistent with the honor and interests of the country, to secure such peace, re-establish the Union, and guarantee for the future the constitutional rights of every State."

This paragraph shows the entire difference between the present Administration and the Democracy. In it, it is proposed to exhaust all the resources of statesmanship to end the war honorably to both sections. To hold out the olive branch with one hand, whilst the sword is grasped firmly by the other. It too calls submission, not submission to an arbitrary edict, but to the laws and the Constitution as interpreted by the good and wise men of the past. In effect it says: consent to the Union and you yourselves shall aid in determining upon what condition it shall exist hereafter. This is the submission which will be required by the Democratic party, from those who have taken up arms against the government. And when such submission is yielded by the rebels, the object for which the war was prosecuted is attained, the Temple of Janus will again be closed, and peace once more dispense its blessings over a re-united, prosperous and happy people. "The Union is the one condition of peace. We ask no more."

VII
The End of War

1. Augusta County

Staunton Vindicator, "Public Meeting," March 24, 1865

The Vindicator *prints a list of resolutions passed in support of the Confederacy at a public meeting held at the Staunton courthouse in late February 1865. Expressing defiant support for the Confederate cause, the resolutions reflect the depth of commitment many in the county felt for their Southern nation, as well as their desperation in the spring of 1865 to stave off the likely defeat of the Confederacy.*

At a large and enthusiastic meeting of the citizens of Augusta County, held at their Court House on Monday the 27th day of February 1865, General Kenton Harper was called to the chair and Wm. H. Tams. Wm H.H. Lynn and Richard Mauzy were appointed Secretaries.

Gen. H. on assuming the chair forcibly explained the object of the meeting.

Col. Wm. H. Harman, in behalf of the committee appointed by the primary meeting held in Staunton, and which called this meeting, reported the following Preamble and Resolutions:

Whereas, The people of these Confederate States have had a distinct and unmistakeable issue presented to them by the Despotic Ruler of the United States, We are emphatically informed that the abject surrender of our liberty as a people is demanded, and further contumacy and assistance is to be visited with all the horrors of a subjugation which carries in its brain deprivation of personal freedom for ourselves and children; confiscation of our property, and the destruction of every right we hold dear. The Government created by us and fairly representing us, has met this insolent demand with a manly defiance, which we re-echo and endorse. Placing our trust in the Lord of Hosts; relying upon the justice of our cause; preferring death to dishonor—determined to bequeath the precious boon of Independence which we inherited from our Fathers, to our children, or die in the effort; willing to lay *our all* if need be upon the altar of our country, resolved never to submit to the yoke of such a people as those with whom our brothers and sons have been engaged in deadly struggle for four years, and who have delighted in sacking and destroying our houses, devastating our lands, insulting our women and murdering our citizens; the People of Augusta County have assemble[d] in primary meeting, and do solemnly Resolve:

1st. That we have a firm and certain conviction of the justice of our cause, and will maintain it at every sacrifice of blood and treasure.

2nd. That the watchfires of Liberty lighted in 1861 burn with undiminished brilliancy in this the 5th year of the cruel war waged against us by our unscrupulous and vindictive foe; and though occasional disasters have and may occur to our gallant armies, they cannot be extinguished until our independence as a people is fully established.

3rd. That the noble, defiant and patriotic resolves coming up daily from our gallant armies in the field and from our people at home, give renewed assurance of unspoken determination to persist in the struggle until that end shall have been attained.

4th. That our subjugation cannot be effected if our people are united—and notwithstanding the vaunted superiority of our enemy in numbers, having full faith in the justice of a righteous God, in the valor of our veteran soldiers and in the patriotism of our people, we may, and do set their threats of *extermination* at defiance.

5th. That we regard reconstruction as but another name for submission to tyranny, and "we pledge our lives our fortunes and our sacred honor never to entertain even the idea of it, but to resist it in the future as we have done in the past, to the utmost extremity."

6th. That our confidence in our Rulers, civil and military and our noble armies is unabated.

7th. That for the sustenance and support of our Government and our soldiers we are prepared to meet all demands which are made upon us, and to this end, if it be deemed necessary, we are willing to open our Store Houses, and reduce our families to half rations, or even less.

8th. That having given our sons and brothers to the cause we would be "less than man," if we were not ready to make any sacrifice of property, or hesitate to respond to the calls of our chosen leaders.

9th. That whilst some of our fellow citizens oppose the arming of our negroes, we are content with the knowledge that we have the sanction of God for using all the means in our power to resist wicked oppression, and if this means of resistance be deemed necessary and available by such men as President Davis and by Gen. Robt. E. Lee, we shall not stop to discuss abstract questions, but will cheerfully give our servants, as we have our sons to our country. * * *

Martha L. Roadcap to a Friend,
April 11, 1865

Martha Roadcap writes to a friend about her distress at the close of the war and relays news of the death of a mutual friend. After enduring occupations by two separate Union forces, many in Augusta shared Roadcap's fears of being "overrun by the vandal foe" in the aftermath of the Confederacy's defeat. Only two days before she wrote the letter, Robert E. Lee had surrendered the Army of Northern Virginia to Ulysses S. Grant, effectively ending the Civil War.

At Home
April 11th/65

My Dear Friend
    It is with a troubled mind I now seat myself to pen you few lines horrible thought that we are likely to be overrun by the vandal foe

what a sad trial to our brave men who have fought so vigorously for nearly four years now to think that all is to be lost but yet I can hardly give up to it nothing but distress prevails now throughout our land hearts are breaking to know the fate of loved friends what has been the fate of your neighborhood boys who are safe & who are lost where is your dear brother I hope he is safe I have not heard a word from my Charlie since you wrote until a few days ago I heard through a letter from one of our neighborhood boys who saw him before the fight he was well at that time but should he happen to get home as you will be sure to see him before I will you must press him to come to see me immediately be sure and find him—I received a letter this week from Mr. Heist it was written from Staunton concerning Johnnies death he has not been home since the sad occurrence but saw a lady who succeeded in obtaining a passport from General Sheridan to pass his lines he was mortally wounded a short distance from the town the ball penetrating his head just back of his ear he requested his friends to have him removed to the Heists house which was accordingly done but before they [illegible word] his house with him he expired & was interred in his lot in the Winchester cemetery he thinks the death of Johnnie's death [sic] has been productive of a change of heart in his son in whom he counciled a reform which his death has caused him to remember & also to practice for which he seems to be very thoughtful indeed—he says his daughter will write to me the full particulars as soon as the way is open I will keep the letters for Charlies perusal you will have to excuse this short letter this time as I feel so unfit for writing but will try and write again when I become more composed give my love to all the family & write to me soon Allie sends love to you

as ever your devoted Friend
Martha L. Roadcap

Diary of Joseph Addison Waddell, April 25, 1865

Joseph Waddell records in his diary the difficulty of procuring reliable news at the end of the war, noting the numerous rumors he has heard recently. Conflict-

ing and inaccurate reports were common during the war, when moving armies and the disruption of communication lines made it difficult for people and newspapers to receive accurate intelligence. The rapid succession of events in the final days of the conflict, as Waddell reported, exacerbated the problem.

Rumors of momentous events came in rounds to-day. First we heard that Gen. Johnston had surrendered. Next that a Federal force of 1200 was coming from Beverly to establish a garrison at Staunton. Then a gentleman arriving from Charlottesville with a report that Andrew Johnson, Lincoln's successor, had been killed, and that Washington, Philadelphia and New York were in flames. Finally, it was reported by some one who came up the Valley, that Grant had been killed, that fighting was going on in Washington city, and that all the troops had been removed from Winchester. We know not what to think of all this. It is not more strange than the intelligence of Lincoln's death, which we did not believe, but can it be that society is broken up, and the whole country in a state of chaos! that assassination, heretofore unknown amongst us, has become a common event! I cannot think so. The man who killed Lincoln must have been a lunatic, and surely a similar act has not been perpetrated since. There has been no confirmation of the report that a mob in Baltimore hung Gen. Ewell and others. We have no mails, no newspapers, and no regular communication with the world. Occasionally some one arrives with a Baltimore or Richmond paper. The Richmond Whig is issued by new hands as a Union paper. * * *

Staunton Vindicator, "Hanging and Confiscation," June 30, 1865

The Vindicator *considers what will become of the South and Confederates now that the war has ended. No one was certain what the postwar repercussions would be for those who had supported the rebellion, although some in the North hoped that high-ranking Confederate leaders such as Robert E. Lee and Jefferson Davis would face trial. The* Vindicator *argued that if the South were to rebuild itself and rejoin the North in harmony, then further punishment of the defeated South should be avoided.*

The penalty of treason is death; and while we doubt the constitutionality of the Confiscation Act as passed by Congress, it may be conceded that forfeiture of property is one of the liabilities incurred by those who can be proven to be traitors. Starting with these premises, a considerable portion of the people of the North have determined that there is only one conclusion to be reached, and that is that a great number of men must be hanged and hundreds of thousands of acres of land must be confiscated. They say, that if Mr. Davis and General Lee had resisted the authority of the Federal Government at the head of fifty or a hundred men, they would unquestionably have been brought to trial, and that it only makes the matter worse that they were the leaders of many hundred thousands.

This statement they seem to think exhaust[s] the argument. We do not propose to discuss these points. No reasoning would probably have any effect upon those persons who can see no difference between the most gigantic civil war on record and the John Brown raid, and who would, at the end of a prolonged contest, signalized on both sides by innumerable feats of heroism, have the Southern soldiers indicted for assault and battery, or trespass. We fancy that if any such soldier should be tried at Gettysburg for shooting at Federal troops in the memorable battles of the 1st, 2nd and 3rd of July, 1863, he would be pretty sure of an acquittal, if any Pennsylvania soldiers who participated in the fights should be upon the jury.

But our present business is with the future rather than the past. In view of the fact that proceedings have been initiated against the persons and property of many of the citizens of the Southern States, it behooves us to look at the effect of such a policy upon the prosperity of the country. The condition of the South is bad enough already. A new labor system is to be organized, railroads and manufactories are to be rebuilt, vast tracts of land which have relapsed into wilderness must be again enclosed and brought under cultivation, and all this is to be done by a people who are nearly bankrupt, and when the able-bodied part of the population has just been largely diminished by the casualties of war. At such a moment comes the rumor that the confiscation law is to be rigidly enforced. This is sufficient notice to eight-tenths of the property holders of the insecurity of their titles, and they feel at once that any further outlay of energy or money may be altogether wasted. Now, the North is, of course, looking to the South to pay her portion of the national debt; and it will be some time, under the most favorable circumstances, before the latter can respond to the demands of the tax-gatherer. What must be the result if a rigorous policy is insisted on which altogether checks the efforts her people are willing to make to restore their olden prosperity?

Again, it may be assumed that it is very desirable that the people of the two sections should live in harmony together. Proceedings have already been instituted in Richmond against the property of three hundred persons, and the officers of the law are daily bringing new actions. If the same course is pursued in all other judicial districts of the South, what must be the inevitable result? A bitter feeling of hostility will be engendered towards the North such as was never developed during the war, and hundreds or thousands of men will be driven to the extreme of recklessness and desperation. A great many patriots will say that Southern rebels deserve all that can happen to them. We do not intend to discuss that question either. We simply presume that the sensible men in the North desire, if only for the sake of their own section, the prosperity of the South, and that they wish to live amicably, if not in friendship, with their late foes. How can this be accomplished? Certainly not by creating a wide spread disaffection and despair throughout all the country stretching from the Potomac to the Gulf. The question at issue touches the pacification of a nation, and we earnestly submit that it ought not be determined by those who regard the matter in the light of a street riot.

Staunton Vindicator, "Since the end of the war . . . ," June 30, 1865

The Vindicator *reports with approbation the recent arrest of all "the idle colored men" in Staunton—apparently by the Union commander in the area—as the newspaper believes they must be "made to labor." The end of slavery in 1865 had entirely upended Augusta's long-established labor and social systems, and many whites in the county believed that ex-slaves would have to be carefully controlled in the postwar South, fearing that blacks would use their newfound freedom to avoid labor of any kind.*

Since the end of the war all our towns have been overrun with the negroes from the surrounding country, who have imagined that freedom gave them the right to live in idleness and be supported by the whites.

This idea was summarily put to flight a few days since by the arrest of all the idle colored men in town, and their being required to find and pursue some means of livelihood. This is a step in the right direction and Col. Stewart, the Commandant of this post, deserves credit for it. Unless they are made to labor there must necessarily be great suffering among this class during the coming winter. We trust that they may learn from the action of the Military authorities that they will not be allowed to live idle and dissolute lives, and may conduct themselves in such a manner as to secure profit to themselves and retain the kindly feelings of their former owners.

Staunton Spectator, "Letter from Alexander H. H. Stuart to Nicholas Trout," July 11, 1865

The Spectator *prints a letter from Alexander H. H. Stuart, a prominent lawyer and politician in Augusta County, to Nicholas K. Trout, the Commissioner of Election for Augusta, on the subjects of amnesty, pardons, and the loy-*

alty oath required of those who wished to run for office in postwar Virginia. Ex-Confederates throughout the South carefully considered their political options in the immediate aftermath of the war, trying to determine who would be eligible to represent them in the new state and federal governments.

Staunton, July 8th, 1865
N. K. Trout, Esq.

Dear Sir:—I have had the honor to receive your note of the 7th inst., requesting me, on behalf of yourself and your Associate Commissioners of Election for Augusta county, to give my opinion as to the legal effect of President Johnson's Proclamation of Amnesty, upon the eligibility to office and capacity to vote of persons embraced by its terms. * * *

* * * It seems to me that if there be any one proposition which has been more firmly established than another, by the terrible struggle through which our country has passed—It is that the Constitution of the U. S. and all laws passed in pursuance thereof, are the supreme laws of the land, anything in any State Constitution or laws to the contrary notwithstanding. As a corrollary to this proposition, it must be conceded, that all proclamations of the President, and other executive action, following up the Constitution and laws of the U. S., and intended to give practical effect to them are of like permanent authority.

If we bear this cardinal proposition in mind it will give much aid in solving the difficulties which surround the subject.

The Constitution of Virginia provides that "no person shall hold any office under this Constitution who has held office under the so-called Confederate government, or under any rebellious State Government, or who has been a member of the so-called Confederate Congress, or a member of any State Legislature in rebellion, against the authority of the United States, excepting those from County officers."

It also requires that every one who shall seek to hold any office under the Constitution of Virginia shall take and subscribe the following oath: "I do solemnly swear (or affirm) that I will support the Constitution of the U. S. and the laws made in pursuance thereof, as the supreme law of the State of Virginia, or in the ordinances of the Convention which assembled at Richmond, on 13th Feb., 1861, to the contrary notwithstanding, and that I will uphold and defend the government of Virginia, as restored by the Convention which assembled at Wheeling on 11th of June, 1861, and that I have not since the 1st of January, 1864, voluntarily given aid or assistance, in any way, to those in rebellion against the Government of the United States for the purpose of promoting the same."

The language of the Constitution and oath, is very broad and comprehensive, and if they be consistent with the constitution and laws of the U. S., the effect will be to disfranchise probably 99 out of every 100 our citizens. For whatever opinions parties may have entertained in regard to the unconstitutionality of secession, and the inexpediency and folly of attempting to dissolve the Union, there is hardly a man to be found, who after the war had been commenced, and his sons and brothers and near relations were forced into it by conscription, did not furnish them with horses, clothing, food, money, and other articles necessary to their comfort and thereby incapacitate himself from taking the prescribed oath.

We cannot disguise the fact that the object and effect of the provisions of the constitution above quoted, were to impose other and onerous penalties on persons guilty of treason, in addition to those imposed by the laws of the U. S. It matters not what the form of the disfranchisement may be: it is substantially a penalty for an offence. * * *

* * * Now it seems to me that where a case is clearly embraced, by the terms of the President's proclamation of amnesty, the guilt of the party with all its penalties and consequences, is removed.— He is made, as it were, a new man, and is restored to every right that he would have possession if had never been guilty of that offence. So far as he is concerned, all laws imposing penalties are inoperative. He is taken out of the sphere of their influence. A pardon is an entire thing. It reaches through the whole subject to which it is applied. It sweeps away, and blots out every consequence of the commission of the offence. It regenerates and makes a new man of this offence. * * *

* * * I take it when the President grants a pardon, it removes every vestage of the offence, and in the language of Bacon "all the consequences thereof."

Those views have been hastily thrown together, (for you informed me a prompt answer was requested,) but I believe they embody, in substance, the true doctrine on the subject.

Hence I conclude that all persons who have been specially pardoned, or who have been absolved by the terms of the amnesty are restored to all their rights as citizens, precisely to as great an extent as if they had never committed any offence, and may thereof, be elected to office or vote for officers, notwithstanding the prohibitory clauses in the Constitution of Va., said clauses being in conflict with the Constitution of the U. S. and therefore of no effect.

Respectfully, your ob't serv't,
Alex H. H. Stuart

Staunton Spectator, "The Oath of Amnesty," July 11, 1865

The Spectator *implores its readers to take the oath of amnesty in order to be eligible for the general pardon issued to ex-Confederates by President Andrew Johnson. Johnson issued a general amnesty proclamation on May 29, 1865, promising a pardon to all Southerners who would swear an oath of allegiance to the United States (although high-ranking and wealthy Confederates were excluded from the offer). Many whites in the South, particularly those who had sacrificed loved ones for the Confederacy, were loath to take an oath demanding loyalty to the United States.*

A strange delusion prevails in regard to the propriety of taking the oath of amnesty. Many seem to think that there is no necessity for taking it and that they can take it or not, as happens to suit the fancy of individuals.

This is a dangerous error, and one which should be promptly dispelled.

Under existing laws of the U. States, every citizen of the Southern States, (with very few exceptions) has been guilty of treason. Treason consists not only in waging war against the United States, but giving "aid and comfort" to its enemies. "Aid and comfort" are very broad terms. They embrace all who have aided or assisted the Confederate Government, during the war. All who have been in the military or civil service of either Government—all who have given horses, arms, clothing, food, or money to any of the Confederate soldiers—every Tunker who has paid $500 to the C. States, to keep out of the service—every detailed farmer who has raised provisions for the C. S. Government, under contract with it has given aid and comfort to the enemies of the U. S., and has, therefore, technically been guilty of treason, and is liable to its penalties. These penalties are confiscation, imprisonment, and death.

The President of the *U. S.* influenced by human motives, has offered amnesty, or pardon, to all, except certain specified classes, on terms prescribed by himself. But the offer is conditional.—He says you may be pardoned *if you will take the oath of amnesty*.

That is the condition and the only condition, on which the pardon is promised. Those who do not choose to take the oath, are not entitled to the pardon—those who do take it, are absolved from the penalties.

It will be seen, therefore, that all who desire pardon, had better take the oath without delay. If they do not, both their property and persons are in danger. They will, at least, be at the mercy of every malicious enemy, until they do take it. The oath squares the account, and relieves the party from all apprehension.

Every man, therefore, who wishes to stand on a safe footing, and to have his life, liberty and property secure from hazzard, had better take it without any hesitation.

If they fail to do so, they may find proceedings instituted against them, in the *U. S.* Court, and then it will be too late—the door will be slammed in their faces. Then they will begin to whine and say: "*I* did not know such would be the consequences; I always intended to take the oath, but was too busy, &." But it will then be too late, and they must take the consequences of their folly. It would be better for them to leave anything else undone to attend to this most important duty.

Let all then take warning in time.—The oath can certainly do no harm. It requires nothing unreasonable, and it will certainly save all who take [it] much trouble and anxiety in the future.

We have thus given our advice to our readers. If they choose to disregard it, well and good. We, at least, have discharged our duty as a journalist.

2. *Franklin County*

Valley Spirit, "Rejoicing," April 12, 1865

The Valley Spirit *describes the celebrations that broke out in Chambersburg when news arrived of Robert E. Lee's surrender of the Army of Northern Virginia to Ulysses S. Grant, a scene that played out in hundreds of communities across the North.*

The news of Lee's surrender reached this place, by telegraph, on Sunday night between nine and ten o'clock. The whole community was at once thrown into a state of wild excitement, the like of which was never before witnessed here. Every one left their beds and gathered on the streets. The bells were rung, guns, pistols and cannon fired, and bonfires blazed at every corner. The excitement continued all night and increasing to a perfect *panic* about morning. The speech-makers were called out and mounting the store-boxes harangued the crowds in the most excited strains—our friend of the *Repository* leading off in a blaze of glory. The rejoicing continued through the whole of next day. The troops stationed here turned out and made a grand parade. The artillery company fired a salute of two hundred guns. We feel assured that no community exceeded ours in its demonstrations of joy over Grant's glorious victory.

Alexander K. McClure to Eli Slifer, April 12, 1865

Alexander McClure writes to his friend, Eli Slifer, about his plans for rebuilding his house and the postwar economic situation. After the war, the greatest challenge facing Franklin residents was in rebuilding all that had been destroyed in the Confederate burning of Chambersburg. The task appeared all the more daunting because many shared McClure's fears that the end of the war could bring with it an economic recession in the North.

Chambersburg, Pa.
April 12, 1865

Dear Col—

I wrote you last evening that I had arranged for my Lumber. A friend who is an old dealer, has kindly consented to supply me at cost, and I will save much trouble & some money by the arrangement. * * *

* * * I am going to rebuild my house this summer also & it is a fearful undertaking. I am sorely perplexed about it & the more I study the more I get confused as to what kind of House I shall build. Mrs McC & I have agreed that the roof shall be on the top & the cellar under the House, but that is about as far as we have got.

My grounds are such that I have but a certain amount of room each way, without interfering with some tree or something else, so that I must locate it about as the old one was & cannot widen out either way. I mean to follow the general plan of yours which is something after the old one, [illegible word] Library, Drawingroom, kitchen &c on one side & parlor on the other.

I will go down to Philadelphia next week, if I can then meet Jno Rice & will stay there until I worry out a plan, & then I will dismiss the subject & put the contractor at work.

It is a jolly time to build. Home & Bain will cost me all of $20,000 & then finishing is to follow.

I think the war is ended, & the Order is safe. In that there is no army in Virginia for [illegible word] to fall back upon, they will soon be compelled to abandon their occupation, as the will be hunted & shot down wherever caught.

There will be no stagnation in answer this year. Gold will be higher Jany 1, 1866 than now, & I doubt whether it will at any time in the next three years touch so low a [illegible word] as it did on Monday last.

Our debt is now $4,000,000,000. It is all very well as long as the gvnmnt delivers $4,000,000 per day: but when that stops, the severe ordeal for government credit will be at hand.

Yours
AK McClure

Valley Spirit, "Funeral of the Late President," April 26, 1865

The Valley Spirit *describes Chambersburg's solemn observance of Abraham Lincoln's funeral. A frustrated Confederate sympathizer, John Wilkes Booth, assassinated Lincoln on April 14, 1865, only five days after Robert E. Lee surrendered to Ulysses S. Grant. Communities across the North held services similar to the one in Chambersburg, as the nation mourned for the first president killed while in office.*

The day set apart for the obsequies of the late President in the city of Washington was observed by our citizens in a manner befitting the mournful occasion. All business was suspended and the solemn deportments of our people during the day evinced that they fully participated in the feelings of grief caused by the atrocious crime by which the Chief Magistrate of the nation was cut off at a most critical conjuncture of public affairs. Nearly every residence, office, workshop and dwelling in the town was draped with the sombre emblems of mourning. Sadness appeared to pervade the entire community and every countenance wore the impress of grief at the loss of a friend. The interior of the different places of worship were appropriately clothed in black and at 12 o'clock, services of the most solemn and impressive character were had in each. In the afternoon a procession of the Military, Fire Companies, the different benevolent Associations and citizens generally was formed which after passing through the principal streets halted at the Depot where an eloquent and appropriate address was delivered by C.S. Eyster, Esq., the orator selected for the occasion by the committee of arrangements. During the progress of the procession through the streets minute guns were fired by a battery of artillery and the toll of the church bells added solemnity to the display.

It is with pleasure that we chronicle the fact that not a single instance of disorder occurred during the entire day. Every one seemed fully impressed with the solemnity of the time and deported themselves accordingly.

Valley Spirit, "The War Over—What Then?" April 26, 1865

The Valley Spirit *ponders the postwar political landscape, arguing that with the war over the Republicans would no longer be able to force their partisan agenda on the public. The Democrats struggled in the postwar years to regain their political might, which had waned during the war, and no one was certain how the political balance between the Republicans and Democrats might shift once the war came to an end.*

The effect, upon parties, of the end of the war is beginning to be much discussed. The Abolitionists cannot but feel that, with the end of the war, must come a terrible shock to their power as a party. They know that it must at once cut off from them hundreds of thousands whose pecuniary interest alone led them to sustain an administration that was profitable, and who, contracts being unattainable, and the myriads of forms which executive patronage can assume only in time of war being no longer available, will abandon the party to which they have for four years been giving a purchased and heartless support. The war has given the party now dominant, engines all powerful for the crushing of its political opponents. These engines will be no longer available, or even have existence, when the strife shall cease. The Abolitionists, while the war lasted, could absolutely control the ballot boxes. They could call to their aid the influence of military officers upon Democratic soldiers in the field, compelling the latter, whose comfort, and even whose lives were at the mercy of their superiors in the military rank, to suppress their own sentiments, or even to assume the political notions of those superiors—which superiors were controlled in turn for their dependence upon an Abolition administration for military promotion. This element of strength will be destroyed by the return of peace. The vast armies of political spies, *mouchards*, government detectives, provost marshals, deputy provost marshals, deputy-deputies, commissioners of drafts, enrolling officers, recruiting officers, examining surgeons, inspectors of horses, inspectors of mules, inspectors of every conceivable thing used in the army, agents to buy and agents to sell, fellows between the two latter in complicity to both and making "good things" out of their jobs, the swarms of officials connected with the machinery by which trade was regulated between "loyal," insurgent and semi-insurgent communities, confiscation agents, additional turnkeys to the densely populated bastiles, petty lords of military hospitals all over the land, dilapidated preachers of easy virtue who had calls to "support the government," not particularly by preaching or praying, but by pocketing with commendable regularity the salaries of the chaplaincies—all these, and thousands upon thousands of others not enumerated, could be relief upon always to labor diligently for the success of the party from whom they had their daily bread, well buttered. All that is over now—if the war be really ended.

Just so soon as the Abolition party shall be stripped of the power to bribe, to intimidate, to force acquiescence in their monstrous wrongs, will come their doom; and when they shall be obliged, unsustained by the agencies of which we have spoken, to confront the disenthralled people at the polls, God pity them!

Democrats might well rejoice to witness the close of the war. Bonfires, illuminations, bell ringing, the loud booming of artillery, would but inadequately express their joy at the prospect of restored vitality to the will of the governed.

Joseph Christy to Mary Jane Demus, April 27, 1865

Joseph Christy, a black soldier from Franklin County, writes to his sister, Mary Demus, about his final days fighting for the Union, how he received word of the end of the war, and his experiences transporting slaves to freedom. Soldiers like Christy wished to return home as soon as possible once the war ended, hoping to resume the lives they had left behind and reunite with loved ones.

1865
George town, S.C.
Aprile the 27th

My Dear sister
    i take my pen in hand to in form you that We ar All Well at present and I hope thes fue lins may find you all Well When i gut your letter i Was on Bord of the steem boat Coming from savannah to georgetown and When i gut thear i set my self down to Ancer it and the nix thing i heard Was fall in Company J in lite marcing orders and the nix thing i hard Was forword March and a Way We went to hunt the Johneys and We found them too and kild a grate meney of them We fot for six days
    We didin lose verry meney We took all old mare meet and every thing he had to eat And burnt down thear houses We Went a but one hundred And fifty nils a bouve george town and We hard that peace Was decleard and then We Cam back to george town a gane think that We Will be home in too months We ar giting a long verry Well We had quite a nice time on the rode We Didin lost enny out of our Companey give my love to all the rest and all the rest

of the boys sends thear love to you all David is Well and george
We Captered A but two hundred Cars and twenty thee lokemotives
and burnt them up and We brot for thousand slaves With us to
george town O J T Was one of the grates sits that i ever seen
We started on the 4th of Aprile and gut back on the 26 and We
march every Day this is all i have to tell you this time so i think i
must Com to a Close this time nothen mor at present but still
remane

your Brother
Joseph L. Christey

Franklin Repository, "Address by Rev. Dr. Harbaugh," May 3, 1865

The Franklin Repository *provides a transcript of Reverend Harbaugh's speech on the death of Abraham Lincoln, delivered in Franklin County on the day of the president's funeral. People held ceremonies in every Northern state to mourn and mark the passing of the slain president. Harbaugh used the occasion to argue that Southern treason led to Lincoln's assassination and that treason had to be dealt with in a harsh and firm manner.*

The citizens of Mercersburg and vicinity had appropriate ceremonies on the 19th ult., the day of the funeral of President Lincoln,
and the following eloquent and touching address was delivered on
the occasion by Rev. Dr. H. Harbaugh, Professor of Theology in
Mercersburg:

It is most difficult, on this solemn occasion, for one to speak for
another, in the way of leading or interpreting his thoughts for him.
This is one of those overwhelming events which make one's
thoughts stand still; and when we feel the truth of the sacred declaration, that the heart knoweth its own bitterness, and a stranger
doth not intermeddle with it. For days past, throughout the land,
friend has met friend with the feeling that, in the presence of so
great a sorrow, silence is the most eloquent word. Even when one

ventured a word of remark or inquiry, it was with the vain hope
that the one addressed might be able to express and interpret for
him his own deep feeling.

When the telegraph first dropped this fearful news into the thousand cities, towns and villages all over the land, men were stunned
and paralyzed with amazement. His implements dropped from the
hands of the laborer; the student cast away his pen and books; the
merchant closed his store; the buzzing of factories ceased; busy
streets were changed into scenes of Sabbatic quiet, and over all this
expressive silence rolled the solemn sound of tolling bells. The land
mourned its fallen chief, as it had not mourned from the first hour
of the Republic till now.

We have sometimes heard of the coming together of a marriage
and a burial—where sorrow tread so closely on the heel of joy that
the joyful bride, on the very day of her happy marriage, was laid
out as a corpse in her wedding robes! In like manner has, during
these last few days, the nation's joy been suddenly changed into
mourning. Scarcely had the bells ceased tolling out their jubilations
in honor of victory, and the prospect of speedy peace, with the
restoration of the supremacy of law and order throughout the land,
when they began to toll in sad harmony with a nation's sorrow. And
though days have passed since this fearful tragedy was enacted, the
national mind still labors under the subduing burden of its momentous grief—still stunned and silent!

What is this all-pervading and steadily continued feeling, but the
mute utterance of the people's sense of the awfulness of the crime
which has been committed. The mind cannot fathom the turpitude
of this crime of *regicide*, or the killing of the ruler of the land. But
the existing unutterable feeling furnishes proof that God, by the
very constitution of our being, has underlaid our deepest life with
a sense of its enormity; our nature thus spontaneously bearing witness to what has been the sense of all civilized—yea, even barbarian and semi-barbarian—as well as Christian ages and nations, that
the highest possible crime is regicide. * * *

* * * Such being the character of the crime which has caused our
present grief, and such the horror with which this crime of regicide
shows itself to be regarded by the whole nation, in harmony with
the deepest sense of all civilized, and especially christianized, na-

tions and ages, the sorrowing millions may well this day lift their hands to heaven, and ask, How is such an awful crime possible? Where is an adequate begetting and sustaining element and basis for such a crime to be found? Certainly it has been in no other way possible for it to appear except as the nursling and legitimate ripe fruit of that spirit of enormous treason which has, during the last four dreadful and bloody years, labored to consummate substantially the same crime by aiming its deadly dagger at the very heart of the Republic itself. Whether formally, and by organized conspiracy or not, still essentially and really treason and rebellion is the legitimate mother of regicide. The assassin of the President and head of the nation, whether thereunto appointed or not, is the organ of that treason which has its embodiment in the great Rebellion. It was the concentrated life of that great treason which nerved his arm and guided the fearful weapon of death. The truth of this fact beats to-day with powerful, harmonious, self-attesting assurance in the patriotic and loyal instincts of millions of sad and sorrowing hearts.

How better can we improve this sad occasion than to possess our souls more fully with a deeper sense of the enormous crime of treason; a crime when, according to the wisdom of all christian nations, can only be adequately atoned for by the penalty of death. We speak our own deep convictions, and we hope the convictions of all present, when we say that no sign of the times portends greater danger to the nation at present than that morbid and unchristian spirit which is in some quarters beginning its endeavors to avert the penalty due to treason. We dread this spirit more than all else that is before us as a nation. Such men as Beecher and Greeley, who are endeavoring to lead off in this miserable effort to degrade and ignore the internal sanctions of divine and human law, and to convert honest but unreflecting people to their crusade against the true idea and end of law and justice, are now emphatically *the* enemies of the Republic. This mawkish sentimentality is called "magnanimity." What a misnomer! Its true name is infidelity to the majesty of law. It offers a premium for treason; and, if successful, will be the greatest unfaithfulness and cruelty to posterity of which the rulers of our eventful age can be guilty. It will be in truth the laying up of wrath, anarchy and rebellion for our children. It will be a comforting precedent for treason in all coming ages of the Republic. It will show that treason and rebellion deserve and shall receive nothing but magnanimity, in a degraded sense of that word. It will ever show that treason, so enormous in its sweep as to people a hundred battle-field grave-yards with the bodies of brave and loyal men, has earned for itself only the right of what is falsely called magnanimous treatment. In pestiferous sentiments like these, be assured, lies deadly poison, which if allowed to work its way into the heart of our rulers and our people, will sooner or later take the nation's life as effectually as the Rebellion itself, had it succeeded, would have done, and as it has actually intended to do by bayonets, cannon, and starvation of thousands of loyal and brave men, and which it has now again attempted to do as by desperation, in the person of the assassin of the President. * * *

* * * To ask that the majesty of law be allowed to have its free course against crime is no spirit of revenge, is no want of magnanimity—betrays no absence of mercy and charity. If so God himself would fall under blame! Justice and judgment are the habitation of His throne. Human governments are a parable and reflection of His own. Human law is a reflection of His will. Human justice is after the pattern of His justice. To abrogate the sanctions and penalties of His law, is to annul one of His own attributes. In the suffering of the penalty of human guilt in the person of His own Son, he has demonstrated to the world that His mercy does not abrogate His justice. Vain is the attempt of man to propose a sickly sentimentalism as a substitute that shall outdo and set aside God's immutable law against crime. Men may be tender, but law and justice are inflexible. We have heard of judges who pronounced the sentence of death on murderers *with tears*—but pronounced it in firm faithfulness nevertheless. The judge who thus discharges his solemn duty to the law and society is twice great in the act; great because he shows that he has all the feelings of the man, and great again because he has all the firmness of the judge. Above all his merely humane feelings rises the solemn conviction that the execution of the law is absolutely necessary for the safety of society. He feels for the criminal, but he does not suffer his feelings to carry him into a current of washy sentimentalism. He pities the criminal, but he pities society more. It is said that Washington signed the death-

warrant of Andre, the spy, with tears! This is proof that he would have spared even him had not a higher obligation to honor the law rested on him. Let our rulers study this example, that the majesty of law be not changed into a mere mawkish feeling. * * *

* * * I attempt no eulogy of our departed President. His earnestness, moderation, kind-heartedness, proverbial honesty and unswerving loyalty and patriotism are well known. Only when generations shall have passed away, and all the seeds of the mighty present of the nation shall come to their full fruits in the future, will his name and fame stand out in full relief on the historic page. What if it should appear, to those who shall study the events of his administration in the light of the future, that he was the leader of a high and holy patriotic purpose, which has delivered the Republic from a bondage as heavy and galling as that from which we were delivered by Washington at the first? What if our children should experience the fact that the names of George Washington and Abraham Lincoln may be sounded together with perfect accord?

Jacob Christy to Mary Jane Demus, May 29, 1865

Jacob Christy, a black soldier in the 54th Massachusetts Infantry, writes to his sister, Mary Demus, about his desire to return home and his encounters with former Confederates on the streets of Charleston, South Carolina. Christy enjoyed his new status as a victorious soldier over the defeated rebels, and wished to march triumphantly through Massachusetts with his regiment before it disbanded and he mustered out of the service.

St. Andrews Parish
Camp of the 54th Mass Vols
May the 29th 1865

Dear sister

I receive your letter dated may the 15th your kind letter found us all well I hope this letter will find you all well

we are garrisons two fort now we are drilling on large cannons now we aint dueing much of anything now thay are agreat many men giting their Discharges out of our Regiment James Crunkelton and David is about to get their discharge but I dont want no Discharge untell the Regiment is all disbanded I want to stay with the old Regiment As long as she is together I come away from Massachuettes with it and I want to go back with it to march through the city of Massachuettes agian Affter our old stars and strips she is all riddle into strings just to look at it any body can tell what we have been dueing we fought hard a many A time for them

I think that we will be home a gain newyear thay are sume talk of us geting home agian the fourth day of July but I dont now how that is it may be so and agian it may not I think more about geting home now then what I did while the war was going on I think that we will get home now before verry long thay are a great many men that did belong to the Rebel army in Charleston City now it goese verry hard with them to give a way under us colard soldiers but we knock them out of our way And if thay dont like that we take them up and put them in the Guard house

We just go into the city And take the hole streets just fer to get them to say something out of the way to us so that we can get at them and beat them all the boys send their love to you all give my love to father And Elizaberth and to Mary and tell them that I think that I will see them all before verry long thay are three men just starting home now out of my Compy which gut their discharge

give my love to all the inquireing friends an like wise to yourself and to all the girls no more at preasant still Remain

your Brother
Jacob Christy

VIII
Emancipation and
Reconstruction

1. *Augusta County*

Diary of Joseph Addison Waddell, July 2
and July 5, 1865

Joseph Waddell, former editor of the Spectator, *fumes in his diary about the treatment of ex-Confederates by Union soldiers in Staunton, and a 4th of July dinner put on by local blacks for Federal officers. For many former Confederates, like Waddell, the presence of occupying Union troops and the willingness of local blacks to assert their new freedom served as constant reminders of the struggle that white Southerners had lost.*

July 2, 1865

Have been thinking much more than I ought to-day about the clerkship. The Yankee soldiers have been enforcing the order for Confederates to strip off military clothing. Some of them have stood at the street corners with shears, to cut off brass buttons &c. Every negro wearing an old Confederate coat or jacket has lost his buttons. Is'nt it ridiculous? U. S. officials seem determined to bring their government into utter contempt. * * * J. H. Skinner was here to-night. He said a young Confederate soldier rode into town to-day, wearing a military coat with brass buttons. Four or five Yankee soldiers gallantly advanced upon him, and surrounding him, proceeded to cut off his buttons. He was doubtless ignorant of any order on the subject, and naturally felt aggrieved by the dastardly insult. The miserable Yankees are only intensifying and perpetuating sectional hate.

July 5, 1865

The *negroes* gave the Yankee officers a dinner yesterday at their barracks. The town was full of negroes of both sexes, who celebrated the 4th by walking about. A number of drunken soldiers were also on the streets. At night a mob of soldiers, and several *officers*, assembled before Hirsh's house and sang a Yankee war song. All of our family except Va and me; were at Mr. Stuart's, on the porch and not *enjoying* the song they went into the house and shut the door. This movement *insulted* the gentlemen Yankees, and they called upon one of their number to improvise a song suitable for the occasion. A miserable affair was then sung, with a chorus, making rude and pointed allusions to Mr. Stuart and his family. There's the *magnanimity* of our conquerors!—I started to make a report of the matter to Col. Fisher, but being detained on the way he set off for Winchester before I reached his quarters. Col. Steward has gone to Lexington with part of the command lately here. * * *

W. Storer How to Orlando Brown, September 29, 1865

W. Storer How, an agent of the Freedmen's Bureau based in Staunton, forwards to the regional headquarters in Richmond the case of James Hamilton, a free black from Maryland who had been captured by Confederates during the war and sold into slavery in Augusta County. Confederates kidnapped hundreds of free blacks during their incursions into Union territory in 1862 and 1863, and many of these people and their families turned to the Bureau for assistance after the end of the war. Established on March 3, 1865, by the U.S. Congress, the Freedmen's Bureau worked to assist the four million ex-slaves of the South in a wide variety of matters, ranging from contract disputes and employment issues to personal conflicts and cases of physical abuse.

Col. O. Brown
Asst. Comr.
Richmond, Va

Staunton Sept 29t 1865

Colonel

I have the honor to submit for your revision the following case
with my action upon it.

James Hamilton, colored, says he was a free man living in Han-
cock Md before the war—was free-born—He was captured by the
rebels while driving a team in the service of the Government
somewhere between Winfield and Cumberland, and taken to Harrisonburg, Rockingham Co, Va, where he was put in Jail and kept
there four (4) months. In May 1864 he was sold to Mr. Wm. J. Shumate and by him taken to Staunton Va where he was kept in Jail (1)
one month. When Genl. Hunter came along and Shumate took
him out of Jail Handcuffed and kept him so (4) four days and
nights. He lived with and worked for Shumate during one year
leaving his service about the last of May 1865.

I sent for Mr. Shumate who appeared and substantiated the
main points of Hamilton's statements.

Shumate said he bought Hamilton of Mr. Trick, Jailer, in Har-
risonburgh for 505, or 510 dollars. He was sold as he understood
by order of Court. Did not see the order knew that he Hamilton
claimed to be free, and that some one in Md had answered to
Jailer's letter to that effect. Knew also that he was a prisoner of war.

Afterwards brought to me the bill of sale, of which the following
is a true copy. "Rec'd of William Shumate—five hundred Dollars it
being in full for the purchase of a Negro man named James Hamilton aged about 30 years. The write and title of which man I sell for
the term of twenty years, at which he is free unless some one claiming proves a write to him as property. Witness my hand and seal this
the 4th May 1864."
Sigd Peter Trick (seal)

Upon the facts as they thus appear and in the view of the fact
that this Shumate was a trader in doubtful "property" of that kind,
and considering that Hamilton would probably have been released
as were the other prisoners in Harrisonburg Jail by the troops

under Genl Hunter had not Shumate gone there and speculated in him, I decided that Shumate should pay Hamilton thirty (30) dollars per month (Hamiltons wages for one (1) year[)]. He demured and thought Trick, if anybody, should pay and wished me to see Trick, which I did, but he is a poor, infirm old man who can recollect nothing except that he sold Hamilton to Shumate for Jail Fees by order of Court—the records of which have been destroyed.

He claims to have been a "Union Man" but was old and could only do as he was bid. I also submit without comment a letter from Shumate's attorney Mr. John B. Baldwin, and respectfully ask Instructions,

Respy &c
W Storer How

W. Storer How to Orlando Brown, November 3, 1865

W. Storer How reports his general assessment of the condition of the freedmen in his district (which included Augusta County) and comments on the disdain local whites held for blacks and the Freedmen's Bureau. The Bureau maintained a presence in Augusta from July 1865 until the agency shut down operations in all Southern states at the end of 1868. Its work during that period was both a great comfort to ex-slaves across the South, who often relied on the Bureau for protection, and a great irritant to white Southerners, who resented the presence of the federal agency in their communities.

Col. O. Brown
Asst. Commr. &c Winchester
Nov 3d 1865

Col.

I have the honor to report that the condition of the freedmen in this district is generally good, and that the operations of this Bureau have positively, and by its presence negatively, added greatly to the attainment of such condition. The freedman having learned that they will be protected in the exercise of unquestionable rights and the former masters now knowing that they may not ill-treat nor unjustly use them with impunity. The freedmen have however a vague dread of being soon deprived of the assistance now given by this Bureau, and are thus repressed in their aspirations for manhood through fears of being left at the mercy of implacable neighbors, who now secretly vaunt the terrible things they will do when "the yankees" and (with undescribable sneers) the "Freedmens Bureau" are gone.

The freedmen are generally at work under verbal contracts terminating at Christmas and are averse to written contracts for a future period, because they can hardly be induced to look beyond that time—though I hope during this and the succeeding months to aid and persuade them to the exercise of forethough and providence—and the prospect now is that effective labor will continue to be required in excess of the supply.

Among the old and infirm and women with three or more little children, there is now considerable suffering which will increase with the approach of winter. Partial issues of rations prevents starvation but wood is also needed to defend them from the cold. The local authorities profess inability to and until compelled by law will not make any provision for the support of colored paupers, and the former masters are only prevented from setting many adrift by the knowledge that it is not permitted; although there are instances in which the old ones are cherished on account of family associations, and for long and faithful services.

The Board of Agents authorized by Circular dated Richmond Septr 27, 1865 has not been organized by all the Asst. Supts. because the citizens will not act, nor serve, and can hardly be compelled to accept an invitation. For Winchester, where there are a few loyal men a Board is in successful operation with business enough for two half day sessions in a week. Its decisions are respected and enforced.

The question of compensation is for the present waived but should be provided for. In Woodstock a Board is organized but is without cases for trial.

The Mil. Authorities afford all the assistance in their power which in men, ways & means is very limited.

I am, Colonel &c
W.S.H.
Capt &c

Valley Virginian, "What Are We To Do?" February 21, 1866

The Valley Virginian, *a newspaper that began printing in Staunton in late 1865, complains about the refusal of Republicans to allow Southern representatives to take their seats in Congress and the rising support for Republicans in the North, asserting that many white Southerners are contemplating leaving the country rather than live under the rule of Radical Republicans. The Virginian hoped, as did many in the South, that the Radicals would be voted out of office by a disapproving Northern public and that their policies concerning the South would be reversed.*

It is useless to deny that the course pursued by the Radicals in Congress and their evident determination to grind the Southern people into the dust, if they can, has caused a general feeling of distrust in the South, and produced the desire among many of our most respectable and worthy citizens to emigrate to Mexico or anywhere, so as to be relieved of the present painful feeling of insecurity for the future. The Southern people went into the war for independence honestly; they staked their all upon the issue and when they lost it they honestly submitted to the arbitrament of the sword. They were willing to give the North all it won in the fight and they have performed their part of the contract. * * *
* * * It was hard to be conquered; it was hard to furl the banner that had floated in triumph over so many glorious fields; it was hard to give up cherished hopes and fond anticipations of a separate na-

tionality; it was hard to reap such bitter fruits from four years suffering and privation and accept the result; it was harder still to trudge over weary miles, with the shout of the conqueror ringing in your ears, to desolated homes—but all this we did and nothing the Southern people endured during the war adds so much to their honor and glory, as the honorable manner in which they have carried out the pledges made to Grant at Appomattox. But now after all; after we have performed our part and accepted the pledges of Grant and Johnson, it is harder still to be threatened with new penalties and forced to live in a constant state of uncertainty and doubt.

It is not that we doubt the will and determination of Andrew Johnson to do us justice, but the fear that the mass of the people North are so imbued with Radicalism, that nothing but our extermination will satisfy them. It is this feeling that creates the desire to leave home and friends and settle in a foreign land. Carry out President Johnson's policy; fulfill the pledges made by Grant at Appomattox and afterwards approved by Johnson, in his amnesty proclamation; then, will the Southern people go to work with a new life and energy and the idea of leaving the country be abandoned. We can not think the people of the North are fools or radicals and we hope soon to see the latter overthrown. If the honest, conservative sentiment, is as overwhelming North as reported we will soon see a change, and we can not see anything for our people to do now but to await the result of the coming conflict between President Johnson and the Radicals as patiently and as bravely as they endured the storms of the last four years. There is much to do in our country; everything is to be "reconstructed" and wealth untold is ours if energy and good sense direct our labors. Let the radicals do their worst, we surely can wait for the development of their policy before we leave our homes and all we hold dear, to be occupied by strangers. And, after all, this is a good country to live in and it is our duty to live and labor here. The widows, the orphans of our dead are left a sacred heritage to us. A land made glorious by the deeds of Jackson, Lee and a host of brave hearts is still ours. By making it prosperous and wealthy; by working as a people never worked before, we can say, come what may, "we have done our duty."

Staunton Spectator, "Lo! The Poor Negro," April 10, 1866

The Spectator *argues that "the emancipation of the negro heralds the doom of his race," and believes that the colonization of American blacks in another country represents their best chance for survival. The idea of colonizing free blacks in a remote country or on the western frontier had been discussed for decades before the Civil War, as most whites in the United States could not conceive of African Americans living among them in equality.*

What is to become of the negro? This is a question which now addresses itself to the minds of all reflecting men. Shall he remain here where he will be brought into ruinous competition with a superior race, or shall he seek a home elsewhere? If he remain here, poverty, wretchedness, and ultimate extinction will be his sad fate. If it were not that we have the kindest feelings for the negroes, we should like to see them move into the Northern States, that they might test the friendship of the Northern people for them. We are satisfied that the best friends of the negroes are the people of the South, who, with few exceptions, have for them none other than kind feelings. The Southern people do not blame the negroes for anything which has occurred. Their emancipation, which we believe to be a curse instead of a blessing to them, was effected without any agency of theirs. They, as a mass, acted well and faithfully during the war, and have comported themselves remarkably well since the war. No blame attaches to them, and this the Southern people appreciate and acknowledge, and hence attach no culpability to the negro.

If the negroes are to be considered the *wards* of the Government, and this guardianship is to continue for an indefinite time, we think that they should be distributed among the several States of the Union, North and South, in proportion to the population of the several States. In this way, the *blessing* would be equitably distributed, and none could complain that they were denied their just share of it.

But as we know, notwithstanding their loud professions of friend-ship, that the people of the Northern States do not desire, the ne-groes to become residents of their States, would treat them worse than the Southern people ever did, or ever will do, we must decide whether it is better for them to remain in the Southern States, in unequal and ruinous competition with the whites, or to seek a home in some favorite clime where they can live to themselves and for themselves alone. If the latter could be, it should be done. We confess that we fear the emancipation of the negro heralds the doom of his race. Are they willing to be colonized, and can colo-nization be rendered practicable? We will recur to this subject in future.

Staunton Vindicator, "When the Southern Armies surrendered . . . ," June 8, 1866

The Vindicator *argues that even though Southerners have faithfully met their obligations under Reconstruction, the proposed Fourteenth Amendment to the Constitution would prevent most ex-Confederates from holding national political office, effectively excluding white Southerners from representation in the federal government. Among other things, the law prohibited most of the South's politi-cal elite from elected positions while allowing ex-slaves to run for office, thereby helping the Republicans retain control of Congress and making the amendment highly unpopular among white Southerners.*

When the Southern armies surrendered it was with the idea that they and their people would be allowed all the rights they had in the Government prior to accession. This then was the ultimatum of the northern leaders and found an authentic mouth-piece in President Lincoln, who frequently declared that with the laying down of arms and cessation from hostilities, the full restoration to rights, &c., would and should follow, Congress, on several occasions, ex-pressed in strong language, its sentiments on the subject declaring that the war was waged, not for conquest, but for the preservation of the Union. More than a year has elasped since the brave spirits commanded by Lee and others gave up the contest and betook themselves to the peaceful pursuits of life, and yet the States forming the late Confederacy are admitted to no rights they formerly possessed, which was frequently promised them. They are simply vouchsafed the onerous privilege of paying taxes. It would seem but just that the object for which the war was commenced and prosecuted to successful consummation should be carried out in good faith. On the contrary, the spirit of fanatical hate and vindictiveness seems to be more rampant than during the war. This is plainly patent to all who have scrutinized the acts and doings of Congress and shines forth conspicuously, in all the glare of violent partizanship, in the report of the Reconstruction Committee. Their unjust attempt at a wholesale disfranchisement of the Southern people met a just fate in the Senate, by the unanimous disapproval of that particular clause in their proposed Constitutional amendment, yet an equally unjust substitute was offered and adopted as follows:

Section 3. That no person shall be a Senator or Representative in Congress, or Elector of President or Vice-President, or hold any office, civil or military, under the United States or under any State, who, having previously taken an oath as a member of any State Legislature, or as an executive or judicial officer of any State, to support the Constitution of the United States, has engaged in insurrection or rebellion against the same, or given aid and comfort to the enemies thereof. But Congress may, by a vote of two-thirds of each House remove such disability.

This substitute would exclude the very best men of the South, who being men of merit were forced into public positions and office, and in a great measure took part in the rebellion. Aside from this it is unjust to single out and cause to suffer, for a whole people, any particular class of community. They are no more guilty than those of us who have thrust their positions upon them. They were the mere servants of the masses and did but their bidding. For the same reason we have urged the injustice of trying the Southern people in the person of their late chief magistrate, Jefferson Davis, who is doubly endeared to them at this day from the sufferings already endured for obeying their behests.

We are unrepresented and can simply protest against such injustice but we say to the implacable, disfranchise all and eternally—confiscate and impoverish—send forth as homeless exiles, or behead, if the Gods fanaticism can be propitiated in no other way, but for the sake of justice and right, take no revenge upon any particular man or class of men for the acts of a whole people.

Nelson Irwin to John M. Schofield,
October 8, 1866

Nelson Irwin, an African American in Augusta County, writes to General John Schofield, the military commander of Virginia, pleading for protection and justice on behalf of the freedmen. Citing the recent imprisonment of several black men in Staunton, Nelson argues that freedom for blacks under such circumstances remained "meaningless tyranny." For ex-slaves in Augusta, as in most parts of the South, the Freedmen's Bureau was usually the only government agency they could appeal to for protection—and even the Bureau could not prevent much of the violence that freedmen endured during the postwar era.

Staunton
Oct. 8th 1866

General
    Living within your military department, I am forced to appeal to you in my own behalf. My case and cause are those of thousands and just as I am effected they will be effected also. There is a deep laid organization here that governs and controls every thing by might in defiance of truth and justice. On any, even the least pretense a black man is taken up and imprisoned. His color is his condemnation, and every lawless act committed he is accused of. At present my brethern are living in a reign of terror and many of them are locked up in Stauton Gaol.
    An act of theft has been committed here by one or two black men and lo! four are taken up and all of us are accused. Some of

us had to fly, who were and are as innocent of the crime as you are. The Freedmen's bureau is ineffective, laughed at and despised. On the first Monday of November these men are to be tried, and in view of their case we cannot expect justice unless the strong arm of military protection is reached out to us. We gave to the rich white man our best years, our strength, our youth, our sweat, and now that we are free, we get in return meaness, tyranny and injustice.

And now General, instruct the officers of Bureau and let them insist on justice. Some of our men are in a state of perpetual terror. If you turn your back on us, who can we appeal to. If we have committed a violation of law let us be judged impartially by the laws, but let us not be condemned with out a cause. From this depth of degredation we look to you, and in the name of suffering humanity, I trust I do not write in vain.

The name of those imprisoned are Reuben Hill, James Burgy, Joe Wilson is out as State evidence, and mind you a black man's oath before the war would not be believed and now they would degrade him to be a liar. General we only ask for justice. See that we will have it and all will be yet well. There is no accusation against me and there never was. I am black but in my heart there is not stain of infamy.

I am General
Your very humble Srvt
Nelson Irwin

Statement of Isabella Burton, January 17, 1868

Isabella Burton provides information to the Freedmen's Bureau office in Augusta about her two sons, who had been sold by her master before the end of the war, in hopes of finding her children. Ex-slaves across the South sought desperately to find loved ones who had been sold away from their families during slavery, and often appealed to the Bureau for assistance in their searches. Isabella still lived alone in 1870, when the census officials for Augusta came to her home, and there is no record that she ever found her children.

Isabella Burton (Mother)

Horace Bucker sold my two sons (seven & five years age) Benjamin & Horace, sold to Larke & Wright in Maddison County Va. Johnny Gilgarnett & Jeremiah Gilgarnett were playmates.

I am living in Staunton Now a widow & alone, would like very much to see them.

Thomas P. Jackson to Orlando Brown,
March 24, 1868

Thomas Jackson, agent for the Freedmen's Bureau in Augusta from April 1867 to March 1868, reports to the regional office in Richmond about the general condition of the county, the problems faced by the freedmen, the persistent antagonism between local blacks and whites, and current divisions within Augusta over the political future of Virginia. Field agents such as Jackson were required to file monthly reports detailing local conditions in their jurisdiction.

Brig Genl O. Brown
Asst Comr District of Va. Richmond (Through HdQrs 9th Sub Dist Va)
Staunton, Va.
March 24, 1868

General

In compliance with C.O. No. 6 S. 1866 B.R.F.&A.L. I have the honor to make the following report of condition of Bureau Affairs in 4 Div. 9 S. Dist Va. comprizing the counties of Augusta & Highland.

Settlements of wages for labor in 1867 are generally concluded, still this office is much sought by freedpeople asking aid and advice on the many questions of account which ever arise between employer and employed. With some exceptions, more than is desirable, but less than could be expected, considering their recent condition of ignorant servitude, freedmen in this Division are industrious and orderly. Surplus earnings of last year have been largely expended in bridging over the long winter, but save in cases of sickness or desertion there has not been much actual suffering. There is much diversity of employment in this Division—farming, coaling, in connection with iron mining, rail road repairs, and supplies of fuel, &c, preparing material for building, such as brick, lumber &c and this causes more regular demand for labor than in a purely agricultural district. If freedmen could but better understand the value of time and short intelligent money reckonings, they would advance much more rapidly in material prosperity. The desire to own a homestead is general, but the plan pursued by many freedmen is fraught with great danger, if by any disaster present system kind officers should retain power. Purchases are made with agreement to make so many annual payments and when purchase money is all paid then a deed to be received. Unless where I can influence them, most take but a simple receipt and may have to sue for title, but I advise all to have a legal contract drawn executed and recorded, but many do not. Written contracts for labor by the year for 1868 are not so general as usual. As I have before reported I think the change to casual hire will in the end prove a disadvantage to the laborer and have advised permanent contracts through this office. The social and moral condition of freedmen is not what it should be. The vices engendered by slavery are too deeply rooted to be easily eradicated and I fear until the community at large realize that the freedman is a citizen and seek to elevate him by example and precept, he will in many respects disappoint his friends. The relations of freedmen and whites to each other is in an unsatisfactory condition. The pernicious teachings of the conservative leaders and press have unbounded effect on ignorant whites, who look upon the freedmen with contempt and hate and do not hesitate to use violence where their leaders use abusive language. Assaults on freedmen during this month have been trifling except attack on Jefferson Davison (c) by William Hite and Joseph Trimble. The wounds caused by a stone, the pistol though drawn not fired. This case is referred to Mr. Joseph Wilson J. P. for investigation. The political relations of white and colored to each other are directly antagonistic. The conservative leaders have through District Superintendents, Chiefs of 50 & Captains of 10 fully organized themselves to defeat the Constitution about to be submitted to the people of Va. I do not anticipate there will be any armed and organized public demonstration to drive voters to or from the polls but every effort short of what would necessitate military interference will be used to secure the defeat of the Constitution no matter what its provisions. No progress has been made by me in organizing Temperance Associations in this Division. I have striven earnestly to establish such societies but without any success. There is not much drunkeness among freedmen here but there is more spirits drank than is good for them even were their circumstances better than they are.

I have the honor to be, General
Your obt servt
Thos P Jackson
Asst Sub Asst Comr

John W. Jordan to John A. McDonnell, May 4, 1868

John Jordan, Freedmen's Bureau agent in Augusta from April to August 1868, reports to his commanding officer in Winchester on the appearance of the Ku Klux Klan in Staunton. The Klan emerged during the late 1860s as a loosely organized movement that served as a means for frustrated white Southerners to influence local political and social development through terror and intimidation.

Capt. Jno A. McDonnell
Sub Asst Comr
Winchester, Va

Staunton, Va.
May 4th 1868

Capt.
    I have the honor to call your attention to certain demonstrations made by an organization here known as the "Ku Klux Klan" and

which have caused a vast deal of dangerous excitement, especially among the colored population and which if not promptly suppressed will culminate in serious and deplorable disturbances of the public peace.

This Klan made their appearance in the Streets of Staunton about 1 o'clock Sunday morning last, mounted and the Klan being enmasked in white sheets or something of the kind, and being armed caused no little consternation among the colored people and much serious annoyance to the respectable whites. Their operations were attended with the discharge of pistols and also by cheers or yelling, which of course occurring as it did almost in the center of the town aroused almost the entire population.

On yesterday I addressed a formal communication to the Mayor upon the subject who has informed me that every effort is being made by the Civil Authorities to ferret out the guilty parties in the matter, who I am assured will be brought to punishment and the operations of the Klan suppressed at once.

The colored people are very much excited upon the subject and but little is needed to bring about a serious state of things here. I would also remark that I have reported the facts to the Military Comr for this Division also.

I am Capt
Your obt Svt
Jno W. Jordan
A.S.A.Comr &c
B. of R. F. & A. L.

2. Franklin County

Franklin Repository, "Freedmen," February 8, 1865

With the war nearly over, the Repository *considers what will become of blacks in the United States once the slaves of the South are all liberated. Arguing that blacks will make good citizens (as evinced by their distinguished service as soldiers, and their accomplishments as a race), the* Repository *argues that freedmen should be educated, provided moral instruction, and given economic opportuni-*

ties. While many Republicans believed that the freedmen deserved support in the postwar era, others in the party were also motivated by the fact that the Republicans depended heavily upon black votes in the South to remain dominant in national elections.

Since the skies of our national horizon are beginning to look bright, and the dark and threatening clouds of war disappearing, the question is often asked, what shall be done with the freedmen? We confess the question easier asked than answered, yet it may be never so difficult, it must be answered, and that too, in a way becoming a free intelligent and christian people. Whilst the war lasts, but one duty remains, that is, to keep up our armies to their full complement, and supply them with every thing necessary to prosecute the war vigorously and successfully. We have Generals the ablest and bravest in the world, and who have the full confidence of the people. The last election was but a warrant to them from the people to use all means necessary to suppress the rebellion, and conquer a lasting and permanent peace. This they are doing as fast as the most sanguine could ask. Victory everywhere perches proudly upon our banners and as the southern traitors are yielding and our armies marching unmolested through their borders; the civil authorities are tacitly seeking terms of compromise and peace honorable to themselves if possible. Whilst the affairs in the field stand so favorable, we find nearly one million of freedmen, and the number daily increasing, accessible to the people of the loyal States. They are ignorant, stupid in many cases, and passive recipients of the first influences which strike them. The transition from slavery to freedmen has doubtless jostled their minds a little, and developed new hopes and desires, and prepared them to hear and think as they never could before. The proper instruction will elevate them rapidly—wrong influence will make them more miserable than they were before emancipation. If we do not carry them light, truth, strength and courage, they will inevitably sink under the flood tide of vices which follow an army. Their usefulness has been fairly tested, they have entered the ranks, have shown good capacity in acquiring knowledge sufficient to make good soldiers, and at Fort Wagner; in front of Petersburg and elsewhere, they have shown themselves equal to the best soldiers. No one who speaks dispassionately upon the subject will say that they will not make courageous and available soldiers. They have on more than one occasion received the commendation of their Generals for valuable and efficient services.

That they make good mechanics is fairly proven by the fact, that many of them are such, even in the degraded condition of Slavery. They are found in almost every one of the rougher trades, and skilled equal to any even of our own race, who labor in the same occupations. In many parts of the South, it was no unusual thing for planters, to have all the necessary mechanics among his slaves, and the slaves were valued according to their skill in whatever trade they were taught. They are proverbial for their powers of imitation. They are as a general thing fond of music and acquire it easily, and always where they have the least opportunity become excellent performers. We find even some without the advantages of instruction, or much opportunity for practice become quite proficient.

But we need not stop here, we find them entering the learned and honorable professions. We have them in the ministry, and doing much honor to the profession. We have them in the profession of medicine, editing newspapers, and but a few days since on motion of Hon. Charles Sumner, one Brooks was admitted to practice law in the Supreme court of the United States. This man Brooks is admitted to be gifted with extraordinary intellectual powers, and although young in years, stands at the head of the profession he has chosen for himself.

What then shall be done with the freedmen? Shall we allow them to look out for themselves and provide for their wants as best they can? Shall we keep open our stables and employ them as hostlers, use them as waiters at our dining tables, servants anywhere and everywhere? Or shall we colonize them and send them to some other part of the globe, as an inferior and useless race. No, none of these. There is a higher duty required of us, and our own national salvation demands it. We must come to their help, and pour in upon them the inspiration of a higher and better life; they must be taught to read and write, under the tuition of religious teachers, and in this way, they will be elevated very rapidly and enjoy the blessings of liberty.

We are bound by many considerations to come to their help. They are a part of our fallen race, and from this part, we are required by the spirit and aim of the religion we profess to save all the lost that is possible. They have been degraded and oppressed by our nation, and we have for years denounced the institution that bound them to the earth. We therefore owe them more than common benevolence to amend for the injury we have done them. If we therefore at once fit them for the position of freemen; if they are made intelligent, virtuous, industrious, they will prove a great blessing to themselves and the nation, but if they are left in ignorance, the victims of loose and vile men, they will prove a curse to themselves and our country.

In many parts of the country societies are organized for the purpose of raising funds to send teachers among them. This is a step in the right direction. Let the right kind of teachers among them. This is a step in the right direction. Let the right kind of teachers be sent, and plenty of them, and it will not be long until a new era shall dawn upon our country, and we can truthfully say, that our country is, "the land of the free" "and the home of the brave." If history be true, our own race were as degraded intellectually when the Romans invaded Britain, as ever the African race was, yet by moral and intellectual training, it has surpassed all others, and now stands the most powerful and enlightened race upon the face of the earth.

What may be done with the African race in the future we cannot tell. We know they have capacity, and this being the land of their birth, our duty is with the present. That they have giants among them even in their degraded condition does not admit of a doubt. In this broad land of ours, under the blessing of our Government, they can be made useful to themselves, the country and posterity. Let it the effort be fairly made.

Valley Spirit, "Tricks of the Radicals," August 9, 1865

The Valley Spirit, *a Democratic Party newspaper, complains that Republicans are attempting to thwart President Andrew Johnson's plans for Reconstruction in an effort to force "negro suffrage" on the South. Johnson's lenient approach toward the defeated Confederacy, combined with efforts among white*

Southerners to prevent blacks from enjoying full citizenship, enraged Radical Republicans, who subsequently attempted to wrest control of Reconstruction policy away from Johnson.

The radicals having been completely "flanked" by President Johnson's reconstruction policy are now endeavoring to force the President to abandon his position by the circulation of the most absurd falsehoods. The plan is to systematically libel the Southern people by originating stories of great dissatisfaction among them as unwilling on their part to submit to the conditions laid down by the President. They hope by this means to retard the work of pacification and reorganization in the South until they can perfect their plans to force negro suffrage upon the people of the Southern States as a condition of the return to their Union. If they can induce the President to believe these fabrications they imagine he will abandon his present position and adopt the radical view of the case. Even "conservative" Republicans, who but a few weeks ago were loud in their praise of the President's policy of restoration, are now heard to say that "the South will *compel* the President to hold them as conquered provinces," when they well know it is the Northern radicals that are attempting to do the "compelling." This transparent trick will fail if President Johnson is made of the stuff we think he is.

Franklin Repository, "Who Shall Dictate Terms?" October 31, 1866

The Repository *argues that the Southern states gave up their rights in the Union when they seceded, and so must accept the terms of Reconstruction and pass the Fourteenth Amendment to the Constitution. The amendment was proposed on June 13, 1866, and mandated that states provide equal protection and due process to all persons living within their borders, provided penalties for any state that withheld the right to vote from eligible citizens, disqualified many ex-Confederates from holding national public office, and repudiated all Confederate war debt.*

Enough is now known of the sentiment of the North to convince the most obdurate, that the people will consent to no policy of reconstruction that falls short of the acceptance of the proposed constitutional amendments. The issue was fairly made in the great States, and they have with one voice demanded the adoption of the proposed change in our organic law.

Had the elections been but half as decisive in favor of the Democracy, the verdict would have been pronounced a condemnation of the amendments, and they would have fallen. But, since the people have decided for the amendments and against the policy of Andrew Johnson, the President and the leading journals and managers of the Democracy, persist in advising the South not to accept the amendments. The President, in his singular blindness, advises against the adoption of the amendments even in the face of the palpable fact that during his entire term he will be as powerless as he is now, to bring about any more favorable adjustment to the rebels. * * *

* * * The issue is therefore plainly presented to the rebellious States. They have made causeless, wanton, bloody war. Their own arbiter has given its fearful judgement against them, and from it there is no appeal. They have, by the constitution and the laws, forfeited citizenship, property and even life, and their rights are only the rights of disfranchisement, confiscation, or the right to die as the law demands. They have not, either by moral or legal rules, any voice in the government they spurned and sought to dismember by the sword. They have no claim other than that which appeals to the magnanimity of the victors, and reminds us that we are all of one nation and should be again one brotherhood.

But the North desires to welcome the rebellious States again into the folds of the Union, and while it would be boundless in its generosity, it dares not be entirely forgetful of justice. It seeks no wanton humiliation, no measure of vengeance; but it must make treason and rebellion odious, and must protect the living and those who are to live hereafter from a repetition of the bloody drama that has just shadowed the land. It asks the adoption of the constitutional amendments and the modification of local laws in conformity therewith, as South Carolina has already done, and the work of reconstruction will be finished. * * *

* * * The North is firm to the point of its demand—beyond that it would allow no mere sectional feeling to retard the complete restoration of the rebel States. It demands the amendments. It demands

universal justice—equality for all before the law and submission to the paramount authority of the general government. It wants no more—it will take no less; and that once given it will seek to heal our common wounds, and invite all sections, in interest and affection, to our free institutions.

The South cannot dictate other terms of reconstruction, even though they come from the very throne of prostituted power itself. If it will not assent to the propositions made in generous and patriotic purpose by the North, it will only arouse and make more exacting the supreme power of the government—the twenty millions of people who have preserved their government by countless sacrifice. They will *enforce* what the South fails to concede, and they will enforce it with penalties. They will bring the South into loyal harmony with the logical teachings of the war—kindly if they can, but otherwise if they must. They have now submitted to all the people engaged in rebellion the determination of this question—disfranchising the only class [in the] South that was true to the Union. If the vanquished white man will not accept the proffer of the North, he will thenceforth be voiceless in the reconstruction of the rebellious States, and the measure of the penalties will be the measure essential to the prompt and enduring solution of the problems left as the legacies of the war.

We entreat the South not to be willfully blinded to their best interests, and to the interests of all. They can restore these States any day on better terms than delay and agitation can possible give them. Have they not been deceived and betrayed enough by the defeated and powerless Democracy? Have they not seen enough of the invincible determination of the North to counsel a prompt and cordial assent? If they have not, then are they strangers to wisdom, and their own worst foes. Let reason resume its sway and we shall soon have enduring Peace and universal Justice.

Valley Spirit, "Negro Government," October 2, 1867

The Valley Spirit *complains bitterly that Republican control of the U.S. Congress ensures that blacks rather than whites will dominate the governments of the*

Southern states, a situation the newspaper asserts is ill-conceived because of the ignorance of the freedmen. Most Democrats deplored the disfranchisement of whites and enfranchisement of blacks in the South, both because of attitudes toward race and because a large base of black voters in the South would add political strength to the Republican Party.

It is now being demonstrated to almost a mathematical certainty, that the governments of the late rebel States will soon be under the absolute control of negroes. All the legislation of the last Congress seems to have had that end in view. The registration of the voters now going on in these States shows that the black population entitled to vote will far exceed the white. Congress intended to disfranchise the great majority of the white, and it has succeeded in doing so. * * *

* * * And who are to take their places? Who are to hold the reins of government in the South? Who are to control the destines of States which have given to our National history some of its brightest names? The negroes. They are now declared to be the only loyal people in the South except the loud-mouthed cowards who, under military protection, have emigrated thither from the New England States since the war. The loyal negroes, who cheerfully dug the ditches and labored in the trenches at the bidding of white rebels— the loyal negroes, who, while their masters were away in the field, worked on the plantations and raised the bread which fed the rebel armies—the loyal negroes, who clung to the rebel officers through the hardships of the camp and the dangers of the battle-field, in preference to accepting the blessings of freedom under the emancipation proclamation—*they are the loyal men who are to found loyal State governments.* These negroes too, have just been emancipated from a state of slavery. But a few years have elapsed since the horrors of that accursed institution were being constantly portrayed. What vile epithet was too strong to be applied to the slave-holder? Slavery was denounced as the "sum of all villainies," and as one of the "twin relics of barbarism." It was asserted that the negro of the South was not above the level of the brute. The opportunity for elevation was never afforded him. No ray of light was allowed to penetrate into his intellect. He was kept in the grossest ignorance.

[P]retended philanthropists appealed to the charities of the public, by picturing the worse than Egyptian darkness in which he was enshrouded. He was denied the advantage of schools. It was alleged that he was shut out from the light of christianity, and left to follow the promptings of the passions of his own wicket heart, and that thus slavery, a monster in itself had given birth to the black monsters of iniquity in the shape of these ignorant, uncivilized blacks.

And yet, these same blacks, thus imbruted by slavery, kept in intellectual darkness, and excluded from the civilizing influences of Christianity, have been suddenly invested with the highest political rights, and are expected to make and administer the laws for their intelligent superiors of the white race.

This is not a fancy sketch. It is not a dream. It is not a Rebel canard. It is not a Copperhead lie. The figures on the Registration lists show that the negro voters are largely in the majority in the South. They have thus the power in their own hands. They may elect whites or blacks to office as they deem best. Who imagines that they will be contented to allow the whites to enjoy the emoluments of official positions when they may just as easily flow into the pockets of men of their own race? The negro is naturally impudent. Encourage him to "get above his business" and he soon developes a saucy disposition. So, being petted by Radical place hunters and caressed by Radical strong-minded women, he will soon reach after higher honors, and never rest satisfied until he enjoys them.

Pennsylvanians: Let but the old Keystone State endorse the policy of the Radicals, and before another year rolls around, negroes will hold the chief positions in the Southern States and the *Congressional Globe* will be publishing the speeches of negroes made from their seats in the Halls which once resounded with the eloquence of Clay, Webster and the honored white statesmen of the past. Are you ready for this? If not, cast your ballot for those who are in favor of having this government administered by white men for all time to come. Vote the Democratic ticket and you need to have no fear of negro governments.

IX

Remembering the War

1. Augusta County

Valley Virginian, "Honor the Fallen Brave," May 9, 1866

The Valley Virginian *implores the people of Augusta County to honor those who died for the Confederacy by assisting in the decoration of graves at a local Confederate cemetery. Memorial days devoted to tending the graves of soldiers became common in postwar Southern communities, as people grieved for those they had lost in the war.*

To-morrow is the sad anniversary of the death of Virginia's bravest and best loved son. To-morrow three years ago, Stonewall Jackson, the Christian, the Soldier and the greatest military genius of the age, passed from earth to Heaven. And it is but meet that the people of his loved Valley should consecrate the day and hold it sacred—devoting their minds, hearts and hands to the work of decorating the graves of his soldiers and paying proper respect to his memory. The Ladies Cemetery Committee call upon the people of Augusta to join them in this "labor of love," and we feel confident that, though the notice is short, the demonstration will be worthy of old Augusta. Let our farmers aid the ladies, and let evergreens and flowers be brought in by wagon loads. Over two thousand "dead heroes," from every State in the South, lie uncared for and unnoticed in Thornrose Cemetery. Brave hearts and true, they lost all, even life, for us, and it will gladden the hearts of many widows and orphans in the far distant South, to know that the remains of their loved ones are not neglected by the fair women of the Valley.

In the more Southern States, the 23rd of April, was devoted to this holy purpose, but by common consent the 10th of May has been set apart in Virginia to preserve and perpetuate the memory of our martyred dead; to freshen their graves and to renew, from year to year, these offices of love and attention that make green the memory of those who once "trod the path of glory." Our Merchants and business men will observe the day by closing their places of business, and it is hoped that all will unite to pay that respect due those who gave all for their country and their principle.

It is but little that is left to us of the South, but surely we can devote one day to the honored memory of those that sleep in soldiers' graves. Then cover their graves with flowers; make the barren hill that disgraces our Cemetery, for one day at least, "blossom as the rose," and give an earnest of what you intend to do, to beautify and adorn the last resting place of our best and bravest. Come, if only to shed a tear over the graves of those, who for you, now lie in that neglected spot. * * *

Staunton Spectator, "The Whites and Blacks," April 16, 1867

The Spectator *argues that since blacks now have the right to vote, it is in the political interest of whites to treat them with "friendly feelings." In making its case, the newspaper asserted that almost all slaves had supported the Confederacy during the war and would have gladly served in the rebel armies if given the chance. While many whites in the postwar South came to believe that slaves had willingly supported the Confederate cause, the idea had little basis in fact. During the war, blacks seized their freedom by running away to the Union lines whenever the opportunity presented itself—many of them enlisting in the U.S. army in order to fight against the Confederacy.*

We have always been kindly disposed to the blacks, and have believed that such was the case with most of our people, and, consequently, have uniformly maintained that the best friends they have are the people of the South. None but friendly feelings should exist between the whites and blacks of the South. We concur with the *Houston* (Texas) *Telegraph* that it is all important in view of the new right of suffrage conferred upon the negroes by Congress. Those among us who are inclined to impose upon negroes, or to treat them in such way as to engender strife between them and the whites are, without thinking of it, the worst enemies of the country. We have but few such men, but we have some, and we owe it to ourselves to discountenance them. It is true, the conduct of some negroes is often vexatious in the extreme; so is the conduct of many white men. And our own theory, that the negroes are an inferior race, should cause us to treat them with forbearance. It is no credit to any white man to have quarrels with negroes, under present circumstances especially. And, then, there are many things to be said in favor of the negroes. Nine-tenths of them were staunch Confederates during all the war, except where armies of invasion demoralized them. Three-fourths of the able-bodied blacks would have volunteered in the Confederate army had it been permitted. And they are not at all responsible for their emancipation, nor for the effort to place them upon an equality with the whites. Whatever their faults—and all races have faults—they are the most docile people in the world, and are as true as steel to their friends. Those of the Southern people who manifest kindness and friendship for them can exercise a stronger and better influence over them than any other class. And it is now the highest patriotic duty, as it was a humane and Christian duty before, that every Southern man should be a friend to the negroes; and to have influence with them, and seek to guide them for good in their new position. Otherwise, they will fall into the hands of bad men, and mischief will be the result. "A word to the wise, etc."

Valley Virginian, "The 21st," July 22, 1868

The Valley Virginian *notes the anniversary of the first battle of Manassas— the first major engagement of the Civil War—and mourns the memory of*

soldiers from Augusta County who died for the Confederate cause. On the an-
niversaries of battles, many Southerners and Northerners took time to remember
those who had died during the war. In later years, reunions held on the anniver-
saries of great battles, like Gettysburg, provided an opportunity for veterans to
reunite with old comrades and reconcile with former enemies.

Yesterday, seven years ago, the first battle of Manassas was fought. The individual gallantry of the South triumphed over the disciplined masses of the United States and the incompetency of our generals! Yesterday, the Staunton Artillery, under General J. D. Imboden, (then Captain) gained its first laurels! Yesterday the "Stonewall" and Bee's Brigades gained their immortal names! Yesterday Wm. E. Woodward and Joab Seally, the first martyrs from Staunton, gave up their lives for the Right—Woodward shouting "Give me liberty or give me death!"

Oh, the hot and weary day! How it breaks upon our memory! How it fires every fibre of our heart! How it tingles each pulsation, and casts a halo of glory around and about the cloud of darkness that now enshrouds us!

Let it forever be sacred! Treasure it up in your hearts, and sadly cherish the memories of the boys who we lost—those gallant boys who represented all that was good, brave and noble in humanity! And the "Old Stonewall," the "West Augusta Guards," the "5th"— all—Baylor, Harman. Harper, and a host of others, the peerless and free! all gone! God help us! we cannot pursue the subject. They are gone. * * *

Staunton Vindicator, "Thursday last . . . ," June 17, 1870

The Vindicator *reports on a recent memorial celebration held at the Thorn-*
rose Confederate cemetery in Augusta County. In the decades that followed the
Civil War, memorial celebrations became increasingly elaborate and ritualized,
as different associations formed—often headed by the women of the local com-

munity—in order to take responsibility for such things as tending the graves of veterans and erecting monuments in their honor.

Thursday last was the day appointed for paying our annual tribute to our "loved and lost," who sacrificed themselves for us, and now "sleep their last sleep" in the Confederate Cemetery near this place. The day was most unpropitious, the rain falling in torrents during the morning.—Nevertheless, a large crowd assembled at the Town Hall, and, although the managers deemed it advisable to postpone the ceremonies to a more pleasant day, formed a procession, headed by the famous Stonewall Band, and, amid the rain, proceeded on foot and in carriages to the Cemetery. The procession was composed of the Stonewall Band, Fire Companies, the Pioneers, Councils of Friends of Temperance, a number of Ladies, volunteer Band and citizens generally, all bearing wreaths and boquets. Arriving at the Cemetery, the Bands discoursed sweet and appropriate music and the crowd, about 2000 persons, decorated the graves, not one of which but had its tribute of love and affection. It was the more satisfactory to see, through this most disagreeable weather, so large a crowd in attendance, and evidences the fact that the heroism, devotion and self-sacrifice of those who gave their all to the "lost cause," are held in the dearest remembrances by those of us who live to lament it and their fall. In rain or sunshine our annual tribute is due, and in rain or sunshine, our people are determined it shall be paid.

The Pioneers, with shovels, spades &c., proceeded to fix up those graves most needing it, but, satisfied that concerted labor and means were necessary to put in proper condition the last home of our buried brethren, have instituted a movement, noticed elsewhere, to form an association to take charge of and beautify the grounds of the Confederate Cemetery. This will meet with the hearty accord of every well-wisher in the county, and we hope to see the Association an immense affair.

The graves fixed up and decorated, the crowd slowly moved back to town, the Bands discoursing appropriate music while passing through Thornrose Cemetery and on their way back.

In the evening, the young ladies of the Deaf & Dumb and Blind Institution moved in procession, with flowers, headed by their Band, to the Cemetery, and paid their tribute to their lamented Confederates whose "Silent tents are spread on Fame's eternal camping ground." A mute and touching appeal to the feelings and sympathies of all who witnessed it.

Altogether, the ceremonies of the day were most satisfactory. Although there was not the usual number present, yet there was a very large number, and the spirit, which induced the attendance of those present, was, itself, a most appropriate tribute to their comrades and friends who fell in the great struggle, in which nearly all of us participated or deeply sympathized.

Confederate Veteran, "Gay to Grave in the Army of Northern Virginia," 1903

A member of the "Valley Rangers," a unit organized in Augusta County at the beginning of the war, recalls some of his experiences as a Confederate soldier in the Army of Northern Virginia. Stressing the excitement of the period and the joys of camp life, this veteran's magazine account downplayed the tedium, terror, and hardship that marked so much of army life for soldiers during the war, recalling instead the time as "the four gayest and jolliest years of life."

* * * What a thrilling time it was in that spring of 1861 when a "nation was born" and a most glorious chapter in human bearing and daring was written! The Southern Confederacy, that inspiration of cavaliers and righteousness, that inspirer of heroes, who pricked their names on the pages of history with sword and bayonet point; of poets, who "wreathed around with glory" the Southern cross; of matrons and maidens, who gave more than life to its defense!

Then began the assembling of that Southern manhood and boyhood who were to go "sounding down the ages" as the Confederate army. Among the first to enroll themselves under its banner were the Valley Rangers, a voluntary cavalry company composed of the very best of the young men living along the eastern side of Augusta County, who under their first captain, the brave Patrick (who later as major of the Seventeenth Battalion was to die gloriously on the plains of Second Manassas), met in historic Waynesboro to go to the front. It was then the comedy parts in the great opening drama commenced. How exercised we were about our uniforms, how we had to send off for the material, and get just the right shade of color, and the exact buttons, braid, etc.! * * * How we formed in line on Main Street, and, as we mounted our horses for the last time, of the motherly caress and cautions, the father's advice, the sister's proud smile, and the admiring looks of the younger brothers and servants; and then, the sly embrace of the sweetheart behind the parlor door, when we rushed in to say goodby for the twentieth time! Last came the presentation of our flag and farewell address from our good and true "Old Parson" Richardson.

Then from our captain came, "Attention, company! By two, march! Head of column right!" and away we marched for Harper's Ferry to fight Yankees, and without a gun. (Pure comedy that, with no chance for a tragedy.) What an enjoyable march it was! To us boys it was as when school closed and we reveled in the sense of freedom and dreamed of the great and daring deeds we should perform. The march down the valley in that lovely April was enjoyed ever so much. How we laughed and chatted by the way, and now and then tried the speed and mettle of our horses, and how we were cheered and admired by the girls all along the route! And the great event, our arrival at Harper's Ferry, where was forming that grand army that later, as the Army of Northern Virginia, was for the coming four years to perform the deeds of heroism that make it the honor it now is to be a Daughter of the Confederacy! Camp life was a revelation and delight to the boys who had been so strictly reared at home, and we threw ourselves into and enjoyed it to the full. How we smoked, played cards, frolicked, tussled, and let ourselves out in gay abandon! O, but it was jolly!

Pretty soon our camp at the Ferry was broken up, and the war began in earnest. Then our company—now known as Company E, First Virginia Cavalry—made the first fight in the Valley by a skirmish with a lot of Yankees across the Potomac at Williamsport, and in a few days we had our first man shot—Sam Dalhouse—and then we fought along with the West Augusta Guard of Staunton and the Rockbridge Artillery and the other troops under Jackson (the building Stonewall Brigade) at Falling Waters, and under J. E. B. Stuart, our major then and afterwards our great cavalry general. We captured the very first company of Yankees and had one of our company—Zach Johnson—wounded. Both Johnson and Dalhouse died in a few months, partly from their wounds. * * *

* * * So it was we lived our soldier life, from grave to gay and gay to grave, and as time passed the fighting was more frequent, and there was more of tragedy and less of comedy, for after each fight some gay spirit of fun would be missing from around a camp fire. Yet those who were left got all the pleasures possible out of life, and without any disrespect for the missing comrade we kept up the fun and frolic to the end. And to some of the survivors those were the four gayest and jolliest years of life.

One of them, "Fish."

A. F. Robertson, "My Childhood Recollections of the War," January 19, 1915

The daughter of Alexander H. H. Stuart, one of Augusta's most eminent and influential politicians, A. F. Robertson records her childhood memories of the Civil War fifty years after Appomattox. Her account reflects the nostalgia and romantic imagery that informed much of how white Southerners remembered the war by the beginning of the twentieth century, including the honored position that Confederate leaders like Robert E. Lee held in the minds of former Confederates.

* * * Even at the early age of five years the terrible events of war were burnt into my memory with fire and blood. No account of these days would be correct without the relation of domestic life as it then existed, nor could the younger generation understand a child's life in Confederate times without a knowledge of his envi-

ronments. I shall, therefore, tell the story as I first remember it—at the beginning of the war and again when nearing its close.

Born in the days of slavery and my childhood having been spent under the old regime, no picture of it would be complete without its background of black people among whom I was raised. My brother and I were the youngest of a large family of grown children, and arrived in this world greatly to the regret of the whole connection. Our white family was largely outnumbered by the colored. The servants connected with the town houses were Aunt Kitty, the cook, and her assistant, Uncle Davy, Uncle Peyton, the carriage driver, John, the butler, Millie, the housemaid, Aunt Rachel, Nancy Ballard, Sarah and Mat.

* * * Our old black mammies had all died off, and I never remember to have been crooned to sleep on the ample bosom of a faithful slave. My earliest recollections are of being put to bed by two half grown negro girls, Sarah and Mat, by the light of a wood fire in the nursery. If we had been particularly good throughout the day—had helped to carry chips or tote wood—we were rewarded by charming stories of wild "critters and hants and sperrits" while we trembled in bed, and the little darkies lay full length in front of the crackling fire. Had we been mean and stingy—like po' white trash—refusing to share our taffy or horsecakes—woe betide us!

* * * Uncle Jerome brought us partridge eggs from the harvest field, and at twilight Uncle Jeff—a silent little yellow man, played for us on the fiddle. Every Saturday "Monkey Jim" came from the farm with the cart. My sister called it her "Ship Africa." "Monkey" drove old Kit at the rate of three miles an hour. "Kit" was a fat, freckled, white mare; "Monkey" was a little black, bald-headed old man. His small flat head was covered with an old slouch hat which rested on a pair of enormous outstanding ears; small furtive eyes, a great wobby nose and scattered rows of teeth set in the kinky hairy face of the little old dwarf, made up an appearance singularly grotesque. * * *

* * * The early days of the Confederacy were very gay and interesting to a child, for we lived on excitement and "little pitchers" heard and saw all that was going on. There was music in the streets and gay, young soldiers drilling in their handsome uniforms. The girls cheered them on, throwing flowers and kisses while the band played "Dixie" and the troops went marching by. Indoors they

laughed and sang bright war songs, and made haversacks and tobacco bags. My pretty cousin sewed on a beautiful silk flag for "her
captain" and my sister said she was making a petticoat for Billy
Blank because he wouldn't go to war! Sometimes "Sears Hill" and
"Dogwood" were full of tents, and we children used to watch the
soldiers standing guard or dragging cannon from the arsenal opposite the Mary Baldwin Seminary. Often they said the Yankees were
coming, and one night at home I heard most curious noises under
the floors and in the garret, something like spirits—only louder.
When I went there, my mother and sisters were stooping down over
a candle, and with hatchets were pulling up the floors; back in the
cracks and corners they were poking bacon and silver and all sorts
of things. I crossed my heart I would not tell, then made all the children wretched by saying that I knew grown up people's secrets
which even the Yankees could not find out! But they did come and
search the house and steal everything that was left in the smoke
house and store room, and all the bacons except old Brutus, and
he was hid in the cellar. Then they cut the spokes in Papa's fifteen-
hundred dollar wood wagon! We children went out and cursed the
Yankees, and seesawed on the back fence and sang loud as we
could;

> "Jeff Davis rides a white horse,
> Abe Lincoln rides a mule.
> Jeff Davis is a gentleman,
> Abe Lincoln is a fool."

At that time I was very proficient in songs and oaths, which
seemed perfectly justifiable on such occasions.

We had very plain fare in those days, so whenever we had
"Secsh" pudding or other dessert, some one raised a little Confederate flag on the dinner castors to celebrate the event. There was a
scarcity of everything, and the women went to work knitting socks,
and making gloves, and dresses from the lindsey which was woven
on the farm. I thought my sisters looked beautiful in their red flan-
nel garabaldi waists and the hats which they made of plaited straw
and trimmed with rooster tails. * * *

As I grew older it seemed to me the house and the town were always full of soldiers coming and going; tents on the hills one day,

the next day, done in great wagon trains. About that time two charming girls came to stay with us. My father called them "refugees," and said the Yankees had driven them out of Winchester because they did so much for our soldiers and were so brave and kind. They made our house very gay and lively with their music and all they had to tell about the war.

One day a boy told me that "Old Jube" was in town, and that General Lee was in our parlor to see my mother. All of us had heard of General Lee and I determined to see him for myself. Stealing into the front hall and hiding behind the partly open door, I peered into the room. And there, according to my childish fancy I saw *a king*, a grand and beautiful man with gray hair, gray uniform and wonderful dark eyes! There was no crown on his forehead or golden sceptre in his hand, yet he was the realization of all that I had read in story books,—it was His Majesty, the King! He saw me peeping through the door, and, rising from his chair, he took me by the hand and led me into the room. He placed his hand upon my curls and said they were pretty, then lifting me upon his lap he gently kissed me on the lips. I was but a child, yet I felt as I did in after years when the Bishop laid his hands upon me—that I had been blessed and consecrated by his touch.

* * * Hope grew dim but war went on. The V. M. I. cadets were ordered to the field and the battle of New Market was fought. A brave young cousin was brought back to us wounded, and my boy soldier brother limped back on blistering feet, only to have his mother wash them with her tears and bind them up for longer marches and watches in the dreadful trenches around Richmond. Our food was low, our servants had gone, some to heaven—some to freedom. * * *

* * * One day in early spring I was skipping along the road from my grandmother's house when I saw a young man coming quickly towards me. He was greatly excited and out of breath, and as he drew near called out "General Lee has surrendered!" Hot indignation boiled within me and I exclaimed "That's a lie, and you know it." Then I ran rapidly homeward. The tears were streaming down my father's face, but the women sat stolidly gazing at each other and said "The war is over." Yes, the war was ended.

Confederate Veteran, "Distinguished Soldier and Citizen," 1922

Published in Confederate Veteran magazine, this obituary of George Imboden praises his distinguished service as a soldier in the Confederate army, as well as his active participation in memorial organizations during the postwar era. As veterans died in the decades after the Civil War, tens of thousands of similar obituaries appeared in newspapers and magazines across the nation, for both Union and Confederate veterans, praising the deeds and memory of those who had fought in the war.

Col. George W. Imboden, noted lawyer, soldier, and public citizen, departed this life from his home at Ansted, Fayette County, W. Va., on January 8, 1922, in the eighty-seventh year of his life.

He was born in Augusta County, Va., and practiced law at Staunton till the breaking out of the War between the States, when in April, 1861, he enlisted and was elected first sergeant of the Staunton Artillery, and second lieutenant in November. On its re-organization, he was chosen major of the 62nd Virginia Infantry, and in December, 1862, was elected colonel of the 18th Virginia Cavalry, with which he served till the close of the war.

He and his four brothers—Gen. John D. Imboden, Capt. F. M. Imboden Capt. J. P. Imboden, and Maj. James A. Imboden—all gained distinction for bravery in the Confederate service, and all continued in service till the surrender of General Lee.

Colonel Imboden was a gallant soldier, leading in many battles in a quiet way and with sound judgment. He kept his own counsels and often sprung surprises on the enemy. At one time he captured a wagon train of fifty-four mule teams, newly equipped and loaded with provisions and corn. When the front wagon was upset and caused a stampede, he ordered all to turn, and at Summersville they ran an old grist mill all night and had a royal feast in the morning. In June, 1863, he surprised and entered Cumberland, Md. Through his noble example of faithfulness, courage, and self-sacrifice he won the respect and confidence of his followers, and with honor and humanity he was always kind to his captured prisoners. He was wounded at Gordonsville in December, 1864, had his jaw broken and was shot in the shoulder. He ever had the confidence of Generals Lee and Stonewall Jackson, who could safely rely on him to carry out the plans intrusted to him.

* * * Politically, Colonel Imboden was a staunch Democrat and a great admirer of Woodrow Wilson and his administration. He was always interested in the development of his State, his county, and especially his own home town, Ansted, where he lived fifty-one years. He was a student, well posted in ancient and modern history, a subscriber to the CONFEDERATE VETERAN, which he always read with great interest. He was a member of the Jeb Stuart Camp, U. C. V. and Commander of the Camp from 1913 until failing health caused him resignation. In faith he was a Presbyterian, and in early life gave his heart to God and became occupied in Church work. He was elected a ruling elder in 1867 and served faithfully in his duties in Kentucky and in Virginia. He was a Sunday school superintendent for forty-seven years. He was not a sectarian, loved all of God's children and joined heartily with them in advancing the kingdom.

At his funeral ministers of the Presbyterian, Methodist Episcopal Church, South, and Baptist lovingly joined in paying tribute to his memory, after which he was laid to rest, dressed in his Confederate gray, in a gray casket, at the Ansted Cemetery, near the tomb where lie the remains of the sainted mother of Stonewall Jackson. * * *

Weevils in the Wheat: Interviews with Virginia Ex-Slaves, "Interview with Mrs. Mary E. ——wsey," circa 1936–38

Mary ——wsey (her last name remains unclear) recalls her early life as a slave and how her master—William Marshall, who appeared in the 1860 census of Augusta County as the owner of eight slaves—sold one of her aunts during the war. During the Great Depression, the New Deal Works Projects Administration contracted unemployed writers and researchers to conduct interviews with ex-slaves like Mary from 1936 to 1938, recording firsthand accounts of the lives of enslaved men and women.

My mother belong to William H. and Susan Marshall. She was born 1835. Mary Grason she was—

* * * Yes they were good when you could work but when you got sick they sold you.

I had an aunt took fever in war time—left her feeble minded. She wandered off sometimes. They sold her. They knew at big house traders was coming—kept it from her. Answer was, when they broke news to her she said, she just as soon belong to one white man as another. Tole us all good by like she was going on a visit. We never saw her no more.

2. Franklin County

Franklin Repository, "Horrors at Andersonville," July 26, 1865

The Repository *reports on the appalling number of Union deaths that occurred at the Confederate-run prisoner-of-war camp at Andersonville, Georgia. Conditions were often poor in prisoner-of-war camps on both sides—particularly in the later years of the war—but the situation at Andersonville was by far the worst, where about 13,000 died. The great suffering endured by soldiers, here captured by the problems at Andersonville, informed much of how people in both the North and South chose to remember the war in the early years after 1865.*

A statement carefully prepared by one who had access to official documents, and who was a prisoner himself, has been made out, showing the number of deaths among Union prisoners at Andersonville, Georgia, from February, 1864, to February 1865. The grand total is twelve thousand, eight hundred and eighty four! The highest number of deaths in a single day was one hundred and twenty-seven, the date being August 23, 1864, at which time thirty-two thousand one hundred and ninety-three prisoners were confined there, being the highest number ever imprisoned at that point. The statement was prepared by Charles Lang, hospital steward of the 101st Pa. Regiment, who was captured at Plymouth, N. C. Governor Curtin, who has been eagerly seeking for a list of the Pennsylvania soldiers who died at Andersonville, has received the full roll of Pennsylvania victims from this considerate soldier, and it will be found on an inside page of our double-sheet to-day. The list will also be published in pamphlet form by Surgeon-General Phillips. We understand that the bodies of the victims cannot be removed until October, and before that time Governor Curtin will probably announce the best and most convenient way of securing such removals. The Governor is engaged at this time in an effort to procure full lists of Pennsylvania soldiers who died in other rebel prisons, and it is hoped that a list more or less complete will soon be ready for publication. A statement of those who died at Salisbury, N.C. will probably soon be made public.

Nothing has made so deep an impression on the heart of the loyal people as the treatment of Union soldiers who fell into the fiendish hands of the Southern military authorities. The evidence that a deliberate system of starvation was practised accumulates every day. * * *

* * * The history of the civilized world cannot furnish a more atrocious record than that made up for themselves by the leaders of the rebellion, and among our greatest reasons for thankfulness at the close of the war and the death of slavery, is the fact that such horrible outrages on humanity can never more be perpetrated. The oligarchic system which tended to sanction such indescribable cruelties has been ground to powder, not a vestige of it is left, and the entire world has cause to sing to a paean of rejoicing at its destruction.

Valley Spirit, "Democratic and Conservative Soldier's Club," June 17, 1868

The Valley Spirit *reports on the formation of a Democratic veterans' association in Franklin County, encouraging former Union soldiers who disapproved of the course of Reconstruction under Republican leadership to join. Debates in the North about why the war was fought, and what its legacy should be, often pitted Democrats against Republicans in the postwar years, as Republicans continued to dominate the federal government and Democrats attempted to regain their party's former political strength.*

In pursuance of a call, as announced in these columns, there was a large assemblage of our citizens and soldiers in the Court House on Thursday evening last. The Citizen's Band was present and entertained the audience with some well executed national airs—such as many of those present were accustomed to hear on the "tented field," and in the deadly strife and tug of war. Once more the gallant survivors of many a hard fought battle field met side by side, and they who shared the fight mean to share the peace they helped to make.

The meeting was organized by calling Dr. R. Rush Senseny to the chair, and Thomas Donavan as Secretary.

The Dr., to the great delight of all present, in stating the objects of the Meeting, delivered a brief, eloquent, earnest and highly appropriate speech, in very fine style, and was loudly applauded by the audience, showing their high appreciation thereby.

Capt. Geo. W. Skinner, being called upon, delivered in a clear, forcible and earnest style, a speech of some length, in which he hurled back the slander, so oft repeated, that there were no Democratic or conservative soldiers in the late war.

The speaker then pointed to the honored graves of our dead soldiers, on a hundred battle-fields and in a hundred grave-yards and cemeteries, to prove the fact that there were thousands, aye! hundreds of thousands of democratic soldiers in the late war, who proved their devotion to their country and sealed it with their blood.

The soldiers present this night, he said were living witnesses also to the fact that Franklin county did send out some democratic soldiers; and many obscure mounds, and many a marble monument on Southern soil shows that many never returned. This slander was refuted with some warmth by the Captain, and justly—for, as he says, it is a base and cowardly attempt of the Radicals to rob the honored braves of the blood-bought glory they now so richly merit. The Captain in vindicating the brave defenders of our national honor from this defamation, did it in a scholar-like and soldierly manner.

The issues involved in the present crisis of our country were dwelt upon, and clearly presented by the orator, and he demonstrated that the soldiers who fought for union and peace abroad, from a sense of duty, have the same duty still resting upon them to fight for the same ends at home—then with bayonets, now with ballots. He clearly defined what was the position of the Radical party in the reconstruction policy, by which, in times of peace, they have established a military despotism in violation of the constitution. That to-day, in this land, we have a despotism, more galling and absolute than was ever set up in the old world by the boldest tyrants that ever cursed or oppressed a people. We are, of course, unable in a brief notice to do the speech of the Captain anything like justice.

The Captain during the delivery of his remarks, was frequently, loudly and enthusiastically applauded by the audience, who heard him with much pleasure for the first time in this town.

The organization of the Club was effected, and about sixty-seven names were appended to the list. The list has since swelled to over one hundred. The meeting was more numerously attended by citizens and soldiers than was anticipated by the movers; and the interest manifested by the soldiers present, and the enthusiasm shown, were highly gratifying to all who love their country and their country's good.

There are still more soldiers who desire to join the Club. They are requested to report themselves to one of the officers who will take measures immediately to introduce them into full membership. The soldiers of this "neck of woods" didn't fight to make negroes their equals, or to establish military governments over any portion of the Union. All such are earnestly requested to join.

Valley Spirit, "A Monument to Our Dead," December 2, 1868

The Valley Spirit *draws attention to an address in the newspaper from a memorial association seeking funds to erect a monument to memorialize the Union dead. As in the South, Northerners formed groups and committees to tend the graves of veterans and establish markers to honor their sacrifices. Often these groups raised money and solicited donations in order to build memorials on the battlefields where many of those who died had been hastily buried in unmarked graves.*

Each one of our subscribers in the county will find to-day enclosed in his paper, an admirable address from a Committee appointed by the Monumental Association. We bespeak for it a careful perusal. It may draw tears from the eyes of many a father as it recalls to his mind sweet recollections of the noble boy who laid down his life for the Union. Or, it may carry a pang to the widow's heart as it calls up before her vision the manly form of him to whom she plighted her troth and who was found "dead upon the field of honor." Or, it may harrow up the feelings of orphaned children as they remember the kind father who was their protector and their guide and who fell beneath the starry banner upon "the perilous ridge of battle." Or, it may pierce the inmost soul of the widowed mother who has stood beside the open graves of both husband and only son, who breathed out their lives amid the rattle of musquetry and the roar of cannon. Or, it may to many, call up old friends of their youth to whom they were bound by golden cords that were ruptured by the mailed hand of war.

But whilst, in reading this address, sad memory may throw the light of other days around each and all of these, yet, into their disconsolate hearts must steal the consolation that their friends, who have fallen, bore the national ensign through many a bloody battle and came out without a stain upon their honor. The thought must, to some extent at least, alleviate their anguish that their beloved dead, when in life, performed their duty nobly on the march, in the camp and on the field of battle. And if this be consolation, what a thrill of joy should run through their hearts when they learn that, in recognition of the patriotism and heroism of our gallant soldiery, a grateful people propose to rear a monument to their memories! Here the opportunity is afforded to pay a lasting tribute to those who went from our county to rally round the flag wherever it should be borne.

How will their living friends and relatives respond?

Public Opinion, "The Burning of Chambersburg," August 2, 1870

The Public Opinion *marks the sixth anniversary of the burning of Chambersburg. The destruction of the town in 1864—the only one burned by the Confederates—remained a bitter memory for most in Franklin after the war, as the county attempted to rebuild the homes and businesses that Confederate raiders had destroyed.*

On Saturday last, the 30th of July, was the sixth anniversary of the burning of Chambersburg at the hands of the rebel incendiary, M'Causland, and his horde. On the morning of that day, just six years ago, twenty-six hundred rebel veterans (cavalry) occupied the out-posts of Chambersburg, in supporting distance of the four or five hundred delegated and commanded to apply the torch. Promiscuous plundering was indulged in by the soldiery from the hour of the possession of the place until the command was given for applying the torch. We were one of a party of eight—T. B. Kennedy, Wm. M'Lellan, J. M'D. Sharpe, Dr. J. C. Richards, W. H. McDowell, W. S. Everett and E. G. Etter, who were ordered under arrest, and held for the raising of five hundred thousand dollars in greenbacks, or one hundred thousand dollars in gold, failing to do which in fifteen minutes, we were to be taken to Richmond and the town burned. Dr. Richards informed the rebel general that it was out of the question to comply with the demand, when the general (Gilmore) said that we could "consider ourselves released for the present but to report again to head-quarters in twenty minutes." The party didn't report. The enemy were stationed and appropriated over the town with torch in hand, ready for the order to burn, which was now given. In fifteen minutes smoke might be seen arising from buildings in every direction, and in half an hour the heart of the town was one body of flames.

We shall not attempt a picture of the horrid scenes that followed. All here are familiar with these heart-sickening details. As a summary of what was done, we give the following from Dr. Schneck's history of the "Burning of Chambersburg." "Residences and places of business consumed, 278; various other buildings, 271; total number of buildings consumed, 549. In a few hours, the major portion of Chambersburg, its chief wealth and business, its capital and elegance, were devoured by a barbarous foe; three millions of property sacrificed; three thousand beings homeless and many of them penniless; and all without so much as a pretence that the citizens of the doomed town, or any of them had violated any accepted rule of civilized warfare. Such is the deliberate, voluntary record made by Gen. Earley a corps commander in the insurgent army."

B. J. Bolding,
"What of the Negro race?" 1906

B. J. Bolding, a black minister from Chambersburg, responds to a series of newspaper articles written by a white minister in Chambersburg, G. C. H. Hasskarl, who had questioned the humanity of African Americans by arguing that science proved that blacks were biologically inferior to whites. Bolding attempted to discredit Hasskarl's assertions and assumptions, at various points using the history of American slavery and the Civil War to illustrate his own arguments.

I have read carefully a series of articles under the caption, "What of the Negro Race?" by Rev. G. C. H. Hasskarl, D. C. L., pastor of the second Lutheran Church, Chambersburg, Pa. On behalf of my race and the great interest manifested in them by the good philanthropists of this country, I cannot refrain from replying to his argument from a scientific and ethnological standpoint.

* * * The Negro has proven that he has a *mind* that is capable of the highest developments. Give the Negro an equal chance in the race of life and remove the barriers of prejudice he will demonstrate his kingly power of mind. Has the Negro a soul? I answer unhesitatingly yes for it is the soul that *loves* and is loved. For mere genius we have respect, and bow before it, but we find there no bosom whereon to rest. In the soul, on the other hand, we can place confidence, and for it we can conceive affection, and look for its sympathy in return. The soul can sympathize both with the intellectual and what is apparent to the senses the heavenly and the earthly, the infinite and the finite because it is itself the marvelous central being which is the union of both. The divine "Logos" Jesus Christ, had a human soul so that he could have sympathy with *our* infirmities and draw us to Himself. It will not take a philosopher to discern that the Negro has will, sentiment or perception. The faculties of the soul are delineated in Dr. Hasskarl's argument. If the Negro has these elements or attributes of the soul he must according to logic have a soul. I believe that souls are created. "Every man is an eternal individuality framed in the image of God, and bears within *himself* the possibility of eternal life in bliss; he is not merely a continuing link in the long series of the human race, a repetition of what has gone before with inherited properties, but moreover at the same time a fresh point of commencement in this series." When the chains of slavery clanked on our ankles and the cry of mothers and fathers could be heard [in] the South the slaveowner allowed religious instruction, (though meager), to be given their slaves. They believed that the Negro had a soul and some owners felt it their duty to teach them there was a God and they had souls to save. They were taught that while the body belongs to me your owner, your soul belongs to God and is destined for heaven or hell.

It is a matter of little concern to me whether I am a descendant of Adam or no, I know that I live, move, feel and enjoy all the advantages of the soul. But when a philosopher, and minister of the gospel strikes at my people I cannot keep silent. * * *

* * * Is the Negro the subject of State? asked Dr. Hasskarl. I answer in the negative. There was a time when he was a subject of the State. He was held as a slave. You remember the struggle between the North and South in regard to slavery. The *civil war was not fought to free Negroes.* But rather to preserve the Union and if the Union could have been preserved without emancipating the Negro we would still be in chains and sold from the auction block. God who rules the destiny of men as well as of things, put it into the hearts of the President of the United States and a part of his cabinet and others "to let my people go." Too much praise can never be given to the great Abolitionists of bygone days for agitating and making sentiment that caused the Negro as a slave to become a man. According to the rights invested by the amendments to the Constitution of this country the Negro is not a subject of the State. * * *

* * * From Ethnological, Philological, Exegetical research I am forced to conclude that the Negro is a (1) human being, (2) he has a soul, (3) he is made of same blood as other men, (4) he is not subject of church or state, (5) he is capable of the highest intellectual development, (6) he is a part of the great Hametic race, a descendant of Adam by the line of Noah.

Kauffman's Progressive News, "Reminiscences of the Underground Railroad," May 7, 1915

Horace G. Kauffman, a former resident of Greencastle, Franklin County, writes an account of his family's involvement in the underground railroad in the years before and during the Civil War. Many postwar Northerners, mostly Republicans, recalled with pride the role they had played in opposing Southern slavery, even though abolitionists like Kauffman represented a very small percentage of the Northern population at the time of the Civil War.

Oregon, Illinois, April 28, 1915.

To the Editor:—I have read with interest the reminiscences of a late contributor to the NEWS, wherein our father, the late John

Kauffman, is referred to as having been an agent on the Underground Railroad in the years immediately preceding and during the Civil War. * * * I am induced to give an item from recollections of my own of that period of sectional bitterness, political upheaval and fratricidal war, when even as a lad of tender years I had experiences which are as well remembered after the lapse of half a century as if they had occurred only a few days ago.

Greencastle was the first station on the Underground Railroad in that neighborhood in a free state, being but four miles north of the historic boundary between the North and the South—"that crimson scar of honor across the brow of our country which divides the land of cold bread from that of hot biscuit." The town was for that reason a place of importance and inspiration to the fugitives. Hope rose within them as they found themselves in the coveted North, nor did Greencastle disappoint them. The sentiments of a Randolph, a Calhoun, or a Toombs, however they grew and flourished in the Halls of Congress, ninety miles away, fell upon stony ground for the most part in the district represented at Washington by the great commoner, Thaddeus Stevens. And why should not the Cumberland Valley have been known for its abolitionists—its people the descendants of colonists from two of the most liberty-loving countries of Europe, Scotland and Switzerland? Greencastle's roll of honor, inscribed here from memory, includes the names of Major John Rowe, George W. Zeigler, William Ward, John Wilhelm, Thomas Pauling, John Kauffman, William Ward, in 1859, acted as guide from Greencastle to Harpers Ferry for John Brown of Ossowatomine, when that brave, though mistaken, champion of the slaves rested in Greencastle on his way south with his pasty and their wagons.

To act as an agent of the Underground Railroad was to risk one's peace and safety, since giving aid to runaway slaves was in violation of the Fugitive Slave Law, of 1850. This enactment was never respected by the more radical of the Abolitionists, who chose conscience as their guide, and which they continued to follow even when in his first inaugural address the enforcement of the obnoxious law was recommended by Mr. Lincoln—the recommendation which drew upon Mr. Lincoln from Wendell Phillips the famous words of opprobrium, "the slave-hound of Illinois."

* * * Political feeling was intense and bitter. In 1854, father left the Whigs and joined the newly-organized Republican party, opposed to the extension of slavery. He was also an Abolitionist. He became therefore, in the vernacular of the day, a "black-Republican," in favor of "nigger equality," and had put to him that clinching question believed to triumphantly dispose of any abolitionist's argument, to-wit, "Do you want your daughter to marry a nigger?"

My first recollection of politics is in that connection, and pertains to an incident which occurred in 1862, I when I was seven years of age. Father had bought the goods for a suit of clothes for me, and took me with him to a tailor to have my measure taken preparatory to cutting out the pattern. The tailor in this instance was a pro-slavery Democrat, jocular, hardshell and complacent, to whom the agitation of the question of abolishing slavery was most objectionable in that it aimed to destroy an existing legal institution of long standing upheld by a majority of the party of his political faith. He had heard father denounce "the league with death and covenant with hell," while not sparing pro-slavery leaders, including President Buchanan. As he stood behind me and drew the measuring tape from my shoulder to my wrist, he took a lock of my hair between his thumb and finger and pulling it gently, said, "Do you know that your hair is getting kinky?" Instantly, I was aflame, of course. I answered, "My hair is a bit curly, but it is not kinky, and it will never be, either."

The pro-slavery joker laughed, enjoying my ire, but he was unintentionally assisting then and there in the making of another Republican and Abolitionist. He himself was joined to his idols, even the convulsion of war passing over him without clearing his mental atmosphere.

Horace G. Kauffman

Kauffman's Progressive News, "The Election of Lincoln," June 25, 1920

Kauffman's Progressive News *recounts how word of Abraham Lincoln's election as president in 1860 first reached Franklin County, and how it then spread from Chambersburg to Greencastle. Though highly criticized during the war itself, even by members of his own party, Lincoln became the great hero of the Civil War in the minds of many Northerners and black Southerners during the postwar era.*

The Election of Lincoln: How the News Came to Greencastle and by Whom Brought on a C. V. R. R. Hand Car from Chambersburg

* * * It is always with interest that we note anything associated or connected with the life of Abraham Lincoln. He was not only the highest and best type of American manhood but one hundred per cent American. His simple life brought him close to the people. It is an inspiration for every American boy however humble his home in entering upon or fighting the battle of life to remember and compare advantages with Lincoln. Few will find the obstruction, such as lay in his path, but many will be the advantages favorable to the young of this day and generation.

His life of earnest endeavor and never tiring will to accomplish something in life worth the effort, overcome his lack of education, admitted him to the bar, brought him face to face in a joint discussion with Douglass, from his own state, Illinois, and introduced him to the people of the United States, which secured him the nomination for president in 1860. To know Lincoln was to be his friend.

His was the second nomination by the Republican party. Feeling ran high. The Democratic party was in power and the South was in the saddle. Every energy of the Republican party was mustered for victory and when it came Greencastle like all other sections of the country was prepared to give it promptly to the people with the least loss of time.

In order to do so, and as the towns telegraph service was not so perfect as today, Jacob Stover, David Ziegler, Samuel Illgenfritz, Daniel C. Stover and Michael McHogan, secured the C. V. S. R.

hand car and worked their way to Chambersburg in time to be present and hear the election returns as they came into the office of the late Colonel McClure, who was state chairman of the Republican party, where they were given out to the crowd that had assembled both on the in and outside. According to Uncle Jacob's story the returns were slow in coming in but finally the tick of the instrument was heard that relieved the wires that carried the news which formed the basis of Lincoln's election. "New York City twenty-five thousand democratic.," read the telegram. Colonel McClure sprung to his feet and said; "That insures the election of Lincoln. The Republicans will come to Harlam river with from seventy-five to a hundred thousand of a majority." Three cheers for Lincoln, and before the excitement had died down every piece of furniture in the office was broken to pieces.

As the news came in it proved the wisdom of his judgment and when the returns assured the election of Lincoln beyond all question of doubt the hand car was again pressed into service and with all speed rushed to Greencastle to make known the result, which was awaited in suspense by the people. On arriving in Greencastle the news of Lincoln's election was made known and a crowd soon assembled among which was Doctor Davison in his night clothes. There was great rejoicing and a demonstration followed.

X
Conflicting Scholarship

How Different from Each Other Were the Antebellum North and South?

Edward Pessen

How different from each other were the North and South before the Civil War? Recent work by historians of antebellum America throws interesting new light on this old question. * * *

The terms "North" and "South" are, of course, figures of speech that distort and oversimplify a complex reality, implying homogeneity in geographical sections that, in fact, were highly variegated. Each section embraced a variety of regions and communities that were dissimilar in climatic, topographical, demographic, and social characteristics. If, as Bennett H. Wall has written, "there never has been the 'one' South described by many historians," neither has there been the one North. Historians who have compared the antebellum South and North without referring to the diversity of each have not necessarily been unaware of this diversity. Their premise, in speaking of the North and South, is that the Mason-Dixon line divided two distinctive civilizations, the basic similarities within each of which transcended its internal differences.

The modern discussion is a continuation of a scholarly controversy that has engaged some of the giants of the American historical profession. Charles A. Beard, Ulrich B. Phillips, Allan Nevins, David M. Potter, C. Vann Woodward, and other scholars of stature have been drawn to the theme because it is inextricably related to perhaps the most fascinating of all questions in American history: the causes of the Civil War. Many historians attribute that "irrepressible conflict" to the fundamental differences between the two civilizations that were parties to it. Even those scholars who have played down the role of sectional differences in bringing on the war have found themselves unable to avoid comparing the ways of life and thought of the two belligerents.

Unsurprisingly, the discussion has produced a variety of interpretations. Some scholars have emphasized the similarities of the North and South, a much greater number have stressed their dissimilarities, and others have judiciously alluded to their significant likenesses—"commonalities," in Potter's terminology—and unlikenesses. The greater popularity, among scholars and laity alike, of comparisons that emphasize differences is doubtless due, in part, to the fact that the war heightened our perceptions of those supposedly irreconcilable differences and, in part, to the fact that several dissimilarities were so striking, so unarguable, so obviously significant. While much of the scholarly controversy has concerned subtle sectional distinctions, whether in values, ideals, or other complex intangibles that might be read one way or the other, depending on the predilections of the interpreter, other disparities transcend subjectivity, based as they are on hard, quantifiable evidence.

Here were two sections containing roughly equal areas for human settlement. Yet on the eve of the Civil War the population of the North was more than 50 percent greater than that of the South. The most dramatic disparity concerned racial balance: roughly one-quarter of a million Northern blacks comprised slightly more than 1 percent of the Northern population; the more than four million blacks in the South constituted one-third of the Southern population. And almost 95 percent of Southern blacks were slaves. Although the value of agricultural products in the two sections was almost equal, Northern superiority in manufactures, railroad mileage, and commercial profits was overwhelming, far surpassing the Northern advantage in population. Similarly, Northern urban development outdistanced Southern, whether measured by the number of cities or by the size and proportions of the population within them. What did these and other, harder to measure, differences signify? To what extent were they balanced out by important sectional similarities? These are among the questions this essay will consider.

In comparing the great antebellum sections, it is useful to remember that all powerful, complex, and viable contemporaneous societies are likely to converge or be similar in some respects, dissimilar in others. It would be lovely were we able to estimate precisely the relative significance of the various criteria of comparison, the points at which similarities or differences become critical, and the nature of the balance between likenesses and unlikenesses that would justify appraising two societies as "essentially" different or similar. Alas, we cannot. A society or civilization is a complex Gestalt. The subtle reciprocity binding together its elements cannot be understood by mechanically attempting to weigh the significance of each of these elements and then adding up the total. The impossibility of contriving a simplistic calculus for measuring societies does not, of course, mean that a sensible comparison is impossible. It means only that such a comparison will inevitably be subjective and serve, at best, as a point of departure to those who evaluate the evidence differently.

A comprehensive comparison of the two sections would overlook nothing, not even the weather, which, according to Phillips, "has been the chief agency in making the South distinctive." In the space available here I shall focus on what our sociological friends might call three social indicators: (1) the economy, (2) the social structure, and (3) politics and power.[1] In selecting these matters for examination, I do not mean to suggest that they are more important than values, ideals, the life of the mind, or any number of other features of antebellum life. Tangible phenomena may be easier to measure than intangible, but they offer no better clue to the essential character of a place and a people. I emphasize economic, social, and political themes because all of them are clearly important, the evidence on them is substantial, and each has recently been re-examined to interesting effect.

* * * Gathering from the manuscript census schedules, probate inventories, and tax assessors' reports statistically valid samples or, in some cases, evidence on every family in the community under

---

[1] The section on the economy has been omitted.

study, modern scholars have been able to arrange the antebellum Southern and Northern populations on a wealth-holding scale. While it is close to a statistical inevitability that the distribution of wealth in the South and North would not be precisely the same, the most striking feature of the evidence is how similarly wealth was distributed—or maldistributed—in the two sections.

On the eve of the Civil War one-half of the free adult males in both the South and the North held less than 1 percent of the real and personal property. In contrast, the richest 1 percent owned 27 percent of the wealth. Turning from the remarkable similarity in sectional patterns of wealthholding at the bottom and the very top, the richest 5 to 10 percent of propertyowners controlled a somewhat greater share of the South's wealth, while what might be called the upper middle deciles (those below the top tenth) held a slightly smaller share in the North. The South also came close to monopolizing wealthy counties, the per capita wealth of which was $4,000 or more and, despite its smaller population, the South, according to the 1860 census, contained almost two-thirds of those persons in the nation whose worth was at least $110,000. According to Lee Soltow, the leading student of this evidence, these sectional disparities "could be attributed almost entirely to slave values. . . . If one could eliminate slave market value from the distribution of wealth in 1860 . . . , the inequality levels in the North and South were similar."

In view of the centrality of slavery to the antebellum South, it is idle to speak of "eliminating the market value" of slaves from the sectional comparison. Northern free labor, rural and industrial, also represented a form of "sectional wealth," if a much overlooked form. Although as individual human beings they did not add to their own private wealth or to the wealth of the employers they served, their labor created wealth for themselves and for these same capitalists at rates of productivity that, I believe, even Robert W. Fogel and Stanley L. Engerman would concede compared favorably with the rates of the most efficient slaves. In other words, the North had access to a form of wealth, free labor, that was roughly as valuable per capita as was slave wealth, however absent this Northern wealth was from the reports prepared by census takers and assessors. Given the known habits of these officials to overlook small property holdings—precisely the kind of holdings that would have been owned by Northern working people—and to accept as true the lies people swore to as to their worth, it is likely that the fairly substantial cumulative wealth owned by small farmers and modest wage earners was almost entirely omitted from the wealth equation. Such groups were far more numerous in the North than in the South. Had slaves been treated as part of the potential property-owning Southern population to which they actually belonged, instead of being treated as property pure and simple, the total wealth of the antebellum South would have been diminished by several billion dollars: the product of multiplying the number of slaves by the average market price of almost $1,000 per slave. The addition of nearly four million very poor black people to the number of potential propertyowners in the South would have increased its rate of inequality (and the Gini coefficient of concentration that measures it), although not everywhere to the same extent.

Wealth in both sections was distributed more equally—perhaps the more apt phrase is less unequally—in the countryside than in towns and cities. While the rural North has been less intensively investigated than its Southern counterpart, enough research has been completed to disclose that the North was hardly a haven of egalitarian distribution of property. Rural Wisconsin (which had a Gini coefficient of inequality as high as that of antebellum Texas), the Michigan frontier, and northwestern New York State were centers of inequality and poverty. At mid-century, the proportion of white men who owned land in any amount was substantially lower in the Northwest than in the South. The percentage of free males owning land in the North as a whole was slightly smaller than in the South. Owing to the absence of slaves and to the relative paucity of very large farms, wealth was somewhat less unequally distributed in the rural North than in the South.

In investigating the distribution of wealth in the antebellum rural South, scholars have probed data on different states, counties, and regions. The patterns throughout are remarkably similar, whether for wealth in general, land and real estate, or personal and slave property. Accentuating the maldistribution of landed wealth—whether in Alabama, Mississippi, Louisiana, Texas, the "cotton South," or the agricultural South as a whole—was a fact of life that the Owsley school neglected: the dollar value per acre of large farms owned by slave-owning planters was substantially greater than the value per acre of the small farm. And yet, regardless of the nature of the soil or the proportion of large farms in a given region, the rates of wealth concentration were remarkably similar as well as constant during the decades before the war. Paralleling the recent finding that in antebellum Texas, no matter what the differences were "in climate, soil, and extent of settlement, the most striking fact is . . . the high degree of concentration in wealth-holding across all the regions," another recent study reports no great differences in "the degree of inequality" between the cotton South and the other "major agricultural regions" of grain, tobacco, sugar, and rice production in 1860.

The distribution of slave wealth closely followed the pattern of other forms of Southern wealth. During the decade before the war, slaveownership was confined to between 20 and 25 percent of white families, and maldistribution of this form of property was the rule within the slave-owning population. Half of all slaveowners owned five or fewer slaves, with only one-tenth owning the twenty or more slaves that by Ulrich B. Phillips's definition made them "planters." Less than one-half of 1 percent owned one hundred or more slaves. As with other forms of wealth, the concentration of slave wealth increased slightly between 1850 and 1860.

While the South had long lagged behind the North in urban development, recent scholarship has unearthed evidence that Southern cities grew at a remarkable rate during the antebellum decades. If the Southern rate of urban expansion still did not match the Northern quantitatively, Southern cities, old and new, were qualitatively not unlike their Northern counterparts. Antebellum cities in all latitudes were amazingly similar in the roles they played in the political, administrative, financial, economic, artistic, and intellectual affairs of their regions. Antebellum cities were also alike in the types of men who ran them, in the underlying social philosophies guiding those men, and in their "social configurations." Not the least of the similarities of cities in both great sections was in their distribution of wealth. * * *

Nor do sectional rates of vertical mobility appear to have been much different. In 1856 Cassius M. Clay told an Ohio audience that "the northern laboring man could, and frequently did, rise above the condition [into] which he was born to the first rank of society and wealth," but he "never knew such an instance in the South." Recently unearthed evidence on the social origins of the men in the "first rank" does not sustain Clay's surmise, so popular with contemporary yeasayers. In the South, "increasing barriers to slaveownership resulting from higher slave prices and the growing concentration of wealth" left "lesser planters," not to mention laboring men, with their "aspiration thwarted." And in the North—whether in Wayne County (Michigan), Newport, Stonington, small towns in Massachusetts, Chicago, and Brooklyn, or the great cities of New York, Boston, and Philadelphia—eminent and rich men of humble birth were a rarity. Evidence on the more likely movement from a lower social position to an adjacent one, rather than to the very top, remains in pitifully short supply. In antebellum Philadelphia, small New England counties, and rural Georgia, even the modest movement from one plebian level to another appears to have seldom occurred. * * *

Carl Degler has recently observed that Southern society "differed from northern in that the social hierarchy culminated in the planter, not the industrialist." At mid-century, great Northern fortunes, in fact, owed more to commerce and finance than to manufacturing. What is perhaps more important is that a sharply differentiated social hierarchy obtained in both sections. In Degler's phrase, planter status was "the ideal to which other white southerners aspired." A good case can be made for the equally magnetic attraction that exalted merchant status had for Northerners. If the fragmentary evidence on Virginia, Georgia, and the Carolinas, which Jane H. Pease has so effectively exploited, is any indication, then great planters lived less sybaritically and consumed less conspicuously than historians have previously thought. If Philip Hone's marvelous diary—two dozen full-to-the-brim volumes of life among the swells during the antebellum decades—has broader implication, then the Northeastern social and economic elite commanded a lifestyle of an elegance and costliness that, among other things, proved irresistably attractive to the aristocratic Southerners who graced Hone's table, pursued diversion with other members of Hone's set, and married into its families—the Gardiners, Coolidges, Coldens, Bayards, Gouverneurs, and Kortrights.

That the social structures of the antebellum South and North were in some important respects similar does not, of course, make them carbon copies of one another. In this as in other respects the chief difference between the sections was that one of them harbored a huge class of enslaved blacks. John C. Calhoun, James H. Hammond, George Fitzhugh, and other influential Southern champions of white supremacy never ceased reminding their antebellum audiences, therefore, that in the South "the two great divisions of society [were] not the rich and the poor, but white and black, and all the former, the poor as well as the rich, belong to the upper classes." Several historians have recently agreed that great planters and small white farmers in the South shared common interests, for all the disparity in their condition. The interests of the different social classes will be considered in the discussion of influence and power that follows. Whatever these interests may have been, Southern whites, rural and urban, lived as did Northerners—in a stratified society marked by great inequalities in status, material condition, and opportunity. * * *

By mid-century the American political system was everywhere formally democratic. Notorious exceptions to and limitations on democracy persisted, but they persisted in both North and South and for largely the same reasons. If blacks could not vote in the Old South, with rare exceptions neither could they vote in the Old North, where they were barred by statute, subterfuge, custom, and intimidation. The South initiated the movement to limit the powers and terms of office of the judiciary and substitute popular elections for the appointment of judges. When Fletcher M. Green reminded us a generation ago that antebellum Southern states created new, and modified old, constitutions that were fully as democratic as those in Northern states, he concluded that by this "progressive expansion in the application of the doctrine of political equality . . . , the aristocratic planter class had been shorn of its political power." Power, he claimed, had now been transferred to "the great mass of whites." As Green's critics were quick to point out, popular suffrage and theoretical rights to hold office are not synonomous with popular power. Yet these are not empty or hollow rights. That they have often been made so testifies not to their insignificance but rather to the importance of the larger context in which democratic political gains are registered. It remains neither a small matter nor a small similarity that on the constitutional level the antebellum North and South were similarly democratic and republican. * * *

Abundant data have been accumulated on the occupations, wealth and property ownership, church affiliations, education, and other social indicators not only of antebellum officeholders in several dozen cities equally divided between South and North and in counties in every Southern state but also of state officials in all of the Southern and most of the Northern states and of Congressmen from most of the states in the Union. The resultant picture inevitably is not uniform. Humble county and town officials, for example, were less likely to be drawn from the highest levels of wealth and from the most prestigious occupations than were men who occupied more exalted state and federal positions. Aldermen and councilmen usually did not match the mayor either in wealth or in family prestige. But the relatively slight social and economic differences found between men at different levels of government or between men nominated by the parties that dominated American politics from the 1830s to the 1850s were not differences between the North and South. In the South as in the North, men similar in their dissimilarity to their constituencies held office and exercised behind-the-scenes influence. In contrast to the small farmers, indigents, laborers, artisans, clerks, and shopkeepers—the men of little or no property who constituted the great majority of the antebellum population—the men who held office and controlled the affairs of the major parties were everywhere lawyers, merchants, businessmen, and relatively large property owners. In the South they were inordinately men who owned slaves and owned them in unusually large numbers. It may well be that a society that is stratified economically and socially will confer leadership on those who have what Robert A. Dahl has called substantial material "advantages." It is not clear that this is an iron law. What is clear is that the Old South and the North awarded leadership to precisely such men.

More important than the social and economic backgrounds of political leaders are their public behavior and the ideologies or "world views" underlying this behavior. Not that the thinking or action of powerful men is totally unaffected by their material circumstances. But, in view of the complexity of any individual's ideology and of the diverse elements that help shape it, the effect of these circumstances cannot be assumed and is likely to vary from one individual to another. Although the political philosophies of men do not lend themselves to quantitative or precise measurement, the burden of recent scholarship is that most Southern and Northern political activists were similarly ambitious for worldly success, opportunistic, materialistic, and disinclined to disturb their societies' social arrangements. Men with values such as these were ideally suited to lead the great pragmatic parties that dominated antebellum politics.

Many parties flashed across the American political horizon during the antebellum decades. That the Antimasonic Party, the Liberty Party, and the Free Soil Party almost entirely bypassed the South is an important difference between the sections. The South was not hospitable to organized political dissent, particularly dissent hostile to the expansion of slavery. These parties were small and ephemeral organizations whose leverage stemmed not so much from any great voting support they were able to command as from the nearly equal strength in both sections of the great major parties, the Democrats and the Whigs. Whoever would evaluate the actions of those who held executive or legislative office in antebellum America must, almost invariably, evaluate Whigs or Democrats—at least until the mid-1850s, when a new party emerged during the great controversy over the extension of slavery in the territories.

The Democrats and Whigs were national parties drawing their leaders and followers from both sections. They could usually count on intersectional support for the national tickets they presented quadrennially to the nation at large. Interestingly, the presidency—whether occupied by Southerners Jackson, Tyler, Polk, and Taylor and the Southern-born Harrison or Northerners Van Buren, Fillmore, Pierce, and Buchanan—was in the 1830s, 1840s, and 1850s in the hands of Whigs and Democrats who displayed great sensitivity toward the political and economic interests of the slaveowning South. In the 1840s Congressmen voted not by region as Northerners or Southerners but primarily as Whigs and Democrats. Party rather than sectional interest prevailed in the roll calls on most issues reaching the national political agenda. In the 1850s, as Thomas B. Alexander has reported, "forces greater than party discipline . . . were evidently at work . . . , forcing party to yield to section on a definable number of issues." Yet, even in the 1850s, "both major parties maintained a high level of cohesion and inter-sectional comity" with regard to the range of issues not bearing on slavery and its right to expansion.

The great national issues of antebellum politics, culminating as they did in Sumter and the ensuing war, were of transcendant importance to Americans. A good case can nonetheless be made that local and state politics touched the lives of people more often and more directly than did national politics, particularly during an era when the men in the nation's capital were inclined to treat laissez faire as an article of faith. State governments in North and South, by contrast, engaged in vigorous regulation of a wide range of economic activities. Local governments taxed citizens and, if with limited effectiveness, sought to provide for their safety, regulate their markets and many of their business activities, look after the poor, maintain public health, improve local thoroughfares, dispose of waste, pump in water, light up the dark, and furnish some minimal cultural amenities through the exercise of powers that characteristically had been granted by state government. States chartered banks, transportation companies, and other forms of business enterprise, determined the scope of such charters, themselves engaged in business, disposed of land, and regulated local communities. The great question is how did the actual operations of local and state governments in the North and South compare during the antebellum decades.

Antebellum state government was almost invariably controlled by either Whigs or Democrats. The major parties were essentially state parties, bound together in the most loosely organized national confederations. Citizens divided not by geographical section but by party preference within each state. The parties were in all latitudes characteristically controlled by tight groups of insiders that sometimes monopolized power, sometimes shared it with rival factions, in the one case as in the other controlling nominations and conventions, hammering out policy, disseminating and publicizing the party line, organizing the faithful to support it, enforcing strict discipline, and punishing those who dared challenge either the policies or the tactics pursued by the leadership. While party policies could conceivably have been infused with the noble principles proclaimed in party rhetoric, such infusion rarely appears to have been the case. The "Albany Regency," the "Richmond Junto," the "Bourbon Dynasty" of Arkansas, and similar cliques in control elsewhere have been described as realists rather than idealists.

To call attention to the gulf between the pronouncements and the actions of antebellum state political leaders is not to indulge in cynicism but simply to report the facts as historians have recorded and interpreted them. J. Mills Thornton's recent description of antebellum Alabama's political leaders as demagogues who felt a "secret contempt for the voters" they publicly extolled and whose "primary function was to gain as many offices as possible for the party faithful" is not unlike historians' characterizations of other leaders in other states, both in the North and in the South. In New York as in Alabama, in Michigan as in Georgia, in Pennsylvania as in Mississippi, in Illinois as in Missouri, the "compelling aim" of the major parties and the groups that ran them appears to have been "to get control of the existing machinery of government" and to dispense to party loyalists the jobs that attended electoral success. While seemingly preoccupied with patronage and gerrymandering or with keeping from the agenda of state governments issues that posed a "threat to property and the social order or which threatened . . . stability," the major parties did not sidestep altogether economic, social, and cultural issues of some moment. The most germane feature of roll call evidence on such issues is how little there is to choose between legislative voting patterns in the South and the North. * * *

Power is not, of course, confined to control of government. Control over banks, credit, capital, communications, and voluntary associations, which in an era of laissez faire often exercised more influence than did public authorities over education and culture, crime and punishment, social welfare and poverty, gave to those who had it a power that was barely matched by those who held the reins of government. The burden of recent research is that small social and economic elites exercised a degree of control over the most important institutions in the antebellum North that bears close resemblance to the great power attributed to the great planter-slaveowners by William E. Dodd a half century ago and by Eugene D. Genovese more recently. Influential voluntary associations and financial institutions appear to have been run by similarly atypical sorts on both sides of the Mason-Dixon line.

Shortly after secession, Governor Joseph E. Brown told the Georgia legislature that in the South the "whole social system is one of perfect homogeneity of interest, where every class is interested in sustaining the interest of every other class." Numerous Southerners agreed with him, and many scholars concur. In their failure to challenge planter supremacy, small farmers—slaveowners and non-slaveowners alike—ostensibly demonstrated the unique identity of interest that was said to bind all whites together in the antebellum South. The interest of a group is a normative term, known only to God (and perhaps to Rousseau in his capacity as authority on the General Will), in contrast to its perceived interests, as stated in its words and implicit in its actions. There are, therefore, as many interpretations of the "true interests" of Southern—or, for that matter, of Northern—small farmers as there are historians writing on the subject. The South's large enslaved black population doubtless affected the perceptions of all Southern whites, if in complex and unmeasurable ways. Recent research indicates that poorer and nonslave-owning Southern whites were, nevertheless, sensitive enough to their own social and economic deprivation to oppose their social superiors on secession and other important matters. Whether the acquiescence of the mass of antebellum Northerners in their inferior social and economic condition was in their own interest will be decided differently by conservative, reformist, and radical historians. Our admittedly insubstantial evidence on the issue suggests that the degree of social harmony coexisting with subtle underlying social tensions was, racial matters apart, not much different in the North and the South.

* * *

Having examined economic developments, social structure, and politics and power in the antebellum sections, let me now return to the question of capitalism in the Old South. Several historians have recently argued that Southern planters constituted a "seigneurial" class presiding over a "pseudocapitalistic" society, a class whose "world view" ostensibly set them "apart from the mainstream of capitalist civilization." By this analysis, the Old South, though influenced by modern capitalism, belonged (as do early modern India and Saudi Arabia, among others) to the category of "premodern" societies that have been the economic and political dependencies of the dynamic industrial world that exploits them. The antebellum South's banking, commercial, and credit institutions did not in this view manifest the section's own capitalistic development so much as they served to facilitate the South's exploitation by the "capitalistic world market." This argument can be accepted uncritically only by accepting Eugene D. Genovese, Barrington Moore, Jr., and Raimondi Luraghi as the arbiters and interpreters of what represents "every normal feature of capitalism."

Capitalism is not a rigid system governed by uniform economic practices, let alone inflexible definitions. The economy of the antebellum United States, like capitalistic economies in Victorian England and other nations, was composed of diverse elements, each playing a part in a geographical and functional division of labor within the larger society. As Lewis C. Gray and Thomas P. Govan long ago and other scholars more recently have observed, Southern planters had the attitudes and goals and were guided by the classic practices of capitalistic businessmen. The antiurbanism and antimaterialism that Genovese has attributed to the great planters is unconvincing because thinly documented and contradicted by much other evidence. Some people, including planters themselves, may have likened the planter class to a seigneurial aristocracy. Unlike the lords of the textbook manor, however, Southern planters depended heavily on outside trade, participated enthusiastically in a money economy, and sought continuously to expand their operations and their capital. Marx once said that the limits of the serf's exploitation were determined by the walls of the lord's stomach. The limits of the slave's exploitation were determined by the expanding walls of the world cotton market.

That slavery is not the classic labor system associated with a Marxist definition of capitalism is, of course, true. The problem with Marx as Pundit of capitalism, for all the undeniable brilliance of his interpretation, is that he was, as he conceded, more interested in changing the system than in explaining it. Those of us content with merely understanding so complex a phenomenon as capitalism know that, whether in its labor system or in other respects, it is a flexible and constantly shifting order, susceptible of diverse definitions. The Southern economy did differ in important respects from the Northern, developing special interests of its own. Yet, far from being in any sense members of a colony or dependency of the North, the Southern upper classes enjoyed close ties with the Northern capitalists who were, in a sense, their business partners. The South was an integral component of a wealthy and dynamic national economy, no part of which conformed perfectly to a textbook definition of pure capitalism. In part because of the central place in that economy of its great export crop, cotton, the South from the 1820s to the 1860s exerted a degree of influence over the nation's domestic and foreign policies that was barely equalled by the antebellum North. India within the Empire indeed! The South's political system of republicanism and limited democracy, like its hierarchical social structure, conformed closely to the prevailing arrangements in the North, as they also did to the classic features of a capitalistic order.

The striking similarities of the two antebellum sections of the nation neither erase their equally striking dissimilarities nor detract from the significance of these dissimilarities. Whether in climate, diet, work habits, uses of leisure, speech and diction, health and disease, mood, habits, ideals, self-image, or labor systems, profound differences separated the antebellum North and South. One suspects that antebellum Americans regarded these matters as the vital stuff of life. The point need not be labored that a society, one-third of whose members were slaves (and slaves of a distinctive "race"), is most unlike a society of free men and women. An essay focusing on these rather than on the themes emphasized here would highlight the vital disparities between the antebellum South and North. And yet the striking dissimilarities of the two antebellum sections do not erase their equally striking similarities, nor do they detract from the significance of these similarities.

The antebellum North and South were far more alike than the conventional scholarly wisdom has led us to believe. Beguiled by the charming version of Northern society and politics composed by

Tocqueville, the young Marx, and other influential antebellum commentators, historians have until recently believed that the Northern social structure was far more egalitarian and offered far greater opportunity for upward social movement than did its Southern counterpart and that white men of humble position had far more power in the Old North than they did in the Old South. In disclosing that the reality of the antebellum North fell far short of the egalitarian ideal, modern studies of social structure sharply narrow the gulf between the antebellum North and South. Without being replicas of one another, both sections were relatively rich, powerful, aggressive, and assertive communities, socially stratified and governed by equally—and disconcertingly—oligarchic internal arrangements. That they were drawn into the most terrible of all American wars may have been due, as is often the case when great powers fight, as much to their similarities as to their differences. The war owed more, I believe, to the inevitably opposed but similarly selfish interests—or perceived interests—of North and South than to differences in their cultures and institutions.

It is a commonplace in the history of international politics that nations and societies quite similar to one another in their political, social, and economic arrangements have nevertheless gone to war, while nations profoundly different from one another in their laws of property or their fundamental moral and philosophical beliefs have managed to remain at peace. The Peloponnesian War, which, like the American Civil War, was a bitter and protracted struggle between two branches of the same people whose societies were in vital respects dissimilar from one another, appears to have owed little to these differences. In Thucydides' great account, Athens and the Athenians were profoundly unlike Sparta and the Lacedæmonians, whether in "national" character, wealth, economic life, ideals and values, system of justice, attitudes toward freedom, or lifestyle. But to Thucydides, as to the leading spokesmen for the two sides, these dissimilarities were one thing, the causes of the war quite another. Athens and Sparta fell out primarily because both were great imperial powers. "The real cause of the war," concluded Thucydides, "was formally . . . kept out of sight. The growth of the power of Athens and the alarm which this inspired in Lacedæmon, made war inevitable." None of this is to say that sectional differences had no influence whatever on the actions of those influential men that in April 1861 culminated in the outbreak of the American Civil War. The point rather is that, insofar as the Peloponnesian War throws any light whatever on the matter, wars between strikingly dissimilar antagonists break out not necessarily because of their differences, important as these are, but because of their equally significant similarities.

Late in the Civil War, William King of Cobb County, Georgia, reported that invading Union officers had told him, "We are one people, [with] the same language, habits, and religion, and ought to be one people." The officers might have added that on the spiritual plane Southerners shared with Northerners many ideals and aspirations and had contributed heavily to those historical experiences the memory and symbols of which tie a people together as a nation. For all of their distinctiveness, the Old South and North were complementary elements in an American society that was everywhere primarily rural, capitalistic, materialistic, and socially stratified, racially, ethnically, and religiously heterogeneous, and stridently chauvinistic and expansionist—a society whose practice fell far short of, when it was not totally in conflict with, its lofty theory.

From *The American Historical Review,* Vol. 85, No. 5 (Dec. 1980), 1119–1149.

Antebellum Southern Exceptionalism
A New Look at an Old Question

James M. McPherson

The theme of American exceptionalism permeated writing about the United States from its beginning but has come under attack in recent years. Ever since Hector St. John Crèvecoeur asked his famous question in 1782, "What Is the American, This New Man?" native and foreign commentators alike have sought to define what supposedly makes the United States exceptional, indeed unique, among peoples of the world. Reaching the height of its influence in the 1950s, the exceptionalist school argued that something special about the American experience—whether it was abundance, free land on the frontier, the absence of a feudal past, exceptional mobility and the relative lack of class conflict, or the pragmatic and consensual liberalism of our politics—set the American people apart from the rest of humankind. During the last three decades, however, the dominant trends in American historiography have challenged and perhaps crippled the exceptionalist thesis. Historians have demonstrated the existence of class and class conflict, ideological politics, land speculation, and patterns of economic and social development similar to those of western Europe which placed the United States in the mainstream of modern North Atlantic history, not on a special and privileged fringe.

While the notion of American exceptionalism has suffered considerable damage, another exceptionalist interpretation remains apparently live and well. Even though America may not be as different from the rest of the world as we thought, the South seems to have been different from the rest of America. In this essay, "Southern exceptionalism" refers to the belief that the South has "possessed a separate and unique identity . . . which appeared to be out of the mainstream of American experience." Or as Quentin Compson (in William Faulkner's *Absalom, Absalom!*) expressed it in reply to his Canadian-born college roommate's question about what made Southerners tick: "You can't understand it. You would have to be born there."

The idea of Southern exceptionalism, however, has also come under challenge. The questions whether the South was indeed out of the mainstream and, if so, whether it has recently been swept into it have become lively issues in Southern historiography. The clash of viewpoints can be illustrated by a sampling of titles or subtitles of books that have appeared in recent decades. On one side we have *The Enduring South, The Everlasting South, The Idea of the South, The Lasting South, The Continuity of Southern Distinctiveness,* and *What Made the South Different?*—all arguing, in one way or another, that the South was and continues to be different. On the other side we have *The Southerner as American, The Americanization of Dixie, Epitaph for Dixie, Southerners and Other Americans, The Vanishing South,* and *Into the Mainstream.* Some of these books insist that "the traditional emphasis on the South's differentness . . . is wrong historically." Others concede that while the South may once have been different, it has ceased to be or is ceasing to be so. There is no unanimity among this latter group of scholars about precisely when or how the South joined the mainstream. Some emphasize the civil rights revolution of the 1960s; others the bulldozer revolution of the 1950s; still others the chamber of commerce Babbittry of the 1920s; and some the New South crusade of the 1880s. As far back as 1869 the Yankee novelist John William De Forest wrote of the South: "We shall do well to study this peculiar people, which will soon lose it peculiarities." As George Tindall has wryly remarked, the Vanishing South has "staged one of the most prolonged disappearing acts since the decline and fall of Rome."

Some historians, however, would quarrel with the concept of a Vanishing South because they believe that the South as a separate, exceptional entity never existed—with of course the ephemeral exception of the Confederacy. A good many other historians insist not only that a unique South did exist before the Civil War, but also that its sense of being under siege by an alien North was the underlying cause of secession. * * *

Many antebellum Americans certainly thought that North and South had evolved separate societies with institutions, interests, values, and ideologies so incompatible, so much in deadly conflict that they could no longer live together in the same nation. Traveling through the South in the spring of 1861, London *Times* correspondent William Howard Russell encountered this "conflict of civilizations" theme everywhere he went. "The tone in which [Southerners] alluded to the whole of the Northern people indicated the clear conviction that trade, commerce, the pursuit of gain, manufacture, and the base mechanical arts, had so degraded the whole race" that Southerners could no longer tolerate association with them, wrote Russell. "There is a degree of something like ferocity in the Southern mind [especially] toward New England which exceeds belief." A South Carolinian told Russell: "We are an agricultural people, pursuing our own system, and working out our own destiny, breeding up women and men with some other purpose than to make them vulgar, fanatical, cheating Yankees." Louis Wigfall of Texas, a former U.S. senator, told Russell:

> We are a peculiar people, sir! . . . We are an agricultural people. . . . We have no cities—we don't want them. . . . We want no manufactures: we desire no trading, no mechanical or manufacturing classes. . . . As long as we have our rice, our sugar, our tobacco, and

our cotton, we can command wealth to purchase all we want. . . . But with the Yankees we will never trade—never. Not one pound of cotton shall ever go from the South to their accursed cities.

Such opinions were not universal in the South, of course, but in the fevered atmosphere of the late 1850s they were widely shared. "Free Society!" exclaimed a Georgia newspaper. "We sicken at the name. What is it but a conglomeration of greasy mechanics, filthy operatives, small-fisted farmers, and moon-struck theorists . . . hardly fit for association with a southern gentleman's body servant." In 1861 the *Southern Literary Messenger* explained to its readers: "It is not a question of slavery alone that we are called upon to decide. It is free society which we must shun or embrace." In the same year Charles Colcock Jones, Jr., a native of Georgia who had graduated from Princeton and from Harvard Law School, spoke of the development of antagonistic cultures in North and South: "In this country have arisen two races [i.e., Northerners and Southerners] which, although claiming a common parentage, have been so entirely separated by climate, by morals, by religion, and by estimates so totally opposite to all that constitutes honor, truth, and manliness, that they cannot longer exist under the same government."

Spokesmen for the free-labor ideology, which was the dominant political force in the North by 1860, reciprocated these sentiments. The South, said Theodore Parker, was "the foe to Northern Industry—to our mines, our manufactures, and our commerce. . . . She is the foe to our institutions—to our democratic politics in the State, our democratic culture in the school, our democratic work in the community, our democratic equality in the family." Slavery, said William H. Seward, undermined "intelligence, vigor, and energy" in both blacks and whites. It produced "an exhausted soil, old and decaying towns, wretchedly-neglected roads . . . an absence of enterprise and improvement." Slavery was therefore "incompatible with all . . . the elements of the security, welfare, and greatness of nations." The struggle between free labor and slavery, between North and South, said Seward in his most famous speech, was "an irrepressible conflict between two opposing and enduring forces." The United States was therefore two nations, but it could not remain forever so: it "must and will, sooner or later, become either entirely a slaveholding nation, or entirely a free-labor nation."

Abraham Lincoln expressed exactly the same theme in his "house divided" speech. Many other Republicans echoed this argument that the struggle, in the words of an Ohio congressman, was "between systems, between civilizations."

These sentiments were no more confined to fire-breathing Northern radicals than were Southern exceptionalist viewpoints confined to fire-eaters. Lincoln represented the mainstream of his party, which commanded a majority of votes in the North by 1860. The dominant elements in the North and in the lower South believed the United States to be composed of two incompatible civilizations. Southerners believed that survival of their special civilization could be assured only in a separate nation. The creation of the Confederacy was merely a political ratification of an irrevocable separation that had already taken place in the hearts and minds of the people.

The proponents of an assimilationist rather than exceptionalist interpretation of Southern history maintain that this concept of a separate and unique South existed *only* in hearts and minds. It was a subjective reality, they argue, not an objective one. Objectively, they insist, North and South were one people. They shared the same language, the same Constitution, the same legal system, the same commitment to republican political institutions and a capitalist economy intertwined with that of the North, the same predominantly Protestant religion and British ethnic heritage, the same history, the same shared memories of a common struggle for nationhood.

Two proponents of the objective similarity thesis were the late Edward Pessen and David Potter. In a long article entitled "How Different from Each Other Were the Antebellum North and South?" Pessen concludes that they "were far more alike than the conventional scholarly wisdom has led us to believe." His evidence for this conclusion consists mainly of quantitative measures of the distribution of wealth and of the socioeconomic status of political officeholders in North and South. He finds that wealth was distributed in a similarly unequal fashion in both sections, voting requirements were similar, and voters in both sections elected a similarly disproportionate number of men from the upper economic strata to office. The problem with this argument is that it could be used to prove many obviously different and mutually hostile societies to be similar. France and Germany in 1914 and in 1932 had about the same distribution of wealth and similar habits of electing men from the upper strata to the Assembly or the Reichstag. England and France had a comparable distribution of wealth during most of the eighteenth century. Turkey and Russia were not dissimilar in these respects in the nineteenth century. And so on.

David Potter's contention that commonalities of language, religion, law, and political system outweighed differences in other areas is more persuasive than the Pessen argument. But the Potter thesis nevertheless begs some important questions. The same similarities prevailed between England and her North American colonies in 1776, but they did not prevent the development of a separate nationalism in the latter. It is not language or law alone that is important, but the uses to which either is put. In the United States of the 1850s, Northerners and Southerners spoke the same language, to be sure, but they were increasingly using this language to revile each other. Language became an instrument of division, not unity. The same was true of the political system. So also of the law: Northern states passed personal liberty laws to defy a national Fugitive Slave Law supported by the South; a Southern-dominated Supreme Court denied the right of Congress to exclude slavery from the territories, a ruling that most Northerners considered an infamous distortion of the Constitution. As for a shared commitment to Protestantism, this too had become a divisive rather than unifying factor, with the two largest denominations—Methodist and Baptist—having split into hostile Southern and Northern churches over the question of slavery, and the third largest—Presbyterian—having split partly along sectional lines and partly on the question of slavery. As for a shared historical commitment to republicanism, by the 1850s this too was more divisive than unifying. Northern Republicans interpreted this commitment in a free-soil context, while most Southern whites continued to insist that one of the most cherished tenets of republican liberty was the right of property—including property in slaves.

There is another dimension of the Potter thesis—or perhaps it would be more accurate to call it a separate Potter thesis— that might put us on the right track to solve the puzzle of Southern

exceptionalism. After challenging most notions of Southern distinctiveness, Potter concluded that the principal characteristic
distinguishing the South from the rest of the country was the persistence of a "folk culture" in the South. This gemeinschaft culture,
with its emphasis on tradition, rural life, close kinship ties, a hierarchical social structure, ascribed status, patterns of deference, and
masculine codes of honor and chivalry, persisted in the South long
after the North began moving toward a gesellschaft culture with
its impersonal, bureaucratic, meritocratic, urbanizing, commercial,
industrializing, mobile, and rootless characteristics. Above all, the
South's folk culture valued tradition and stability and felt threatened by change; the North's modernizing culture enshrined change
as progress and condemned the South as backward.

A variety of statistics undergird the gemeinschaft-gesellschaft
contrast. The North was more urban than the South and was urbanizing at a faster rate. In 1820, 10 percent of the free-state residents lived in urban areas (defined by the census as towns or cities
with a population of 2,500 or more) compared with 5 percent in
the slave states. By 1860 the figures were 26 percent and 10 percent,
respectively. More striking was the growing contrast between farm
and nonfarm occupations in the two sections. In 1800, 82 percent
of the Southern labor force worked in agriculture compared with
68 percent in the free states. By 1860 the Northern share had
dropped to 40 percent, while the Southern proportion had actually
increased slightly, to 84 percent. Southern agriculture remained
traditionally labor-intensive while Northern farming became increasingly capital-intensive and mechanized. By 1860 the free states
had nearly twice the value of farm machinery per acre and per
farmworker as the slave states. And the pace of industrialization in
the North far outstripped that in the South. In 1810 the slave states
had an estimated 31 percent of the capital invested in manufacturing in the United States; by 1860 this had declined to 16 percent.

A critic of the inferences drawn from these data might point out
that in many respects the differences between the free states east
and west of the Appalachians were nearly or virtually as great
as those between North and South, yet these differences did not
produce a sense of separate nationality in East and West. This
point is true—as far as it goes. While the western free states at

midcentury did have a higher proportion of workers employed in nonfarm occupations than the South, they had about the same percentage of urban population and the same amount per capita invested in manufacturing. But the crucial factor was *the rate of change.* The West was urbanizing and industrializing more rapidly than either the Northeast or the South. Therefore while North and South as a whole were growing relatively farther apart, the eastern and western free states were drawing closer together. This process frustrated Southern hopes for an alliance with the Old Northwest on grounds of similarity of agrarian interests. From 1840 to 1860 the rate of urbanization in the West was three times greater than in the Northeast and four times greater than in the South. The amount of capital invested in manufacturing grew twice as fast in the West as in the Northeast and nearly three times as fast as in the South. The same was true of employment in nonfarm occupations. The railroad-building boom of the 1850s tied the Northwest to the Northeast with links of iron and shifted the dominant pattern of inland trade from a North-South to an East-West orientation. The remarkable growth of cities like Chicago, Cincinnati, Cleveland, and Detroit with their farm-machinery, food-processing, machine-tool, and railroad-equipment industries foreshadowed the emergence of the industrial Midwest and helped to assure that when the crisis of the Union came in 1861 the West joined the East instead of the South.

According to a thorough study of antebellum Southern industry, the Southern lag in this category of development resulted not from any inherent economic disadvantages—not shortage of capital, nor low rates of return, nor nonadaptability of slave labor—but from the choices of Southerners to invest more of their money in agriculture and slaves than in manufacturing. In the 1780s Thomas Jefferson had praised farmers as the "peculiar deposit for substantial and genuine virtue" and warned against the industrial classes in cities as sores on the body politic. In 1860 many Southern leaders still felt the same way; as Louis Wigfall put it in the passage quoted earlier, "We want no manufactures; we desire no trading, no mechanical or manufacturing classes."

Partly as a consequence of this attitude, the South received only a trickle of the great antebellum stream of immigration. Fewer than one-eighth of the immigrants settled in slave states, where the foreign-born percentage of the population was less than a fourth of the North's percentage. The South's white population was ethnically more homogeneous and less cosmopolitan than the North's. The traditional patriarchal family and tight kinship networks typical of gemeinschaft societies, reinforced in the South by a relatively high rate of cousin marriages, also persisted much more strongly in the nineteenth-century South than in the North.

The greater volume of immigration to the free states contributed to the faster rate of population growth there than in the South. Another factor in this differential growth rate was out-migration from the South. During the middle decades of the nineteenth century, twice as many whites left the South for the North as vice versa. These facts did not go unnoticed at the time; indeed, they formed the topic of much public comment. Northerners cited the differential in population growth as evidence for the superiority of the free-labor system; Southerners perceived it with alarm as evidence of their declining minority status in the nation. These perceptions became important factors in the growing sectional self-consciousness that led to secession.

The most crucial demographic difference between North and South resulted from slavery. Ninety-five percent of the country's black people lived in the slave states, where blacks constituted one-third of the population in contrast to their 1 percent of the Northern population. The implications of this for the economy and social structure of the two sections, not to mention their ideologies and politics, are obvious and require little elaboration here. Two brief points are worth emphasizing, however. First, historians in the last generation have discovered the viability of African-American culture under slavery. They have noted that black music, folklore, speech patterns, religion, and other manifestations of this culture influenced white society in the South. Since the African-American culture was preeminently a folk culture with an emphasis on oral tradition and other nonliterate forms of ritual and communication, it reinforced the persistence of a traditional, gemeinschaft, folk-oriented society in the South.

Second, many historians have maintained that Northerners were as committed to white supremacy as Southerners. This may have been true, but the scale of concern with this matter in the South was so much greater as to constitute a different order of magnitude and to contribute more than any other factor to the difference between North and South. And of course slavery was more than an institution of racial control. Its centrality to many aspects of life focused Southern politics almost exclusively on defense of the institution—to the point that, in the words of the *Charleston Mercury* in 1858, "on the subject of slavery . . . the North and South . . . are not only two Peoples, but they are rival, hostile Peoples."

The fear that slavery was being hemmed in and threatened with destruction contributed to the defensive-aggressive style of Southern political behavior. This aggressiveness sometimes took physical form. Southern whites were more likely to carry weapons and to use them against other human beings than Northerners were. The homicide rate was higher in the South. The phenomenon of dueling persisted longer there. Bertram Wyatt-Brown attributes this to the Southern code of honor based on traditional patriarchal values of courtesy, status, courage, family, and the symbiosis of shame and pride. The enforcement of order through the threat and practice of violence also resulted from the felt need to control a large slave population.

Martial values and practices were more pervasive in the South than in the North. Marcus Cunliffe has argued to the contrary, but the evidence confutes him. Cunliffe's argument is grounded mainly in two sets of data: the prevalence of militia and volunteer military companies in the free as well as in the slave states; and the proportion of West Pointers and regular army officers from the two sections. Yet the first set of data do not support his thesis, and the second contradict it. Cunliffe does present evidence on the popularity of military companies in the North, but nowhere does he estimate the comparative numbers of such companies in North and South or the number of men in proportion to population who belonged to them. If such comparative evidence could be assembled, it would probably support the traditional view of a higher concentration of such companies in the South. What Northern city, for example, could compare with Charleston, which had no fewer than twenty-two military companies in the late 1850s—one for every two hundred white men of military age? Another important quasi-military institution in the South with no Northern counterpart escaped Cunliffe's attention—the slave patrol, which gave tens of thousands of Southern whites a more practical form of military experience than the often ceremonial functions of volunteer drill companies could do.

As for the West Point alumni and regular army officers, it is true, as Cunliffe points out, that about 60 percent of these were from the North and only 40 percent from the South in the late antebellum decades. What he fails to note is that the South had only about 30 percent of the nation's white population during this era, so that on a proportional basis the South was overrepresented in these categories. Moreover, from 1849 to 1861 all of the secretaries of war were Southerners, as were the general in chief of the army, two of the three brigadier generals, all but one commander of the army's geographical departments on the eve of the Civil War, the authors of the two manuals on infantry tactics and the artillery manual used at West Point, and the professor who taught tactics and strategy at the military academy.

Other evidence supports the thesis of a significant martial tradition in the South contrasted with a concentration in different professions in the North. More than three-fifths of the volunteer soldiers in the Mexican War came from the slave states—on a per capita basis, four times the proportion of free-state volunteers. Seven of the eight military "colleges" (not including West Point and Annapolis) listed in the 1860 census were in the slave states. A study of the occupations of antebellum men chronicled in the *Dictionary of American Biography* found that the military profession claimed twice the percentage of Southerners as of Northerners, while this ratio was reversed for men distinguished in literature, art, medicine, and education. In business the per capita proportion of Yankees was three times as great, and among engineers and inventors it was six times as large. When Southerners labeled themselves a nation of warriors and Yankees a nation of shopkeepers—a common comparison in 1860—or when Jefferson Davis told a London *Times* correspondent in 1861 that "we are a military people," they were not just whistling Dixie.

One final comparison is in order—a comparison of education and literacy in North and South. Contemporaries considered this a matter of importance. The South's perceived backwardness in schooling and its large numbers of illiterates framed one of the principal free-soil indictments of slavery. This was one area in which a good many Southerners admitted inferiority and tried to do something about it. But in 1860, after a decade of school reform in the South, the slave states still had only half the North's proportion of white children enrolled in school, and the length of the annual school term in the South was little more than half as long as in the North. Of course education did not take place solely in school. But other forms of education—in the home, at church, through lyceums and public lectures, by apprenticeship, and so on—were also more active in North than South. According to the census of 1860, per capita newspaper circulation was three times greater in the North, and the number of library volumes per white person was nearly twice as large.

The proportion of illiterate white people was three times greater in the South than in the North. If the black population is included, as indeed it should be, the percentage of illiterates was seven or eight times as high in the South. In the free states, what two historians have termed an "ideology of literacy" prevailed—a commitment to education as an instrument of social mobility, economic prosperity, progress, and freedom. While this ideology also existed in the South, especially in the 1850s, it was much weaker there and made slow headway against the inertia of a rural folk culture. "The Creator did not intend that every individual human being should be highly cultivated," wrote William Harper of South Carolina. "It is better that a part should be fully and highly educated and the rest utterly ignorant." Commenting on a demand by Northern workingmen for universal public education, the *Southern Review* asked: "Is this the way to produce producers? To make every child in the state a literary character would not be a good qualification for those who must live by manual labor."

The ideology of literacy in the North was part of a larger ferment which produced an astonishing number of reform movements that aroused both contempt and fear in the South. Southern whites viewed the most dynamic of these movements—abolitionism—as a threat to their very existence. Southerners came to distrust the whole concept of "progress" as it seemed to be understood in the North. *De Bow's Review* declared in 1851: "Southern life, habits, thoughts, and aims, are so essentially different from those of the North, that here a different character of books . . . and training is required." A Richmond newspaper warned in 1855 that Southerners must stop reading Northern newspapers and books and stop sending their sons to colleges in the North, where "every village has its press and its lecture room, and each lecturer and editor, unchecked by a healthy public opinion, opens up for discussion all the received dogmas of faith," where unwary youth are "exposed to the danger of imbibing doctrines subversive of all old institutions." Young men should be educated instead in the South "where their training would be moral, religious, and conservative, and they would never learn, or read a word in school or out of school, inconsistent with orthodox Christianity, pure morality, the right of property, and sacredness of marriage."

In all of the areas discussed above—urbanization, industrialization, labor force, demographic structure, violence and martial values, education, and attitudes toward change—contemporaries accurately perceived significant differences between North and South, contrasts that in most respects were increasing over time. The question remains: Were these disparities crucial enough to make the South an exception to generalizations about antebellum America?

This essay concludes by suggesting a tentative answer to that question. Perhaps it was the *North* that was "different," that departed from the mainstream of historical development; and perhaps therefore we should speak not of Southern exceptionalism but of Northern exceptionalism. This idea is borrowed shamelessly from C. Vann Woodward, who applied it, however, to the post–Civil War United States. In essays written during the 1950s on "The Irony of Southern History" and "The Search for Southern Identity," Woodward suggested that, unlike other Americans but like most people in the rest of the world, Southerners had known poverty, failure, defeat, and thus had a skeptical attitude toward "progress." The South shared a bond with the rest of humankind that other Americans did not share. This theme of Northern exceptionalism might well be applied also to the antebellum United

States—not for Woodard's categories of defeat, poverty, and failure, but for the categories of a persistent folk culture discussed in this essay.

At the beginning of the republic the North and South were less different in most of these categories than they became later. Nearly all Northern states had slavery in 1776, and the institution persisted in some of them for decades thereafter. The ethnic homogeneity of Northern and Southern whites was quite similar before 1830. The proportion of urban dwellers was similarly small and the percentage of the labor force employed in agriculture similarly large in 1800. The Northern predominance in commerce and manufacturing was not so great as it later became. Nor was the contrast in education and literacy as large as it subsequently became. A belief in progress and commitments to reform or radicalism were no more prevalent in the North than in the South in 1800—indeed, they may have been less so. In 1776, in 1800, even as late as 1820, similarity in values and institutions was the salient fact. Within the next generation, difference and conflict became prominent. This happened primarily because of developments in the North. The South changed relatively little, and because so many Northern changes seemed threatening, the South developed a defensive ideology that resisted change.

In most of these respects the South resembled a majority of the societies in the world more than the changing North did. Despite the abolition of legal slavery or serfdom throughout most of the Western Hemisphere and western Europe, much of the world—like the South—had an unfree or quasi-free labor force. Most societies in the world remained predominantly rural, agricultural, and labor-intensive; most, including even several European countries, had illiteracy rates as high or higher than the South's 45 percent; most like the South remained bound by traditional values and networks of family, kinship, hierarchy, and patriarchy. The North—along with a few countries in northwestern Europe—hurtled forward eagerly toward a future of industrial capitalism that many Southerners found distasteful if not frightening; the South remained proudly and even defiantly rooted in the past.

Thus when secessionists protested in 1861 that they were acting to preserve traditional rights and values, they were correct. They fought to protect their constitutional liberties against the perceived Northern threat to overthrow them. The South's concept of republicanism had not changed in three-quarters of a century; the North's had. With complete sincerity the South fought to preserve its version of the republic of the Founding Fathers—a government of limited powers that protected the rights of property, including slave property, and whose constituency comprised an independent gentry and yeomanry of the white race undisturbed by large cities, heartless factories, restless free workers, and class conflict. The accession to power of the Republican party, with its ideology of competitive, egalitarian, free-labor capitalism, was a signal to the South that the Northern majority had turned irrevocably toward this frightening future. Indeed, the Black Republican party appeared to the eyes of many Southern whites as "essentially a revolutionary party" composed of "a motley throng of Sans culottes . . . Infidels and freelovers, interspersed by Bloomer women, fugitive slaves, and amalgamationists." Therefore secession was a preemptive counterrevolution to prevent the Black Republican revolution from engulfing the South. "*We* are not revolutionists," insisted James D. B. De Bow and Jefferson Davis during the Civil War. "We are resisting revolution. . . . We are not engaged in a Quixotic fight for the rights of man; our struggle is for inherited rights. . . . We are upholding the true doctrines of the Federal Constitution. We are conservative."

Union victory in the war destroyed the Southern vision of America and ensured that the Northern vision would become the American vision. Until 1861, however, it was the North that was out of the mainstream, not the South. Of course the Northern states, along with Britain and a few countries in northwestern Europe, were cutting a new channel in world history that would doubtless have become the mainstream even if the American Civil War had not happened. But for Americans the Civil War marked the turning point. A Louisiana planter who returned home sadly after the war wrote in 1865: "Society has been completely changed by the war. The [French] revolution of '89 did not produce a greater change in the 'Ancien Régime' than has this in our social life." And four years later George Ticknor, a retired Harvard professor, concluded that the Civil War had created a "great gulf between what happened before in our century and what has happened since. . . . It does not seem to me as if I were living in the country in which I was born." From the war sprang the great flood that wrenched the stream of American history into a new channel and transferred the burden of exceptionalism from North to South.

James McPherson, "Antebellum Southern Exceptionalism: A New Look at an Old Question," *Drawn with the Sword: Reflections on the American Civil War* (Oxford: Oxford University Press, 1996), pp. 3–23. Originally appeared under the same title in *Civil War History* 29 (1983), pp. 230–44.

APPENDIX I: POPULATIONS AND ELECTION RESULTS FOR AUGUSTA AND FRANKLIN COUNTIES

TABLE 1: *Population Statistics for 1860*

	Augusta County, Va.	Franklin County, Pa.
Total Population	27,749	42,126
Free Population	22,133	42,126
White Population	21,547	40,327
Free Colored Population	586	1,799
Enslaved Population	5,616	
Slaveholders	811	

TABLE 2: *Results of the Election of 1860*

	Augusta County, Va.	Franklin County, Pa.
Abraham Lincoln *(Republican)*	0	4,151
John Bell *(Constitutional Union)*	2,553	76
John Breckinridge *(Southern Democrat)*	218	2,515
Stephen Douglas *(Northern Democrat)*	1,094	822

TABLE 3: *Population Statistics for 1870*

	Augusta County, Va.	Franklin County, Pa.
Total Population	28,763	45,365
White Population	22,026	42,903
Colored Population	6,737	2,462

APPENDIX II: MAPS OF AUGUSTA AND FRANKLIN COUNTIES

• Map 1: Augusta County, Va., and Franklin County, Pa.: Geographical Location

1. Augusta County

• Map 2: Augusta County, Va.: Residences with Slaves, 1860
• Map 3: Augusta County, Va.: Railroad and Roads, 1860
• Map 4: Augusta County, Va.: Agricultural Production by Precinct, 1860
• Map 5: Augusta County, Va.: Presidential Election of 1860

2. Franklin County

• Map 6: Franklin County, Pa.: Railroad and Roads, 1860
• Map 7: Franklin County, Pa.: Agricultural Production by Precinct, 1860
• Map 8: Franklin County, Pa.: Presidential Election of 1860

Map 1. AUGUSTA COUNTY, VA., AND
FRANKLIN COUNTY, PA.: GEOGRAPHICAL LOCATION

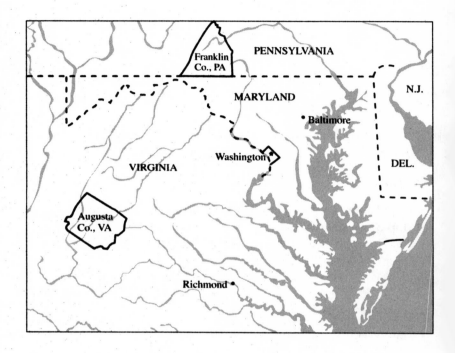

Map 2. AUGUSTA COUNTY, VA.:
RESIDENCES WITH SLAVES, 1860

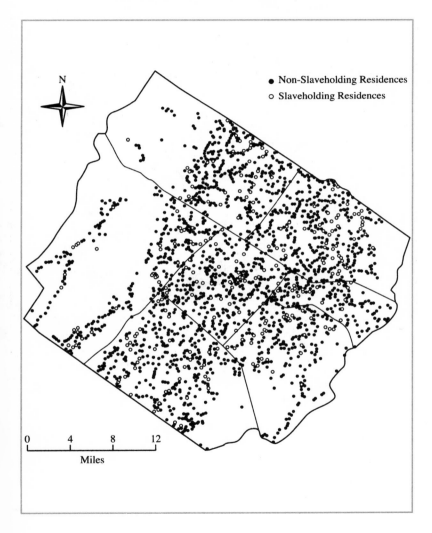

Map 3. AUGUSTA COUNTY, VA.:
RAILROAD AND ROADS, 1860

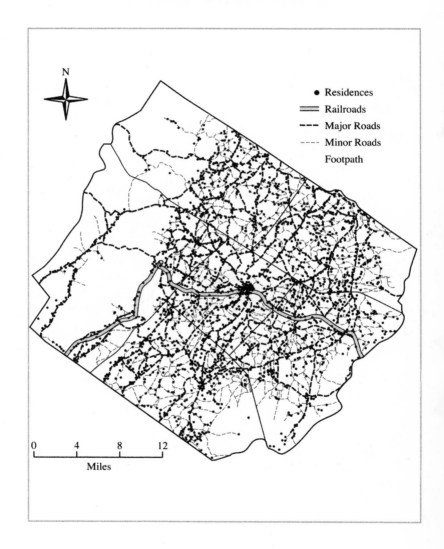

Map 4. AUGUSTA COUNTY, VA.:
AGRICULTURAL PRODUCTION BY PRECINCT, 1860

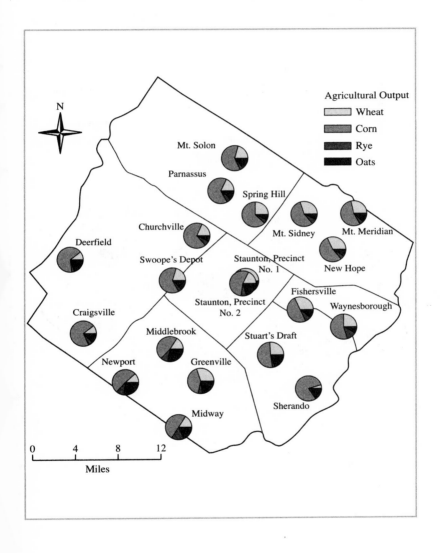

Map 5. AUGUSTA COUNTY, VA.:
PRESIDENTIAL ELECTION OF 1860

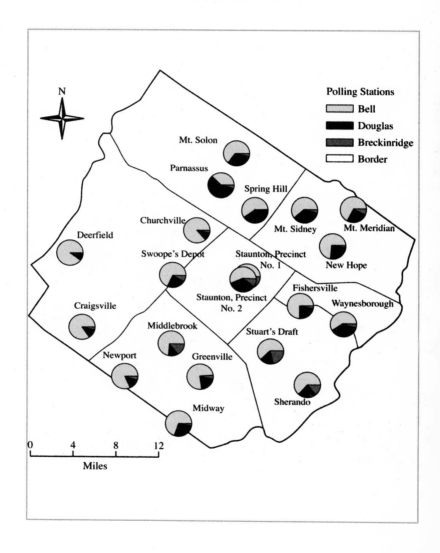

Map 6. FRANKLIN COUNTY, PA.:
RAILROAD AND ROADS, 1860

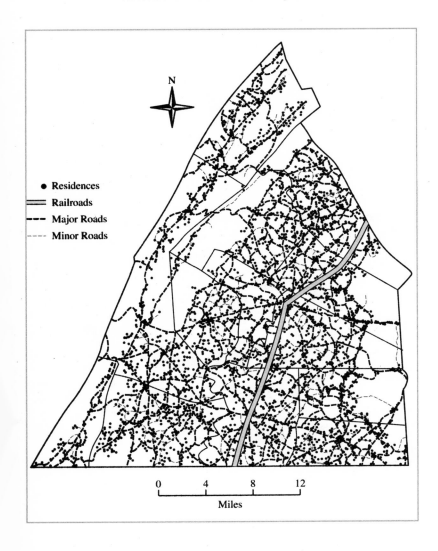

Map 7. FRANKLIN COUNTY, PA.:
AGRICULTURAL PRODUCTION BY PRECINCT, 1860

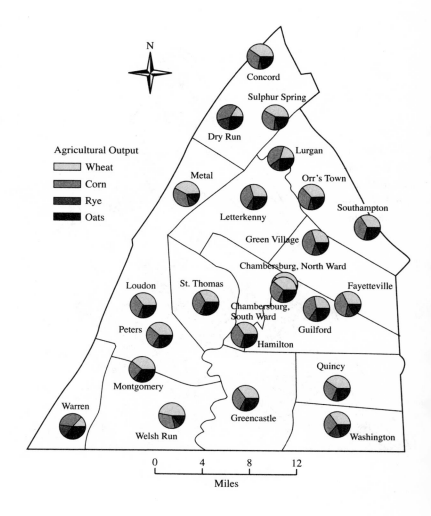

Map 8. FRANKLIN COUNTY, PA.:
PRESIDENTIAL ELECTION OF 1860

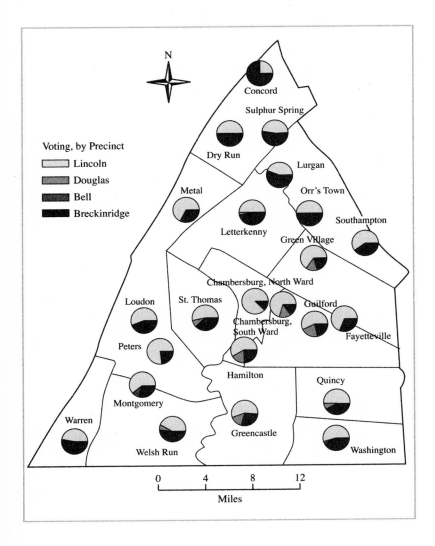

INDEX